JAN 1998

"Whenever I find
myself involuntarily pausing before
coffin warehouses, and bringing
up the rear of every funeral I meet;
and especially whenever my
hypos get such an upper hand of me,
that it requires a strong moral
principle to prevent me
from deliberately stepping into the
street, and methodically
knocking people's hats off—then,
I account it high time to get to
sea as soon as I can."

[HERMAN MELVILLE]

IN THE SLICK OF THE CRICKET

By Russell Drumm

DEDICATION

TO PAMELA DRUMM FOR CO-SUFFERING THE LABOR PAINS
OF THIS BOOK, AND THE PENURY OF A GAZETTEER.

ACKNOWLEDGEMENTS

TO FRANK MUNDUS, A LEGEND IN HIS OWN TIME.

TO HELEN RATTRAY, EDITOR OF THE EAST HAMPTON STAR, THE
BEST DERN WEEKLY IN THE UNIVERSE.

TO ALLAN WEISBACKER FOR HIS SUPPORT AND SHARED VISION.

TO SUSAN POLLACK FOR HER EDITORIAL AND
PISCATORIAL WISDOM.

TO PAT MUNDUS FOR HER LOVE OF
THE SEA AND HER FRIENDSHIP

TO JENNIFER PELTZ FOR HER SHARP EYE.

TO B. MARTIN PEDERSEN, DESIGNER EXTRAORDINAIRE,
FOR SEEING A BOOK IN A PILE OF 8x11 PAGES
AND MAKING IT BEAUTIFUL.

© 1997 RUSSELL DRUMM
ISBN 1-888889-05-5
WINNER OF THE 16TH ANNUAL EDITOR'S BOOK AWARD
BOOK DESIGN BY B. MARTIN PEDERSEN
PUBLISHED BY PUSHCART PRESS, WAINSCOTT, NEW YORK
ALL RIGHTS RESERVED
DISTRIBUTED BY W.W. NORTON & COMPANY, NEW YORK, NEW YORK

"Nothin' on this earth is increasin'.
There ain't as many fish, but
there ain't as many of a lot of
things, like pheasants or buffaloes.
Even the brontosauruses that used to
hang out on the front lawn got '
scarce after I quit drinkin'.
The only thing there's more of
is humans, and some of
them ain't human."

[FRANK MUNDUS]

Chapter

1

H A P P I N E S S

M UNDUS IS WITTY, IN HIS WAY, and grows wittier as this summer storm intensifies. The movements of his six-foot frame are those of his charter boat, Cricket II. He rides Cricket. They are one. He's looking my way, and it's like being observed by Beethoven, same Germanic head with piercing eyes used to looking below the surface— good at it. He sees something in me and smirks like he's going to fix it. □ The first time I saw him, he was hacking at a hanging shark with a machete, blood splattering on a tight ring of tourists. Happy, blood-splattered tourists. His pants were rolled up, the big toe of each foot painted green and red for port and starboard. He wore a gold earring and bush hat turned down, and laughing his high-pitched laugh. The free arm was withered, scarred by what looked like a shark bite. It explained the vengeful hacking. Cricket rocked approvingly at her berth.

A green dragon breathed fire from the door of a walk-in chum fridge, the words "Monster Mash" in bold letters above the flames.

That was 20 years ago, and Frank Mundus was already known as the "Monster Man" because of the big sharks he was bringing into Montauk. His colorful dockings drew as many onlookers as flies. But, despite the reputation for mayhem that had distanced a private man from *"DEM BASTIDS,"* as he pronounced—in his fine, old Brooklynese— the rest of the Montauk charter fleet, Mundus was not a coarse man.

Over the years as waterfront reporter for the local newspaper, I found him to be an uncanny judge of character, both human and piscatorial, a master of subtleties—charter captain defined.

The Cricket II's maiden voyage was made in 1947, with sixteen mackerel fishermen and a Model A Ford on her deck. Forty years later, Mundus would step from this same deck onto the swollen island of a dead whale in order to feed ginger snaps and melon slices to circling white sharks. Even so, I've come to believe that stranger things happened onshore than off in the years between Frank's Model A and his moon walk. Like a once-vivid fading tattoo, his exploits: the years at Fishangri-la, his archers, his kites, the goat sacrifice that fell on deaf ears, they all have been but surface renderings of scary-deep and passionate pursuits. It's why I'm here.

Cricket surfs a huge following sea throughout the night. At one point the automatic pilot fails, and Cricket begins to circle. Frank talks to her, his face cast in radar-screen green.

"Come on now, don't go the wrong way. You're goin' the wrong way. Automatic pilot, you're goin the wrong way, you hear me? You silly son-of-a-bitch, why are you takin' us that way? We'll try to fix you. Otherwise we'll do it the old fashion' way. We only done it 40-some years, twistin' the son-of-a-bitchin' steering wheel around. You're goin' the right way now. You happy now?"

We're heading east again into the night, into a growing storm toward the fishing grounds. The sea is sickening. I flee to sleep.

The sun rises red.

Howard Chong, Frank's charter, snores on. Just hours ago, he arrived at Kennedy Airport from Hawaii, hoping to catch a white shark. If he's dreaming, they are confused dreams. Large seas have him alternately weightless and crushed in one of the Cricket's lower bunks as we head past Block Island toward the place called the Dumping Ground, just west of Nantucket. In normal weather, it's about a six-hour steam from Montauk. When Howard awakes, he may want to get back to his little grass shack—a mondo condo I suspect, in his case.

The Dumping Ground is a 100-square-mile piece of bottom. It got its name because the government dumped tons of bombs, cannon shells, and other unused ordnance there after World War II. The explosive reef became home to bottom-dwelling species fed upon by herring and mackerel, which, in turn, were attacked by schools of bluefish. To this day, the fountain of food attracts the migrating "apex" predators—the sharks, tuna, and swordfish venturing north each year in their cocoon of Gulf Stream eddies and meanders. Frank found the fountain and for 40 years carved out a living by satisfying primordial urges. His greatest discovery was the mammoth white sharks that trail behind migrating whales and tuna.

Peter Benchley, author of *Jaws,* had it partly right; the great white is the Anti-Tourist. In his story, the monster wrecked an otherwise sunny season in the little seaside town of Amity. Frank caught his first big white off Amagansett in the township of East Hampton, New York in 1961. Now he pronounces the two words slowly, "Aaaaamity, Aaaaamagansett," to point up what he considers Mr. Benchley's larcenous authorship. He has never forgiven Benchley for not acknowledging him as the model for Quint, his slightly-mad charter captain.

In *Jaws,* the movie, Amity is an island. But the besieged beaches of Benchley's original are those of the adjacent hamlets of East Hampton, Amagansett, and Montauk on the eastern end of Long Island. Frank never read the book, but was told that following the third shark attack, Benchley's police chief Brody told a newspaper reporter:

"What were we going to do? Close the Amity beaches, and people would just drive up to East Hampton and go swimming there. And there's just as good a chance they'd get killed in East Hampton as in Amity."

The plot grew literal teeth here again in 1986, 11 years after the movie was released, when tiger sharks followed a dead whale to an Amagansett beach.

I was there reporting the day Judith Hope, then the East Hampton town supervisor, ordered the beaches closed and surfers out of the water after witnessing a tiger surf out of its natural environment, take a bite of blubber, and wiggle back into knee-deep water. That night, Captain Mundus pulled one 500-pound tiger shark and another 200-pounder from 30 feet of water down drift of the beached whale. Frank's telling me this story, shouting it against the Cricket's engine growl and the loud flapping of our canvas cocoon on the bridge at dawn.

"We seen that whale a year to the day, Aug. 6, after we caught that big white, Big Boy. I was down below, and Teddy the mate slows the boat down, and I come out and say, 'what's goin on?' Teddy says, 'take a look.' Oh my cussed God, there was this dead whale. It was on the way home, and I look at the cussed clock and says, 'Teddy, we don't have time. We have another party waitin' for us, and we was a shade on the late side already. Teddy says, 'yeah, I know, but I couldn't help but stop to take a peek.' And then he says, 'do you realize it's our anniversary? It's exactly to the day.'

"There was the whale, there was the beach, there was the wind. I says Teddy, 'that sucker's gonna wind up somewheres on the beach if they don't do somethin'. The handwritin' was on the wall. So we go in, and we heard the next day that he washed up on the beach down in Amagansett.

"So Teddy went down to look at him, and they didn't drag him up the beach yet. When they did, the tiger sharks was hangin' on to him. Of all the dumb things. I mean, those people who ordered that whale dragged up and buried— there was never a kid what had a little sand bucket and small shovel and played in the sand that wouldn'ta known better; how the hell they figured they was gonna bury that whale I don't know.

"They got bulldozers to come down but you'd have to make a hole with an atom bomb big enough in sand unless you used bulkheads. So then Teddy went down and looked at it afterwards, and he said you could walk on top of it and feel the whale blubbery underneath. I says, 'My God, man, they're gonna have maggots big enough to shoot with a shotgun.' And that's exactly what happened, and there's nice houses right there. People pay a lot of money for waterfront property, put up a nice house, and then they get a whale buried in their backyard.

"Teddy says, 'whadyasay we go down there and anchor up; maybe we can catch a couple a sharks.' Well I says we have the right party comin' up; they'll try anything. I ask Teddy, 'can you find it after dark?' He says, 'yeah, I got some good ranges on it.' The party comes down that night, so I ask them and says, 'look, it's a gamble, but if we catch fish, we'll probably start a riot.' Oh, that's good, they say. They're all in favor of startin' a riot. We go down there, and Teddy points and says, 'the whale's right in there.'

"I says, 'all right, we want to get as close to him as possible because the juices are still comin' out of the whale, and they're fil-terin' through the sand. The shahks [Frank crushes his r's Brooklyn style] can still smell him, so they'll be there.'

They were there, says Frank, over the rising storm. He said when the Cricket got back to the docks, after newspaper photographers flew over in a chopper to shoot pictures of the monsters hanging from her gin pole, a reporter asked did he see any more. "We didn't see any. We didn't even see these two before they ate the bait," says Frank. The thought of unseen monsters started a riot.

I figure Mr. Benchley dealt with the fear angle well enough. No one is likely to go skinny-dipping in the moonlight after seeing the opening scene in Jaws. Fear of being devoured would seem a given.

But there's another more troubling question to chew on; why is it that for 40 years anglers have flocked to Mundus's 42-foot Cricket II, with her stainless steel stern bits for towing massive carcasses? Why would they travel, in one case illegally across six state lines with a loaded .45-caliber Tommy gun, just to go shark fishing in white ducks and a blazer with the master?

Anger, sure. "Their old man beat the shit out of them, so this is how they get back," Frank suggests in the usual Mundus manner. But you can tell by the sparkle in his eyes that it ain't that simple.

It would seem that for Clyde, as Frank calls he who sat on the Cricket's backdeck, sipping champagne with his Bonnie after re-enacting the St. Valentine's Day massacre on a blue shark, there is more than one way to be devoured.

Perhaps, if bleached life, the great white cope, won't face you like a proper beast, then best to find the nearest thing with real teeth and bare your own. This sentiment, especially in the New York area, was a rich vein which Mundus mined for years before other fishermen caught on.

Frank has a picture of himself up inside the decapitated head of a huge white shark he'd once hung from a dockside gantry. His face is just visible looking out past the animal's big triangular teeth. 'Hyeeeeeeeee,' he laughed, once inside. He says he loved the echo. He was not alone.

The 42-foot Cricket became the conduit to the Dumping Ground, the only charter boat fishing the River Styx on a regular basis. Frank discovered the need shortly after arriving in Montauk in 1951. He was 26.

He knows them all, he says: "the little guinea stone masons and the muscle-building boys who spend their time in the gym. They want to tear them shahks apart with their muscles. The little old lady from Pasadena walks to choych on Sunday. She has no muscles. She knows she has no muscles, so she listens to me and catches fish."

Their captain has taken something from sharks, the fish he understands and loves most. He, too, is a predator and makes no bones about it. It's an honesty aged bronze in the early light of a new age, as the Greenpeace in us tries to sublimate the vicious instincts that have driven us for millions of years.

Good luck. Frank knows we'll likely kill on, if not for food, or God and country, then to avoid having our souls devoured by the comfort monster we've created so pridefully.

The master is retiring after this season and moving with Jenny, his young vegetarian wife, to a house he's bought with a non-ocean view of the Kona coast of Hawaii. He says he's seen enough of the sea. He has an acre there with every fruit tree imaginable, orange, grapefruit, papaya, mango. Nuts, too, almonds and macadamias. He's even found a market for his papayas.

He says sometimes Jenny wants to drive down to the beach in Hawaii. "She looks out at the ocean. I turn around and look into the bushes."

I don't believe him. In the next breath, he's saying he knows how to catch the monsters that live deep around the Hawaiian Islands. Then, as though chasing the monstrous urge to fish back into its cave, his tune changes again:

"I told those Hawaiian charter guys I'll go, but no more than one day a week. If they had their way, they'd have me down there every day." He goes back to bragging about his limes and mac nuts. He says he's learned to get at the nuts through their hard shells by freezing them first before smashing them with a claw hammer on the driveway. He goes on about papayas, but with the beast hunkered way back in his eyes.

Soon he's telling Howard and me about having his arm twisted to go offshore last year with a Kona charter captain who was putting together a tv show. "I didn't even want to do the tv program. What the hell do I want to do it for? You know, I'm gettin' outa this business; what the hell do I need publicity for? But there was a guy down there that done me some favors, so I said, 'look, you wanta do it? I'll do it for you. I don't want to do it for myself.' "

Methinks the captain protests too much.

The Cricket's riding hard. The 35 buckets of ground chum and 20 boxes of mixed fish chunks for the five-day trip add about 5,000 pounds to Cricket, the same number as the dollars this trip is costing the Hawaiian, who's now awake.

Frank, meanwhile, is back in Hawaii, tied up in his mind to "the fishing island," as he calls it, a catamaran called the Double D that's anchored in 6,000 feet of water off the Kona coast. He's talking quicker, and his eyes shine. The monsters have control of his tongue.

He says he didn't know about the Double D before he did the tv show. I suspect he agreed to do the show because he'd heard about it and needed an excuse to investigate.

"We did tie up behind him," Frank says. Howard has just stumbled from his bunk to say he's seen the finished television program Frank's talking about.

"Actually, if you want to know what happened that night—you seen on the tv program that we caught two threshers and a blue shark. We didn't. What we did catch, in reality, was one blue shark. We was tied up on his anchor line. The Double D had two big rigs like that,"

Mundus says, pointing to the heavy-duty rod and golden 12.0 reel
that rise from the Cricket's fighting chair, the rod looking like something between a bishop's crosier and a small crane.

"The captain of the Double D had the two big rigs down deep,
about 200 feet, with heavy leads on them. No chum. I was back there
chummin' and fishin' my regular shark-fishin' way. I raised the one
blue shark. He hooked these other fish and passed us the rods, so it
looked like, on tv, we caught 'em on that boat. There was no mention
of the Double D. Actually, he passed back three. Now the other fish
he passed back had a pair a shoulders on him, cause we wasn't gainin' on him. I don't know what we had a holda, but I know he had
some weight to him. We lost him."

"He was three to my one by fishin' down deep. So then when I got
talkin' to him, I says, 'now let me see what this is all about.' Frank
tells of going again, with Jenny, catching a 200-pound brown shark
and "one of dem shitty ole blue marlins, about 600 pounds— he stole
one of our good shark baits." Frank mocks the Hemingway big-
game-noble-fish ethos one might associate with a 600-pound marlin,
mocks it for class reasons while understanding it completely like a
revolutionary would. In fun— but not really. To me it's one of the
captain's most endearing qualities.

"So I get talkin' to the captain," Frank says, all memory of
macadamia nuts and papayas by this time eaten by the creature within. "I says, 'well, look, if we do get serious and some of my customers want to come down, now much money you talkin'?'"

Frank goes on outlining the deal: The boat picks you up at the pier,
takes you out. It's about a 15 minute ride, only about three miles. Get
on the barge. It's got a big tv room. You can sit there bullshittin'. Its
galley has two full-size ice boxes, a freezer. It's bigger than a regular
kitchen. The coffee pot is on. You're wanderin' around. If you want to
lay down, you lay down. The rods are back there, let 'em go ahead

and fish. For $500 for a night's fishin', from six o'clock at night until eight in the mornin', that ain't a bad deal," he says of the dream oasis— "is it?"

The Cricket's engine growls louder, softer, louder, softer in waves of jealousy.

"She's 80 foot," Frank says of the other woman anchored in the warm tropical water of his future. Cricket's 42 feet and cold today.

"Double D's anchored in SIX THOUSAND FEET OF WATER," he says, his passion growing, going on about how it will be a challenge, because the Double D's captain has had three fish—"OF SOME SORT"—hooked which went all the way and are still going, all their line is still going.

"Now, what did he hook? He don't know this. The Megamouth, which is your new strange shark they found in the last 20 years, was down in the Hawaiian Islands someplace. Aha, what do we have here?" says Mundus, a mystery solved by deduction like his hero, Sherlock Holmes, might have done.

"The funny part about it is," he continues, "if you think a minute, there's nobody that's been able to fish deep because nobody was ever anchored."

"They found just pieces of one Megamouth, right? They never did find a whole fish?" asks a spellbound Howard.

"I think they did find one," says Frank. "It was dead. They got it by accident somehow in the deep-deep. But nobody's ever been anchored in the deep. This is the deepest anchored boat in the world, aaaargh?" says Mundus, using his interrogative grunt for emphasis.

I happen to know, but I'm not going to say because I don't want to break the spell Frank is weaving for Howard, that in 1983 the black carcass of the fish scientists dubbed Megamouth was found on a Hawaiian beach. Like other sharks it's prehistoric in design. It also is a denizen of the deepest waters on earth. The massive body is dark and indistinguishable from the deep, but its mouth, which gapes wide as it swims, is lit, the lighted mouth of a black cave, by the strange neon chemistry of deep-water species called bioluminescence or "photo-force."

"Now, what I'd like to do when I've got the ball started, I'd like to get a government grant. They'll say, 'Okay, Frank, what do you need?' "

As he goes on about the thousands of feet of steel cable, the hydraulic braking system, I see he's already there, 6,000 feet down in his mind and looking into the lighted cave surrounded by darkness. I remember reading in *National Geographic* that Megamouth was filmed underwater, alive. It's a filter-feeding plankton-eater with no teeth. Frank may or may not know this, but I take the point he's making to Howard; monsters are still down there. Alimentary my dear Watson.

It's time for breakfast. We're all braced against the violence of the growing seas.

Megamouth is not alone without ivory. Capt. Mundus is bent over the Cricket's single burner, on the floor of the fo'c'sle, cooking, cussing, and gumming a piece of ham. The godfather of *Jaws* is working with only one tooth, a starboard molar. He speaks of the pain of having his lower jaw drilled and tapped for new teeth only two days before. He explains how the dentist planned to make a handrailing for midgets, in his lower jaw, onto which he'd "snap the new teeth like tools— I'm gonna change my name to Frankenstein," says he.

Frank works magic with a single kerosene burner and a pressure cooker; beautiful steamed vegetables, pot roasts that melt in your mouth. His mother taught him to use a pressure pot when he was a young man after he'd signed on to a shrimper for a season. Only after signing did he learn he was to be the cook. Frank says he thinks most women are afraid of pressure cookers.

The wind has picked up considerably. The sky is black, brown, and green, like an old bruise. We're alone. Howard looks beat up with jet lag, culture shock, and mal de mer strumming Wagner on his gut strings.

Before the trip, Frank had described Howard Chong as a big-game hunter. "Ain't we all," he told me in a rare confidential aside. I find Howard to be a friendly man of Hawaiian and Chinese ancestry, retired from the building trade at the age of 47. He tells us he's chairman of the Hawaiian State Republican Committee. Just before he left for Montauk, the state's Republican candidate for governor, Fred Hemmings, called to ask Howard to be his running mate in the upcoming election. I know that name.

I remember Hemmings. He was once a surfing champion known for his ability to switch stance in the tube, the breaking part of a wave. He was immortalized switching stance, hanging 10 toes over the nose of his board—walking on water, for all intents—and generally defying engulfment in the surfing classic "The Endless Summer." This seems appropriate as big green swells break over Cricket's bow. She shudders. The steel cables used for lassoing monsters rattle against her mast.

I met Hemmings years ago, when he was the doorman at Duke Kahanamoku's restaurant in Waikiki. Now I feel sick.

By the afternoon of the first day, everyone on the Cricket is switching stance, but not with a surfer's grace, as dark green waves grow out of the southwest, rolling the stolid charter boat as she sits broadside on Frank's first drift. The catching has begun, small blue sharks, so far.

If Mundus is the master shark fisherman, it's because he is the master of the chum drift, and he is master of the drift because of his whole approach, both commanding and meditative, to the sea. Like a survivor from slower, bygone days, Cricket boasts a mast whose triangular staysail Frank uses to keep Cricket riding perpendicular to her slick. I sense that for Frank, changing those who come fishing with him, fundamentally and forever, is at least as important as catching fish, although he'd call the idea "happy horseshit," his favorite dismissive.

I'm in and out of sleep, swinging on the great Atlantic hammock, gathering bits and pieces from Capt. Mundus's endless slick of stories. Mine are all jumbled together. Maybe it's the waves, or maybe it was my leafing through the East Hampton Star's morgue before the trip.

A fifth shark is shot, Cricket's lever-action 30/30 delivering the coup de grace. I stir for a moment before falling with Cricket from the top of a wave, back into a dream that navigates gingerly past dangerous outcroppings of fact and recalls the passing of a fisherman named Tom Luby and of Frank's last big white shark.

"The end had come
within months for the big white
and the young fisherman.
The insufficient summaries of their
lives I'd written for the
Star have become one story to me.
I'm sure there's a reason that
"Overdose Ends An Odyssey," and
"The Maw They Came To See"
went and got married in the morgue.
I think they had to."

[Russell Drumm]

Chapter

2

MARRIED IN THE MORGUE

THE STAR

OVERDOSE ENDS AN ODYSSEY, DEC. 10, 1987—Tom Luby had just finished back-to-back fishing trips, almost two weeks of cold hard work offshore. He got back to Montauk on the morning of Dec. 1, cleaned up, and collected some back pay. He hired a long black limousine—no ocean waves, a smooth ride — and was driven out of lonely Montauk, through the Christmas-lit Hamptons, down the length of Long Island, passing a place just this side of the East River his captain would later call "that grotesque sea of tombstones" in Queens. It was there the young deckhand from the fishing vessel Deliverance would be buried three days later. □ Mr. Luby was not quite 25 when he was found in his Montauk apartment at 9 a.m. last Thursday, dead from a mixture of cocaine and heroin, police said. He presumably had bought the drugs in the City. The young man was well-liked, smart, and by all accounts, extremely hard working. He made very good money fishing for tilefish on a boat he had been with for more than a year. His friends and family, however, knew about the dark side.

He learned about drugs early. He had discovered a place where he could feel completely safe, according to friends, where he could feel ecstasy. He had the journey well charted, no problem there, he assured those who asked. He had told his mother he hadn't really needed the oxygen the emergency medical team had given him when he overdosed two years before.

The black limo had picked Mr. Luby up at a Montauk dockside bar at 3 a.m., Dec. 1, only a few hours after he'd returned from sea. The limo drove the tired fisherman to his house on Monroe Street and waited for him while he showered and changed his clothes. En route to the City, Mr. Luby made several phone calls. He told the driver he had an appointment on Bond Street in Soho. He spent about 30 minutes there, and then asked the driver to wait for him at a bar in the East Village.

According to the driver, Mr. Luby asked to be taken to 42nd Street and Seventh Avenue. The driver dropped him and waited 30 minutes for him to return. When he did, the limo drove back to Soho, where Mr. Luby remained until 11 p.m. and then to the East Village bar, where he stayed until 1 a.m. Wednesday. The black limo returned him to his Montauk lodging by 3 the same morning. East Hampton Town police have not released what they know of the circumstances directly preceding his death, except to say he apparently died in the early hours of Dec. 3.

THE STAR

THE MAW THEY CAME TO SEE, AUG. 14, 1986—Celebrity

filled the air and even the bobwhites seemed to have changed

their tune, singing GREAT WHITE...GREAT WHITE, the morning

after the monster was hoisted from the darkness of Montauk

Harbor and into the flash of a hundred cameras. □ It had been a

warm summer night and a local crowd grew through word of

mouth at the Montauk Marine Basin. Captain Frank Mundus was

en route from 20 miles offshore where the fish had been caught

near a dead and floating finback whale. The Cricket II was mak-

ing not quite six knots towing what captain Mundus was calling,

over the radio, a possible world record—a fish that would require

a bigger scale than the one the Marine Basin uses to weigh giant

bluefin tuna and, only two weeks before, a 1,174-pound blue mar-

lin. □ At midnight, before the Cricket came into view, her old diesel gave her away in the dark. The curious pushed forward, those up front with toes over the edge of the dock. The Cricket pulled next to a forklift built for boats from which dangled a scale made to weigh scrap metal. Bagpipe music, the captain's favorite, squealed from speakers aboard the Cricket.

The giant fish was raised by a tail-rope briefly and the needle on the scrap-metal scale rushed past 1,000 pounds. The crowd chanted the number, then 2,000, then three, but the shark's tail began to break under the weight of its body, thick as an old elm. The fish was lowered back under water short of its true weight and with its razor-sharp, bear-trap of a mouth, the maw all had come to see, still hidden beneath the dark waters.

One hour later, after a line with another purchase snapped under the strain, two men dove under the white—there were gasps—to position a cargo net for the final lift. By that time, small boats had closed in on the scene and the jaws-hungry crowd had taken over docks across from the marine basin. Up from the deep it came, danger incarnate, but now seeming to huddle in the yellow polypropylene net, as though afraid of the crowd squealing at the sight of its mortified grin.

His body was discovered at his Montauk apartment about 9 a.m. that morning, and police said a syringe "and other items that may be considered drug paraphernalia," were found at the scene. Fresh needle tracks were evident as well, it was reported.

On Sunday morning the fisherman's mother, father, and sister drove from the Bronx to the home of Dave Krusa, captain of the Deliverance, to pick up their son's belongings. Captain Krusa and friends had packed everything away the day before and moved them to the Krusa garage.

George and Eva Luby, Tom Luby's parents, Susan, his sister, and his girlfriend, were made comfortable around the breakfast table. Stephanie Krusa, the captain's wife, warmed the coffee and passed around the doughnuts. For a few minutes there was a desperate silence, and then captain Krusa, who said he had struggled with a sense of helplessness since his mate's death, broke the ice.

He told of exhausting days at sea filled with the monotonous bating of longline hooks, and the fatigue from endless retrieving of tilefish from the deep. He said it created special bonds among the crew. Fantasies that became theater on the backdeck were shared, deep fears revealed, and those with a sense of humor became worth their weight in gold. In this last respect, "Luby," as Tom was known, was invaluable and would be sorely missed. Captain Krusa shared with the family a moment on the backdeck that was pure Luby, he said, a moment that for him was "stuck in time."

Music piped on deck is perhaps the first defense against boredom on many fishing boats. Captain Krusa had thrown a rock-and-roll tape overboard and replaced it with some Beethoven that seemed to define the isolation of a small fishing boat 100 miles at sea.

"It was blowing hard. Tom did a ballet on the backdeck in a 40-knot wind," captain Krusa said, adding that Mr. Luby often seemed to synchronize his movements unconsciously with the rolling deck, to get into the whole rhythm of the job so that work itself became a kind of ballet. "He would get the moves down, even carrying a basket of fish, and turn it into poetry. He was very positive, but obviously..." The fisherman paused, looking for words.

The following day, crowds chummed up by news reports of the 3,450-pound behemoth circled around its warming carcass with cameras and kids.

Wes Pratt, a biologist from the National Marine Fisheries Service Laboratory in Narragansett, R.I., said it was probably only coincidence when, just after the animal's cantaloupe-sized heart was removed during dissection on Friday, a vicious squall from the northwest broke windows and spit lightning and hail.

News of the white shark had reached Mr. Pratt in the White Mountains of New Hampshire where he was camping on holiday. He made it to Montauk by hiring a small airplane, sparing no expense for a chance to examine the largest white shark to have been caught in the North Atlantic since Captain Mundus landed a 4,500 pound beast in 1964.

Over the roar of a vengeful squall, Mr. Pratt yelled, "763 pounds," the weight of the shark's liver, probably another world record. The livers of sharks tend to make up nearly one-third of their total weight. In a bucket, Mr. Pratt had his 105th backbone sample, a section of about a dozen vertebrae. The vertebrae contain rings, not unlike the annual rings in trees, from which the shark's age can be deduced. Last week's white was between 30 and 35 years old, Mr. Pratt reckoned. The scientist was looking for clues to how big white sharks might grow, how fast they grow and how old they get. He said there was more to know about the animal's sexuality, remnants of which were also contained in his buckets.

Mr. Pratt said the shark's stomach had been inverted; rumor had the stomach and its contents missing because of an explosive charge the shark had been fed. However, Mr. Pratt said, sharks commonly vented their stomachs when stressed. He said he had found a large and unfamiliar copepod, a type of parasite, in the shark's mouth that he would take to a colleague who specialized in such things.

There was skepticism in Montauk that the giant white shark had been "caught by the book" as both Don Braddick, the angler, and captain Mundus reported. How could such a monster have been taken on 150-pound test line with a relatively small hook through the lip, not in the jaw? And, the animal was gaffed and not harpooned. Who would want to be on the other end of that gaff? skeptics asked.

Both captain Braddick and captain Mundus insisted emphatically that the fish was fought according to the accepted rules of rod-and-reel sportfishing. The shark was not harpooned, they said, and was fought by one man with the same equipment from start to finish.

Mr. Pratt said he found no evidence of foul play while examining the animal's skin for parasites.

"He obviously had a problem," Mrs. Luby said, jumping to the captain's aid.

The family looked helpless. The man had been dead only four days and there they sat with strangers, clinging to small pieces of a young life, all that was left, barely enough to keep from drowning in grief. The breakfast table had become an oasis, if only for a short time.

Mr. Luby's girlfriend of two years looked out the breakfast-room window and sobbed. His sister, an Army sergeant who would leave for new duty in Germany the next day, kept a fixed stare.

The Deliverance runs two crews and captain Krusa was out fishing when Mr. Luby died. The boat returned immediately when the news was radioed offshore.

Captain Krusa forged ahead. If the memories were not all pretty, they were at least something.

He said the backdeck of the Deliverance often became a mock classroom to "offset the boredom." There was the "famous person" game, and a vocabulary contest, at which Mr. Luby usually excelled.

Speaking of Mr. Luby and his peers in other walks of life, captain Krusa said he knew they experimented with drugs. While Mr. Luby would clean up and return to innocence offshore, there was also a "terrible recidivism," he said.

"I knew that," Mrs. Luby said softly. "He tried very, very hard."

"We were encouraging on the boat."

"I thought it was this place, that Montauk was the scene of the crime," the mother confessed.

"That didn't matter. He had supportive friends. There is something about injecting at an early age. It haunts. It's a disease," captain Krusa said, going on to talk out his stake in the tragedy, the sense of inadequacy, the feeling that he might have saved the young man.

Tom Luby's mother remarked about how warm the sun was, pouring through the Krusa's breakfast window, and everyone agreed. She said her son talked about the tension that would build before a five-day fishing trip, saying the trip itself was fine, but getting ready mentally beforehand and winding down afterward seemed hard.

And there was a cycle, captain Krusa said, in those with drug and alcohol problems. At the beginning of a trip, everything was okay. Then, after days at sea they would talk about being beyond drugs, followed by a shoreside binge. "I will never do that again," Tom Luby would tell him, captain Krusa said, usually on the fifth day of a hard, yet purifying fishing trip.

According to captain Braddick, the catch had not been easy. He had found the dead whale while tuna fishing on the Fish On with a charter party. When he saw the Cricket II he alerted captain Mundus. Then he returned his charter party to Montauk. Captain Mundus's party, whose day of fishing was over, caught a ride with another boat. When the Fish On returned, the two captains and their mates got down to business. They first saw the shark they came to call, "Big Guy," at 1:30 a.m. on Tuesday and then periodically for the next 30 hours. Another white was hooked at 7 a.m. Wednesday but bit through the wire leader after a brief fight.

Big Guy was hooked at 4 p.m. on Wednesday and during the two hour battle, "he took off at first, came up several times, and rolled around," captain Braddick said. Capt. Mundus said this week that pieces of the fishing line used in the fight with the white shark were sent to International Game Fish Association headquarters in Florida. But, he added, inspection of the tackle was the least of it. He said the IGFA was very active in Australia where the previous record white shark was caught, and there would be interviews and a drawn-out process.

"Australia's gonna fight it," captain Mundus said. "They lost their biggest mako to me, now the white shark, their two best fish."

It was getting late, and captain Krusa took the family offshore again. Tom Luby had come aboard the Deliverance like all neo-phytes, as a "tilette" the lowest tilefish fisherman on the totem pole. He had advanced rapidly to the more experienced "Nova," and final-ly after a particularly hard trip during which the Deliverance landed 18,000 pounds working only three-handed in gale winds in Late February, Mr. Luby became a "Super Nova" in captain Krusa's eyes.

The fisherman looked around the table as if to see whether the people understood that what might seem to be silliness offshore, wasn't really. It was a way to get through something hard, and their son had been good at it.

There was an old Cadillac with an expensive sound system in it, captain Krusa said, getting to the business of his former mate's pos-sessions. Everyone laughed and cried at the thought of a beat-up car with state-of-the-art sound, and the dead man's collection of Beethoven and Haydn tapes.

For a time before the shark took the bait, captains Mundus and Braddick climbed atop the whale as sharks of different sizes fed on its blubber.

He was a philosopher in his own right, and a comedian in high demand. "I never worried when he was on watch," captain Krusa told those at the table.

Capt. Braddick said Mundus fed the big white shark cookies, "and

I fed it pieces of melon right out of my hand."

Mrs. Luby cried as the inventory of all that was left of her son was thought through. "He sent me a card once. It said, " 'Sometimes even a macho man needs his ma.' "

"Sometimes even a
macho man needs his maw."

[TOM LUBY]

Chapter

3

P A N I C   V I E W

ALL THIS CAME BACK TO HAUNT ME last week. It was the day I began

my slide here to the pitching deck of the Cricket. June 30, it was: □

The red-haired girl who sold time-sharing for a local resort, actually

collaring tourists on the street with her pitch, had come up into the

newspaper office where I work to borrow a pen. I got to arguing with

her about the concept of time-sharing—that is, paying for a certain

block of time at an oceanside apartment to which you repair each

year, instead of buying the real estate itself. She was new in town,

another of Long Island's west-to-east migrators who'd found

Montauk like a scared cat finds a tree. □ I'd started out kidding

because she was a lovely-looking girl with long legs, but finally I told

her I thought the whole concept of time-sharing was just this side of

a con job. I said the little flourish upon the old concept of renting—

that is, renting the same place for the same two weeks in perpetuity—was symptomatic of a certain kind of panic. The willingness of people to buy into it, despite its silliness, was indicative of a trend. I said this and more; about how shopping malls had reached critical mass and were spewing stupid gas like volcanos, how they were forming an invisible archipelago across the land. It was too much, I fear. She was so lovely and my desire was just the opposite of offending her. But I did.

She yelled back at me on her way out the door, beautifully mad, red hair blazing, saying, "So what. It's a living. I've got the time, ha, ha [she meant shares of time for sale], if you've got the money."

Sure enough, the paper's secretary downstairs asked me later what the girl had been raving about. I feared she'd heard the words, "I've got the time," etc., and I said, "What girl?" and explained it with a lie; something about a drunken fisherman friend describing in falsetto how a working girl in Gloucester had offered her services.

I think the lie, which oozed out, I guess, because I'm married, set the stage. It made it easier to accept what soon was to follow, the way you might accept the company of a friendly dog or dementia on a long stretch of beach.

After the time-sharess left in a huff, I was sitting alone in my office. The *Star's* eastern bureau, as I like to think of the weekly paper's Montauk office, is only 14 miles from the action—if you can call it that—in central East Hampton. In winter, Montauk, the last hamlet on Long Island, has the feel of an outpost, but not now. Now, in summer, the streets are awash in a tide of tourists. It gives you a creepy, resentful feeling, like what zoo animals must feel.

The waterfront is my beat at the *Star*, and I was thinking about the year just past, important things, things to write the world should know about, when the phone rang.

"Star," I answered.

"I want to place an ad."

"A classified?" I asked.

"Year-round rental."

"Okay, go ahead."

"Two brooms, two bats, and kit on ocean panic view."

"I'm sorry. I don't understand," I said.

She repeated her ad slowly, sounding annoyed.

"Two bedrooms, two baths, and a kitchen, on the ocean, with a panoramic view."

"Oh, you don't have to abbreviate," I tried to explain. "We charge by the word, 60 cents a word, not by the space. There's no need to PANIC," I quipped, trying to brighten the dim transaction. "You may have the ORAM at no extra charge."

"What ORAM, I didn't say ORAM, and I'm not panicking."

"No, no," I said. "I was making a joke. I mean the letters 'O', 'R', 'A', 'M' in panoramic; you get them at no extra charge. You don't have to say 'panic.'"

There was a deafening silence while this sank in, and then: "Oh, okay, then: two bedrooms, two baths, and kitchen, on ocean, panoramic view—ah, which is better, 'scenic' or 'panoramic'?"

"They both cost 60 cents," I said. "It's up to you."

"Okay, wait a minute. HARRY, should we say 'scenic' or 'panoramic'?"

"Scenic," shouted her co-author from a room away. "It's shorter."

"They cost the same," she shouted back at him.

"How could they be the same?" he said. One has more letters. 'SCENIC,' let's see, that's one, two, three ..."

I was left hanging while the creative juices slopped around on the other end of the phone. I feared such times. It's when I begin to doubt my sword of objectivity, my buckler of optimism. I was holding on, forced to eavesdrop on the most pointless argument imaginable and staring at the picture on the wall of Tom Luby standing on the backdeck of the Deliverance, the photo we used for his obituary when something like bagpipes began to drone— first softly, as though from distant, green rolling hills like the waves passing under Cricket today, then growing louder with drums beating:

PANIC

   PANIC

      PANORAMIC—which was when I must have dozed and Luby seemed to appear, looking as he might have looked had he lived. Age had puffed him out, strong drink the puffer. Red, wispy whiskers couldn't obscure his still handsome features.

A greasy baseball cap covered his strawberry hair, rusting gray. Brand-new jeans, with the tags still on, and different-colored socks revealed the constantly distracted mind of a fishing captain shoreside. There he stood, in my dream state waving the "Overdose Ends An Odyssey" story like a broadsheet battle ensign. A missing tooth made him whistle (phone static, in retrospect) as he complained about his own obituary.

"You call this news? This ain't news. It's sentimental shit that stops before the news starts. I sure knew what to buy with the fruits of the sea, didn't I? What a bargain. Millions of years of evolution it took to populate the ocean floor with yellow-spotted tilefish, and I sold my share for 12 hours of deeeeevolution and my corpse. There's a symmetry there, don't you think? Congratulations. Don't it ever occur to you bastards to describe the face of Armageddon? Can't you see the design here, or don't it sell papers?"

"You want news? I'll give you news." He spoke slowly now, deliberately. He rolled his eyes upwards toward a vision. Here's the scoop:

"Babylon Valley's gonna rear up into a giant wave and suck up all this crap: the March of Queens, the titsy cud-chewing mall chicks and their secret sssssssssssprays..."

"It'll be a big green wave, a perfect left-hander, the kind Duke

Kahanamoku would appreciate. It'll tear up the beach like a 100-year nor'easter, purging the time-sharing maggots from the only place of discovery left. Up into the mother tube goes Captain Hader and his little boxes of unsanctified ashes, up go the islands of sewage sludge, all the phony fishing trips by all the phony fishermen, the instant Ahabs and mini-Munduses .... "

"Shhhh," I must have said aloud.

"Whaddaya mean, 'shhhhhh,'" said she who was placing the ad. "Keep your shirt on. We'll be right with you..."

"... including you and your newspaper that ain't worth fishwrap, and including me," continued the ghost of the overdose.

I guess I'd sensed his presence before. But now I knew it was the dead deckhand, among others, behind my fits of gloom, which have been triggered, and with increasing frequency, by a birth announcement, an obituary of man or fish, a press release from the Lions Club, or an interminable classified like this one.

It was as if Luby and the rest of the obits could keep still no longer. Putting up with complaints is part of a reporter's job. You can't please everyone, so a certain amount of harrassment comes with the territory, but this took the cake.

"Extra, extra, read all about it," hailed the doppelganger in my dream state. "One extra letter, the 'w'; and you woulda got my story right. You forgot the W; 'Sometimes even a macho man needs his MAW' is what I meant. 'MAW'— as in hungry, smiling finality. That's what I needed, not MA, although I loved her dearly. You forgot the 'W' and for want of a nail, a horse was lost. There's a whole world between 'mother' and 'maw.'"

"They're just different letters. It's only a word," I pleaded aloud.

"It may be only a word to you, but I'm paying for it, ain't I?" said the would-be landlady, snapping me from my reverie.

"We'll use 'panoramic.' It's the same price as 'scenic', right? Do you think it's a better word?"

"See you later," said Luby, fading back into his picture. "Just different letters, you say?! Only words?! I think you know better than that, but I'll let you go. I see you've got important stuff to do— why don't you get a real job? Who was the redhead? I liked her style."

"Do you have a water view?" I asked Mary Shelley of the classified ad.

"We did," she said, "until someone built in front of us. You can still see the ocean from the bathroom."

"Say 'scenic,'" I advised, and left the office for a drink.

That night the day flooded back like a strong tide. There was logic to this Tom Luby business, something forming — or was it approaching—but I couldn't quite make it out. He was right, of course: there was more to it than stringing letters into words, although I realized this is what newspapering had become to me. I'd forgotten the marrow, had left out the double-you—the other-me, in my case. I was coming apart. It felt like I was treading water.

I tossed and turned in bed, angry at my job, so "cussed," as Frank Mundus would say, boring, tedious and all-consuming, that I felt like a tourist just visiting my one and only, flash-in-the-cosmic-pan, life. Meanwhile, Mundus had fed a monster white shark cookies, by God, from the bloated island of a dead whale—poetry.

There were mountains to climb, but I never would, faraway places with old romantic hotels I would never wake a wild lover in. I was a tourist for life and all I could look forward to was taking my wife and kids to see Mickey at Disney World, and, if I was good, a trip to Hawaii to watch the plastic hula shows.

Slowly, I'd lowered my sights like the rest of the wretches in this overpopulated world. As Frank put it once in his high-pitched Brooklynese:

"Nothin' on this oyth is increasin'. There ain't as many fish, but there ain't as many of a lot of things, like pheasants, or buffaloes. Even the brontosauruses that used to hang out on the front lawn got scarce after I quit drinkin'. The only thing there's more of is humans, and some of dem ain't human."

I'd caught myself marveling at unnatural wonders like city planning and traffic control. In newspapers and on tv the stories were draped in yellow ribbons of paralyzing sentiment and purple hearts of self pity. Weeds had overgrown ideas in our revolution, trivializing the pursuit of happiness. "MICKEY, STOP," I shouted in my sleep that night, my wife told me.

In the nightmare, the Long Island Expressway became a smooth-running, peristaltic, scarlet-brick road, beckoning, jaws gaping wide, like Frank says of the great white shark, "so all you can see looking down is a ring of teeth and daylight from his opened gill plates."

I tried to wriggle free, but Mickey Mouse had me in his clutches, millions of Mickeys, all with huge teeth and no pants on. "No, no," I screamed. "I'm not a tourist. I'm not a tourist."

I woke from the nightmare angry and muttering: "When in the course of human events it becomes necessary..." over and over, until hours later in the dawn's early light, I booked this Fourth of July trip with Captain Mundus and prayed, the blood would be red, the sharks would be white, and the sky would be blue forever and ever.

"Out here you can see
elephants walking in the mud
if you want, but when it goes down,
you'll know it's goin' down."

[FRANK MUNDUS]

Chapter

4

H O M O L E M M U S

CALL ME ISHMAEL IF YOU WANT, but in the year of Frank Mundus's

retirement, on the night of July 2, 1990, having kissed my wife and

young daughter goodbye, I gathered my troubled thoughts and

stepped aboard the Cricket for one of the five-day trips Frank calls

"double overnighters." □ Now I'm here, newspapering, allegedly. The

sky is black. The sea's deep green paws toss Cricket like a giant jade

cat at play. □ The trip is to be one of the last for the Monster Man after

40 years at sea—a good opportunity, I told my boss, for a feature

story. But now, during the half-awake, surreal states one slips into

after only a few hours offshore, I'm beginning to see things in a

whole new light, thanks to Captain Mundus and Luby, my stowaway

companion. □ You see, Frank's stories about the Dumping Grounds

are true. Equally certain, I see now, is the bifurcating effect one decade of reporting on fishy things has had. That is, I've become of two minds about Montauk, a small fishing village named for an extinct tribe of Indians—Frank's home port.

Is it so strange the dead deckhand should help me tell Frank's stories with slightly forked tongue, he on one fork, I on the other, to make the tune ring truer?

If Mundus knew what I'm thinking, he'd call it "happy horseshit," his name for conceits of any kind. But I think I'm safe because they say he can't read. He won't be able to decipher these notes. On the other hand, he's looking at me now like he's having no trouble reading my mind.

So what if he does. Frank himself put wings on the Cricket, special catwalks that fold down on either side, extending 12 feet port and starboard to bait sharks, but also to give photographers the omniscient view of man and beasts in battle. He calls them side pulpits; happy horseshit, if you want to get technical.

I figure he'll forgive me my dead deckhand. He's got a few of his own. Not that I could shake Luby if I tried.

You see, the kid was cocksure. He was good-looking, with a strong appetite for women, and they for him. He made good money. Despite this, and despite having danced to Beethoven on the high seas, he died by his own hand. It seems I've agreed to resurrect him by mine so he can help tell about how it's the sea that's calling us home and away from something terrible.

We eat our lunch with one hand for the boat and one for our plates. Frank's launched into the story of Charles Banks. It occurs to me as the story spreads out before us like the chum slick, that Mr. Banks, Bonnie and Clyde, and all the others over the years have paid Frank their money for a Pied A Mer, a deck from which to bring back real stories, bloody stories, tales of conquest. They built castles in their minds, fortresses with drawbridges they could raise to keep the hordes back home at a safe distance but looking upwards, the way Mr. Banks had them looking.

"But it wasn't a fire escape Mr. Banks had them looking up at," Frank is saying, "the way they made it look in the *Ripley's Believe It or Not* box on the funny pages of the *Daily News* at the time.

"Mr. Banks was the man who used to own Harlem," Frank explains. "He was this colored gentleman who, when we first started shahk fishin', had this social club, and every decent fish he caught, he'd say, 'Head this thing for Haaaalem.'

"Ripley done an article on him— said 'a dusky shahk caught by Charles Banks of New York City was proudly hung by the amateur fisherman from the roof of his home.'

"He got pissed off when he saw 'amateur.' He was a pro, a BIG GAME HUNTA. He started out with a big blue shahk. That was he first decent fish. It goes in and gets hung up.

"In front of his place he had a steel A-frame with tackle so's he could hoist it right up and it could hang. He took me to his place. Upstairs he had a few girls workin' for him. Downstairs was a complete shootin' gallery, with little tin men on tracks and holes in the ceiling where people missed. The main floor was the bar. He took me upstairs and showed me around. I got about from here to there and looked at the hole that's in the door from a shotgun, and I says, [Frank lowers his voice], 'Mr. Banks, did you get 'im?'

"He says, 'I don't know if I gets him or not. He jumped out the winda.'"

"From a blue shahk, the next one was the dusky. Bigger. Then he wanted a giant tuna. We fished for a couple of years. Now he gets a giant tuna. It was all of 500 pounds, and he borrowed my truck to take it in. I said, 'Mr. Banks, it's August, what are you gonna do with this fish?'

"He says, 'I got a friend's gonna Imbalm him.'" Frank lowers his

his voice conspiratorially and puts the emphasis on *Im* like Mr. Banks pronounced the word.

"So he takes the giant tuna in there to his place, the tail stickin' outa the truck, and hangs him up for three days, THREE DAYS. He brings the truck back.

"Nowwwww," Frank growls, "he fishes with us a week or so later. I say, Mr. Banks— always called him Mr. Banks— we're the only two people in the cockpit, and I say, 'Mr. Banks, whadja do with the giant tuna? I know you had him *Im*balmed. I know you can't eat him.'

"He looks over his right shoulder. He looks over his left shoulder. We're 10 miles offshore outa Montauk and still goin'. Frank lowers his voice again mimicking the social club owner. "We throws him in the river.'"

Frank goes on finding joy in the story, spreading it out as the weather continues to deteriorate.

"The following season, I get these cops on the boat," says he. "They start tellin' war stories: what happened up in their district, did you hear about this madman, that goofball, we finally got him, and how'd you make out with that crook. They get to this colored guy in Harlem who has the giant tuna on the fire escape. I don't say nothin'. I'm just listenin,' and they go on: 'Yeah, the son-of-a-bitch he had the fish embalmed all right, but he couldn't embalm the flies, ah ha ha. We had a bitch of a job, took us three days to finally get us a piece of paper to get him to take that thing down, or he'd still have it up there."

Frank said he finally sprang it on the cops. "Hey," I said, "you know where that giant come from?"

"'Whadya mean where it came from?'

"I said, 'where it was caught.'

"'No,' they said.

"I said, 'Right here.'

"'Right where, in this area?'

"I said, 'No, on this boat. Mr. Banks took it in, in my pickup.' They was rollin' around laughin', Jeez that was funny.

"Then Mr. Banks gets himself a swor-dfish," Frank says. "That's what he called it, a swor-dfish. We was shark fishin'. My hands are payin' out line, 50-pound test, and BANG, the swordfish gives it a swipe under water that knocks my hat off, almost gives me a *boydsnest*. I holler, 'Mr. Banks.!'

"'Mr. Banks, you better come here— hurry up, I'm pretty sure we got a swordfish here.' I'm peelin' the line out to the fish. The line starts goin' out nice and neatly. I says, You ready? Come on. You got your belt on?'

"He looks at me with big round eyes and says, 'Maybe you better play with him fo'while.'

"I says, 'Mr. Banks, it's a swordfish. You come all the way out here, you got the fish.' He says, 'You go ahead.'

"The fish is walkin' away from the boat. I put it in gear and wound up. That was a little Penn 68 reel. The line come tight, and I come back on it, and whooaaaaaa, I turn the fish right around, and he comes right past the transom, just got a glimpse of him. We was around an hour and half on that fish. We got him, 300 and somethin'. Mr. Banks hadda take that in, in the truck."

"Nowwwwww," Frank growls the word out, takes a breath, and plants his feet against the Cricket's roll.

"Mr. Banks starts askin a mess of questions. He was a big game hunta. He didn't want to get messed up with the people with the wrong answers, so he says, "How far offshore did we get him?'

"I says, Ohhh, about 20 miles.'

"He says, 'No, no, that ain't far enough— 40 miles—

what kind a tackle we catch him on?'"

"I says 50-pound test."

"'NO, no, no, 30-pound,' he says.

"'Okay.'

"'How long did it take us?'

"I says, 'About an hour and a half.'

"'Oh no—four hours.'

"Now we're back to the dock. 'How heavy was it?' he says.

"I says 360 pounds.

"'No way: 480.'

"He takes it back in there and hangs it up. Next time out I says to him—actually, to Mr. Bieler. He was a fat guy, as round as what he was tall. I think he was Mr. Banks's bodyguard, the way it looked. 'Mr. Bieler,' I says, 'how'd you make out with your questions and answers?' He says, 'We was doin' pretty good, but he says what killed us was one little old lady.'

"I says, 'What was the question?'

"'She comes up and says, 'Whaz that thing?'" (In Frank's telling, the woman has wonder in her voice.)

"Mr. Bieler says, that's a swore-dfish.'

"Wuz the swor-d made outa?' asks the lady.

"Well, er, that's one a them swor-dfish-type swor-ds,' Mr. Bieler says.

"She went away thinkin' she had the answer," Frank recounts, liking the fact that, all the same, the woman wasn't too sure, the sea remaining a mysterious place. Mr. Banks kept his caché—still the unassailable big game hunter of Harlem.

Swordfish and giant bluefin tuna. I think of how the fisheries for these magnificent animals changed from Mr. Banks's time. Both creatures came to be fished very hard by very different types of humans on migrations of their own. The human and fish migrations crossed, in a sense.

Frank's is the story of swordfish and bluefins, as well as of sharks, about their proximity to the village of extinct Indians. All the big fish called "apex" predators because of their place in the food chain, have visited here throughout time on their northerly migrations from the clear, silky waters of the Caribbean and Gulf of Mexico, where they spread their spawn.

This happens in the winter months, before the constant westerlies and equatorial currents pile enough water against the Americas to spring the mighty Gulf Stream loose. It flows hard northward, carrying its army of preadators with attendant whales, jellies, and the fragrant yellow sargasso. The offspring stay behind in the warm tropical nurseries, each tiny animal left suspended at just the right depth by a single tear-like droplet of oil.

The tear is perhaps the essential purpose of the oil which the refined bluefin is driven north to manufacture from the thousands of pounds of oily, cold-water fish it will consume on a journey guided by stars, magnetic fields, and, of course, by God. The migration is made with nary a contemplation, with no doubt born of decision, no ambivalence — only purpose.

Just south of Long Island, the Stream turns right, before heading past the village of extinct Indians, up into the Canadian Maritimes, and out across the Atlantic. Its warm fingers even warm the fjords of Scandinavia.

But it is off Montauk where the army of predators first meets the walls of food it has come for. For the first time after "running" for a thousand miles—feeding, Frank says, only on plankton gleaned from the ocean as it passes through mouths opened to the oxygen-rich water—that bluefins see what they've come for. With their big stereoscopic eyes, they see, and in unknown ways sense, the mountains of silver-sided mackerel and herring shimmering through the shear, cold shards of disintegrating thermocline. It is summer.

In Mr. Banks's day, the fat of the bluefin—even in late summer, when it marbles the red belly meat like the finest bacon—was yet unmined by the Japanese.

It was long before the bluefins grew "wings," as the fishermen say. Before Happy World, the Reverend Sun Myong Moon's fishing company, and its armada of chanting neophytes fished from Montauk after the fat-marbled air freight. And before other people, knowing their own kind had worked through oceans of whales and mountains of forest, cried with, and for, the oily tears of swordfish and tuna babies.

Mr. Banks's was a far more innocent time, when swordfish sunned, to the benefit of harpooners, in full view of Montauk, and bluefins were sold as cat food.

"Then he wants a blackfish whale," I hear Frank recalling of Mr. Banks. "He was woikin' his way up, bigger and bigger and bigger. 'Let me know when they're there,' he says. 'I'll drop what I'm doin', I'm on my way to Montauk.'"

By the time Charles Banks became a regular on the Cricket, Frank had discovered that white sharks tended migrating whales, especially blackfish, or pilot, whales. Chum made of ground whale became a valuable essence. It was 10 years before whaling would be banned by international agreement.

"So I give him a call. I says, 'Mr. Banks, the blackfish whales are out there, and it looks like good weather tomorrow.' He says, 'I'm on my way.'

"Out we go. We harpoon two whales: one for him, one for me. I give him the smaller one. Mr. Banks goes and rents a U-Haul truck, a square truck. We had a bitch of a job slidin' this thing in. We got it in, head-first, but there was no purchase. We had to push and pull and everything else, but we finally got him in, his nose touchin' but his tail hangin' out. So we close the doors, tie them around the tail.

"'How we gonna get him out?' asks Mr. Banks.

"I says, 'Look, take the truck into the city. Keep the whale inside the truck. I'll be fishin' tomorrow. Take this piece of rope, tie the tail up to the piling there, hitch it to the piling, and just go, and the whale stays.

"He takes it into Harlem and gets his carpenter friend to build steps goin' up, so people climb into the U-Haul truck and walk around the whale, and then down the steps on the other side. All night long people go up and down the steps in front of Mr. Banks's club.

"There was a sign in the corner of the truck says if the truck wasn't clean when brought back there'd be a $3 cleanin' fee. Welllll, that oak bed in the truck, they hadda take wreckin' bars and tear it up and throw it away, cause they had 50 gallons of whale blood in there. No way they was gonna clean that thing.

"Before he left, the driver asks me with big eyes, he says, 'Is dat thing dead?'

"'He's dead,' I says. 'Don't worry.'

"'Sure he's dead? I ain't drivin' that truck if that thing come alive.'

"'He's dead. Go.'

"Mr. Banks tells us later the driver stopped in a diner for coffee. So he pulls in for coffee, and a low branch of a tree scrapes along side of the truck and makes this horrible screechin' noise. He just turns the key off, leaves it in first gear, and jumps. He's not even gonna stop. He lets the truck come to a chuggin' halt by itself.

"He finally makes it in and then brings it back. They drop it right where I said. I come in from fishin', and there it is. Mr. Banks tells me, 'That was easy. I wants another one.'

"I says, 'another one? What are you gonna do with another one?'

"He says, 'I'm gonna drop it on Broadway and 42nd Street. Drop it right there.'

"I says, 'Mr. Banks, do you realize how many fines you're gonna get?'

"He says, 'What I takes outa dis pocket, I puts back in dis pocket.'

"He wanted in the worst way to get another one and drop it, tie it to a phone poll, tie it to a fire hydrant, and drop it on Broadway and 42nd Street. He wanted to do that before he left this planet, but the poor bastid never got around to it. He musta died. With all these fish we'd been bringin' in, and no Mr. Banks? He musta died."

We're still on our first drift, which is to last nearly 20 hours. Our chum slick, a calming blend of oil and slowly descending pieces, spreads westward with the current, away from Cricket's starboard side as the wind and sea grow steadily in the opposite direction— into our faces. The engine is off. The radio is off. The silence is mammoth.

"Drives me cussed bananas," Frank says of the radio chatter that comforts most boaters. "What for? Shut that son-of-a-bitch off." He talks slowly at sea to match the speed of time passing. Sleep comes and goes indistinctly. The sky is martian.

What had Mr. Banks seen on the Cricket that kept him inviolate on the ramparts of his social club, that encouraged him to drop a whale on Broadway and 42nd? Insurgency, for sure, but what kind? Against whom? Frank stares aft.

Affixed to the starboard rail of the Cricket is a wooden box. It measures two feet deep by one foot square across its mouth. A wooden-handled ladle is attached to a thin chain, and rests in the box when not in use. Frank says he's tried other chumming techniques, invented most of them: the chum bucket with holes in it that's thrown over the side and works like a tea bag. The chum bag similarly oozes essence of masticated fish. But Frank came back to the old chum box and ladle.

With the box and ladle, chum can be offered judiciously, at just the right speed—slowly, once every couple of minutes to maintain the slick—faster when sharks that Frank senses are in the neighborhood need encouragement.

This ladling has become an art in Frank's hands, a ritual at the core of his approach. I take my turn at it, and, as people will when faced with monotonous occupations, I attach significance to the boredom, once rhythm and purpose unite. Chumming becomes a gentle ritual for me, like tea, while the waves dwarf the Cricket.

I find myself absently whistling the classic 'here-dog' whistle, a quick octave loop. The Cricket rides mountains of water. I think there must be a similar chum slick drifting aft of New York City today, the sewage sludge dumped at the 106-mile ocean site, churned up by the Gulf Stream's warm eddies and meanders, mixing with the tanning oil slipped from the loins of the millions wading at the water's sharp edge.

Frank says sharks don't care for human smells, not even our blood. This may be, but then again, I won't care for the aroma of boiling shoe leather unless I run out of cows and pigs to eat. "Here, big guy," I whistle, "come and get it."

Wonderful how this sticky brown mulch looks so pretty as soon as it hits the water— oil, the finest kind, immediately silver on the blue sea surface, the pieces like the bone ash from cremains I've seen sown from Captain Hader's Devilfish, clean now and descending, still visible deep down and stirred occasionally by the lascivious cruise of a blue shape. Blue tops, white underneath, God's protection, like Frank says. Here's another scoopful, you big mother. Are you there, waiting far back in the slick, like he says you are, or are these oblations for naught. C'mon, the Hawaiian paid a lot to be here.

Howard's in heaven, methinks, a big white on the way, and I bet a girlfriend waiting back at the Merry Mermaid. I whistle again octave loop, a shape like the shapes the Mayans painted coming out of their figurative mouths on the temple walls, each by itself a whistle in the dark, effective perhaps only in the cumulative. Millions of loop notes—here, boy—their slick rising to the surface, the pieces of meat and bone falling like snow or bone ash. Here, boy, or is it girl, come, girl, have a dollop of ground mackerel puree—awful stuff in the formative. These fish were once alive and metallic blue-green in great schools. Now they're brown shiny liquid, like a cheap suit before it's formed upon a man—here, girl—and then they're pure white and falling—for you, red-headed girl.

Soon the blue sharks come, swimming sensuously around the Cricket and nibbling butterfish. Frank seems happier, as though his dogs have arrived. He stands barefoot in his blue union suit, slowly paying out monofilament with a wire leader and mackerel bait from one of the smaller rods. The bait rigged for the big rod—a whole half a blue shark and two "Jap" hooks—is suspended from a grapefruit-sized ball like a child's bobber, and sits farther back in the slick, where Frank says the big sharks typically wait.

"It ain't gonna mean nothin' when he gets his jaw into it," Frank says of the monster bait should a white shark take it with full force. "It's all a joke. He'll stick his head out of the water and shake it back and forth and go away," he predicts. But he says it like a schoolboy double-daring a girl to stay.

"Howid," Frank says, noticing that Mr. Chong is watching the waves expectantly, imagining the giant bobber going down.

"Howid, you may think it's goin' down. Out here you can see elephants walking in the mud if you want, but when it goes down, you'll know it's goin' down."

Mother Carey's chickens, the little black petrels, do a delicate dance on the slick. Graceful shearwaters ride the updrafts kicked off the faces of growing swells, surfing the air currents like the Hawaiian gubernatorial candidate could only dream of doing. Every half-hour, Howard fights a 100-pound blue shark standing up, a dizzying chore on a pitching deck. There is no sound, but for the wind bowing the crosstree shrouds like a fiddle, until the Cricket's lever-action 30-30 sends another shower of sea water and shark flesh into the air.

Frank stares out at the horizon, over the mountains and valleys that will pass under the Cricket for the next four days. The slick extends over them like a smooth carpet.

His dogs have come. Some hang bleeding from the stern-bits, attracting still more in the same way a steak cooking on a grill calls downwind to us. Frank is in his throne room. His fiddlers are playing in the rigging. He doesn't need his pipe and his bowl because he's chewing Red Man rough-cut tobacco and adding the juice to the slick about every fifth ladle.

Hours pass, all eyes on the grapefruit bobber. The day never changes but is ever-changing. It ends with Frank working wonders with his pressure-cooker below and Howard lassoing blue sharks as they swim by. The sunset behind him looks like an atom bomb exploding over the Big Apple.

I first interviewed Mundus for the East Hampton Star in February of 1986, when he returned to Montauk from Saudi Arabia after a stint as shark-fishing guru to Prince Khalid Bin Sultan, then deputy commander of Saudi Arabian air defense. Later the prince commanded all Saudi Arabian troops during Operation Desert Storm. There were no sharks, no booze, no women, and Frank just missed seeing a public beheading because the authorities couldn't distinguish the Filipino culprit from other Fillipinos in the community of roughnecks—not roughneck enough if they'd found him, I reckoned.

Nevertheless, Frank worked little and was paid well. The one extended fishing trip was to the Gulf of Oman, and Prince Khalid brought along a separate, fancy boat to sleep on. It was stocked with Perrier, had a barbecue grill on the gunwale, a microwave, and a regular oven besides.

"When he takes his uniform off, he's just another guy, but being a prince, he's a little demaaaaanding," Frank said at the time, stretching the word out to let me know the man was a bit difficult, even by his standards.

An oil tanker followed along for their fuel needs. The trip sounded like a new chapter of Life on the Mississippi, killing God's creatures for fun and burning precious fossil fuel like it it's going out of style. I thought later the image was enough to get the vegetarian nazis of hope to launch a final crusade.

As it turned out, they did mount a crusade, not against the heathen Mundus, as you might expect, but to halt the trade in bluefin tuna, which had become the most precious flesh in the world. It seems fish, like every other sentient thing, were beginning to enjoy rights, feelings of disenfranchisement they'd never dreamed of. These included the right to be pursued, not only by bigger fish and hungry people, as they always had, but by happiness.

I've been on the Star's fish beat for eight years. The preponderance of my stories during this time have dealt with declining fish stocks and declining fishermen—at least on the surface.

Ah, the surface—refuge to the gazetteer. But I found, like others before, that stories about fishermen begged for depth beyond a newspaper's capacity to plumb. For one thing, there are many more of them. Fishing got popular among those who didn't do it for a living. In fact, it got popular among those who didn't do it at all.

The pull of fish had become a calling. The memory of fighting a fish, the mere thought of it, became as an appendage to millions, an organ of optimisim, a lung with which to gulp a yard of freedom from under the human-flood of city life, a snorkle above the crowded suburbs. It was as though, with this lung (the very thought of pulling against a fish) a new species was evolving. Tribes formed and bought boats. Females were still necessary for reproduction, although the freeing of themselves from other types of servitude during this time made them appear wild and terrible to their mates, but at the same time delicious, like fish.

Oh, to catch a fish, a modest and reasonable expectation for an individual, an insatiable appetite in a multitude.

It might seem I'm hard on fishermen. It's just that it's they I've come to know. They are not alone in their urge to evolve out of the mess. We are of a time when the satisfaction of our simplest wants has become monstrous when multiplied by our great numbers. It's got us scared silly and running, but with only one place left to go. Simple expectations, like our daily bread, its digestion and innocent voiding, have leveled forests, poisoned seas. The pursuit of happiness will surely sink us, but comfortably. Strange how this greatest theme of an age is all but unheard, unseen, until the stories are compressed — squeeezed like whale meat for their essense.

Cricket rocks rail to rail.

From out of the heap of stories I've written for the paper over the past decade, several rise now with the Cricket's rolling. They've merged like the once-pretty school of fish, now gruel in the monster bucket. Today, as the Cricket rocks as though on a bough about to break, they sound odd, but true, like fragments from my daughter's Mother Goose. I hear within the wind's roar and rattling monster tackle:

Once upon a time, as the polar ice caps melted from too much hair spray, a curtain of sewage sludge stopped the bluefin tuna in their migratory tracks and interrupted the flow of sushi to Japan.

Learned people sought to make bricks from the ash of incinerated sewage sludge and use them to build islands in the sea. They even set about to count the number of fish it contained.

During the same time, striped bass and tuna, once only fish, invaded the shallows of politicians like militant grunions yearning to be free.

A charter-fishing undertaker, while sprinkling our departed on the sea as a sideline, helped thousands of swordfish to survive.

No one knew where the white sharks came from that Captain Mundus was catching, but they loved it when he fed them cookies from the back of a whale. They wanted to do the same thing happily ever after.

I see a quickening in the midst of these stories. Unless it's my imagination, We're seeing the dawning of Homo lemmus, the human lemming? Frank is laughing to himself as he pays out the terminal gear from the big rig he's just rebaited.

"A tisket, a tasket," he's singing. I'll call us Homo lemmus, but what's in a name? Mundus has known us, and affectionately, as a special kind of "idiot," for a long time now.

"And the Lord God
of hosts is he that toucheth the land,
and it shall melt, and all
that dwell therein shall mourn;
and it shall rise up wholly like a flood,
and shall be drowned, as by
the flood of Egypt."

[JOB]

Chapter

5

T H E
N E W   Y O R K
B I G H T

THERE IS A BABYLON VALLEY, you understand. It lies just off the Continental Shelf, a nibble beyond the New York Bight, 100 miles southeast of New York City, not far from here. □ Where Frank began his fishing career, in southern New Jersey, the Shelf extends 50 miles from the coast. From there, the whole 50-mile wide plateau sweeps in an arc that parallels the shoreline, turning to the east with Long Island, then angling downward in a long, gradual slope, past where we fish today, to the ocean floor. □ The mouth of the Hudson River, (New York Harbor), gapes wide at the apex of the arcing shelf. From the mouth, the Hudson's prehistoric valleys fan out over the shelf like deep-penetrating tendrils, toward Cape May to the south and toward Montauk to the northeast. The entire succulance is known as the New York Bight. □ It's near the mighty Hudson Canyon, the submarine extension of the Hudson River, which, despite its being 3,000 feet beneath the sea, continues to accept and steer the river's abundance of sweet water and nutrients as they cascade off into the depths.

The Valley was born 10,000 years ago, when water loosed from melting glaciers fell in torrents, scouring its downward path to the sea.

There are other river canyons radiating from the feeder Hudson Gorge, all scribed by rivers unnamed when the East Coast's largest estuary voided the ice of eons. It fell in magnificent torrents, first from the continental land mass, then moving across a shallow continental shelf. The shelf itself rose as it was freed from the weight of the glacier. The rising sea kept pace as the glacier melted, adding its water to a sea that was 350 feet lower than it is today. Water from the glacier's melt forged a wide valley called the Hudson Channel, then moved out onto the shelf itself, and finally off the edge to the ancient sea.

As the glacier retreated and the ocean basin filled, the deepening submarine canyons ran with sweet water, pushing rich river silt and minerals into the water column, feeding plankton, feeding small fish, feeding bigger fish, feeding biggest.

This was not the rain of 40 days and 40 nights, but the suspended life of thousands of cold, seasonless days, freed by the hot breath of a benificent sun. The flood was terrible in its magnitude, nonetheless.

The rivers continued to run through the rising and warming sea past islands long gone and keys populated by birds and seals. As the years passed, the still shallow shelf was rich in whales and fish. It was here on the fertile continental shelf that minerals and salts born by the rivers, met and fed every outrageous manner of saltwater life.

Here the prehistoric lived side-by-side with newly adapted creatures, this because the evolutionary throes of sea beasts were, and continue to be, more forgiving than those of extinction-prone land creatures. Perhaps it was on the shallow shelf that the now-vestigial legs of cetacians once pulled them through swamps of krill, dense clouds of spawning shrimp and phytoplankton. It might have been here the last pleiosaur was disembowled by *Carcharodon megalodon,* white shark progenitor, never to be seen again.

I think the moon has come closer. Its gravitation has made the earth heavier. This is what killed the dinosaurs. It was their own weight that killed them or encouraged some to take to the sea. Gravity was the biggest monster before the birth of the motor vehicles bureau.

The sea rose, swallowing islands and submerging beasts, as it continued to drink from the glacier.

At the eastern edge of the shelf, Babylon Valley lies deep in the past. It runs northwest to southeast, or, like all of the Bight's submarine canyons, a few compass points off the line of its Hudson source. The valley is only 12 miles long, measuring 1,000 fathoms at its deepest point, 500 fathoms at its landward end.

When you see this Bight on a bathometric chart of the kind offshore fishermen know like the backs of their hands, the "contour lines" showing the incremental rise from the bottom of Babylon Valley look like the steps of a giant zigurrat beginning at 1,000 fathoms, where the red crabs crawl, and rising to New York City's twin towers of Babel.

According to ancient Babylonian myth, it was where freshwater met saltwater that the world was created. The god of freshwater and the goddess of seawater married and had children. Freshwater was killed. Then Marduk, the highest god of Babylon killed the god of saltwater and cut its body in half. From one half, he made the sky, from the other, the earth. From the bones of another murdered god, Marduk made man, a savage killer.

On the lowest step, deep in the valley, the hanging gardens of seaweed wave in the upwelling currents. The upwelling lifts clouds of microscopic food above the temple steps like the smoke of burnt offerings, propitiating first the lesser plankton gods. These are consumed, in turn, by the squids, over which the bigeye, yellowfin, and sharks lord as they swim high, near the surface, backlit by the firmament.

The first step on the zigurrat is a big one, 600 feet, up to the plateau of the continental shelf. Here, the seaward edge of the Shelf, where the Hudson Canyon begins, is horseshoe-shaped, like Niagara Falls. Ten thousand years ago, this place surely was a falls, a huge precipice dropping hundreds of feet to the ocean below. At the top of the Hudson Falls was beach, the Hudson delta beyond.

Fossils dredged from the shelf in recent years prove that mastodons roamed here—*eohippus* too, the prehistoric horse. Indians, more likely than not, watched the falls' misty rainbow in the distance as they set their weirs for striped bass or stalked deer.

The earth's melting glaciers quickly filled the ocean basin. After 5,000 years the Hudson Falls were submerged beneath about as much water as there is today. Over the years, ships with all hands have settled quietly onto the ancient beaches where nameless men and women once embraced and died under the mysterious eye of the moon.

The falls continues to spill, mute now, from the head of Hudson Canyon. Heavy, sweet water from the Hudson River sinks beneath the brine, past the Manhattan village of extinct Indians, across the shelf to a quieter but no less precipitous cascade. The clouds of microscopic land food rise from the bottom of the falls as once did the mist to its prehistoric rainbow. Where birds flew, the smoke of nourishing silt swirls upward to placate the storm of transparent jellies through which turtles soar today, beaks agape.

The rainbows, which the Book of Genesis tells us were God's promise never to flood the world again, have drowned. At each beachhead on its creep toward today, the rising sea assured the land of no ill intent—just another step on the shrine to a new god.

Each day was as a thousand years. Slowly, the rocks were ground to sand. The sun warmed the beach and moved people to make people—each beach a fertile crescent, a miniature rocking reprise of civilization's cradle. What's followed from this has always been the same:

When it's time, when enough of us have convinced the rest that we understand everything, and after we have built our towers of pretense, the sea rises again to hide the evil, but not before a lone man is given the word:

"Tear down thy house, abondon wealth, seek after life, build a boat, an ark of gopher wood. Rooms shalt thou make in the ark and pitch it within and without. Bring up the seeds of all kinds of living things, two of every sort, to keep them alive with thee. They shall be male and female."

Of course Frank's were mostly male and often drunk. And as for the rest of the animals, well, there weren't that many left around that part of New Jersey. It's clear to me now that another magic moment was reached on the full-moon night Frank Mundus decided to have the Cricket II built from hearts of pine. Sharks howled. The sea took another step.

It was none too soon, because at the same time old Tiffany Cockrell, Cricket's builder, was pitching the Cricket within and without down in Virginia, the General Electric Company began dumping tons of polychlorinated biphenyls, PCBs, into the Hudson River. The biphenyls eased past Manhattan for 30 years after that, mixing with sewage sliding onto the shelf over the submarine falls, and into Hudson Canyon, Toms Canyon, and Babylon Valley—drool from the New York Bight.

"If one of dem things
sees you comin', he's just gonna
step aside far enough
so you ain't ever gonna see him,
whatever it is."

[FRANK MUNDUS]

6

NOT THE MOST DANGEROUS PLACE IN THE WORLD

IN THE DAWN'S EARLY LIGHT Frank tells Howard, "I've never seen the weather this bad near the Fourth of July." □ The top of one 12-foot wave breaks just aft. We were blown so far to the east during the night, Frank announces, that we'll wind up on the rocks at Nantucket if we don't abandon the drift and beat back. The beating takes four hours. Cricket creaks and bucks. □ There's news from Paul Smith, one of our two mates who last night shared the midwatch: The grapefruit went deep while we were asleep, he said, coming to the surface again with its double stainless steel wires cut clean. □ Frank examines the wires and says nothing for 10 minutes, then recalls the time a white shark cut a double eighth-inch cable leader off at the hooks. "He left teeth marks like Zorro. He made tourists of us," he says. I laugh too loud, so that everybody turns. □ Both our mates, Paul Smith and Jim

Chester, are licensed captains. Frank lost his papers last year, as the press made sure the whole world knew; saying he couldn't read or write well enough to pass the Coast Guard's written exam. He does well enough to have sparked a romance in letters across the wide Atlantic for a year before he and Jenny were married. But audio tapes proved easier, he admitted, as the correspondence grew.

Frank was unhappy about losing his license, at least at first. He'd planned to keep fishing for a year or two at that point. He knew he understood the Atlantic and its rules better than any paper-sea of words could test.

"It's nice not to have a license," Frank told me last night. "you got nothin' to worry about. A guy walks over to side to take a leak in the middle of the night when you're runnin'. 'Go ahead, fall overboard. I ain't the captain. I ain't got nothin' to worry about'— It just takes that big monkey off your shoulders."

Howard lurches across the deck. He says the travail is more than he expected; it reminds him of an elk-hunting trip on horseback in Colorado. He had a clean shot from behind, an "ass shot," the first day on the road going in. He didn't take it, out of principle, and suffered cold rain and discomfort for days, hoping for another opportunity. It was the cold misery that killed the beast of comfort for him, he said, and made the hunt a success.

Four more hours of ladling into the new drift, and there is no sign of life. Not even the blue dogs come when they're called. The grapefruit's out; the two lighter rigs are close in, with Styrofoam floats.

"It's really funny about them blue *shahks,* Howid," Frank says. The Hawaiian hunter thinks a minute.

"Does that mean there's something else?" he asks. Frank says sometimes blue sharks or a school of mackerel on the surface will open a hole for a big shark to swim through; other times, they scatter.

"And that's why the good Lord made their bellies white, and their tops blue, to help the poor bastids hide. Travelin' fish always look up," Frank says explaining how if you're a fish and your belly matches the white light of the sky, you might live. Or, it occurs to me, if you're a human and could just catch a big shark, lash it to the top of your Buick, and drive it down the Expressway like Frank says many of his customers did, you might survive — basic Darwin.

"They'll scatter when they sense the big one is hungry. They can tell by the way he swims," Frank says. "Like an antelope knows when a lion's hungry," Howard adds knowingly.

"Sometimes, when the big boys show, the little ones got to eat fast, they get friskier. But a few times, I've had a white shark out there," Frank declares, "and didn't know it." No one speaks for a long time. The ladling continues 'round the clock. Dreams and wakeful thoughts unite. Somewhere in between, Frank cooks ham steaks with pineapple slices on top in the Hawaiian's honor.

Dinner is a slam-bang affair. The Cricket rolls, and I trip over the chum-buckets. Frank howls a crazy laugh and fixes me another plate and then sets out on what his grin promises will be another funny but unsettling tale.

"... Now Joe gets this tv show for us. "West 57th Street," it's called. He says to the producers, 'we're gonna need a small boat. He suckers 'em into a small boat, a rubber Zodiac. Now, Teddy, my mate, was never in a small boat to catch a big fish. One guy's got a decent-size blue shark. Teddy said, 'you know, it would be a lot easier catchin' that fish out of the Zodiac.' And when he said that to me, I could see his eyes glisten. He wanted to do it.

"I said, 'Go ahead.' So he runs up to the bow, gets the Zodiac, brings it around. He tells the guy, 'Climb in.' So the guy climbs in and they start away. I said, 'Wait a minute. Teddy, come back here.' So he starts up the motor, puts it in reverse against the pull of the fish, which was easy enough to do.

"He says, 'Whataya want?' I says, 'You gotta take the carbine wicha. You gotta have a straight gaff, you gotta have a tail rope. How the hell you gonna get the fish?' So I hand him the carbine, 'here's the tail rope, here's the straight gaff.' And he says funny words; he says, 'No, I don't wanta take the straight gaff, not with this rubber boat. I might poke a hole in it.'

"I laugh, 'All right you don't want the straight gaff, go ahead.' So he's goin' away. I say, 'Hey, when you're ready for a pick-up, when you want me to come, wave your hat; you ain't got no radio on that thing.'

"So away he goes. We're sittin' there, and I'm watchin' him like a hawk, 'cause I've been there. So I says to the party, Looks like everything's all right, he's got the fish stopped and goin' in coicles.' I look down at my other mate, he's riggin up another bait.

"I says, 'Whoa, whoa, don't put no baits in the water, John, we're not gonna fish.' He says, 'Why. '"Why, 'cause if Teddy waves his hat, I wanta go. Now, I says, 'Get the other 30-30 ready, the backup gun, get it ready to go, get the flag buoy ready to go. I'm gonna mash on the starter, you throw the buoy to mark the slick. All right? Pretty soon you're gonna hear a bang. You're gonna hear: bang, bang, bang. Well come on Teddy, let me see your hat.'

"I mash on the starter and away we go. He's maybe a mile and a half away. I'm lookin' at him. Teddy and the other guy what caught the fish. They're sittin' there when I get close. Half of their boat's sunk, and there's a big blue shark, and he's still hangin' on.

"I holler to the camera crew, I says, Hey, fellas, quick, grab the cameras, hurry up.' We just get there in time. We coast up to them, and there's Teddy and the other guy, sittin' on the high side what had air in it. A Zodiac has two separate pontoons.

"What happened was: they had everything under control; the blue shahk is swimmin' around and around the small boat. Teddy says, 'Okay, now I can get a shot,' and he goes bang, bang. He puts two bullets right in his head, good shots, but he said the blue shark kept right on comin', opened up his mouth, and took a big bite outa that rubber boat. The other guy said, 'Yeah, I thought everything was okay, but then I heard PSSSSSSSSSSSSSSSSSSSSS ...

"The blue shark was still hanging on, wouldn't let go. He was lifted by a tail rope, along with the Zodiac. The rubber had to be torn from the dead shark's jaws."

Frank says he's had no serious accidents on the Cricket other than a few broken limbs and hooked customers. The closest call came when Peter Gimbel, heir to the department store empire, had perfected a shark cage for scuba-diving photographers. Tonight it was Frank's bedtime story.

Frank tells about nearly killing Peter Gimbel as the sun begins to set on this, the second day.

"Peter asked me if blue sharks would hurt him if he went in the water," Frank says. "No one did back then. Now you see it, sure, but who's the first one? 'I'll follow you with the 30-caliber carbine,' I told him. Push the shark by his nose, turn him, push him away. What was that, he'll say, a human? My mother told me about them,'" Frank says, taking the shark's part.

"Each time he dove, he got braver and braver. We did what we're doing now, chumming. When we think we have enough blue sharks, we put the cage in the water. Two guys in the cage. Pete just rolled over the side. We'd turn the cage loose, and, with the carbine, I'd follow the bubbles. One day we counted—it was flat calm—a dozen big-mother blue sharks, six smaller ones in the 100-pound class, four or five brown sharks, one tiger, three or four big duskies 400 to 500 pounds, and three makos in the 300-pound class.

"We'd pulled alongside Lenny Babin [a draggerman] who shoveled on 1,000 pounds of bait. We was pickin' whiting and ling, and with all this excitement, the little guys was runnin' around takin' the food.

Didn't see the makos at first. Peter goes in the water. He's on the surface. Then, all of a sudden, there was a mako in the slick. What can I do? The mako jumped right in the middle of the mess.

"When the cage comes to the top, three blue sharks pop up with it, one coming directly at Pete. He bangs him on the nose, but there's one coming directly at his side that he can't see. Another's at his back, aiming at the tank. I know I got to shoot. I'm hopin' for a double-play. I know I got to shoot over Pete's head, but in front of the shark's nose. The whole thing happens in six seconds. If there'd been a coffee cup on his head, I woulda broken it. He hollers, 'You almost shot me.' In five years doing the cage, nobody ever lost their cool. I was pissed, almost blew Pete's head off. He was pissed. I tell him, 'You're kiddin' about almost bein' shot, I'm not.'"

As Frank finishes the story with shark fins circling, Jim the mate shoots a seagull that was stealing chunks of butterfish from the slick. We're edging toward danger, toward the anti-tourist.

I realize that for Frank, there is safety—at least peace of mind—in dangerous places. People pay to feel this in his presence, like they might pay to feel heat provided by the last of a precious oil.

It was Peter Gimbel who, soon after, planted an unforgettable image that seems to dwell in the captain's mind. Perhaps it was payback for the near miss with the carbine. Surely Mr. Gimbel knew the idea of a giant squid's tentacles reaching out from the guts of a sperm whale to strangle humans would coil obsessively in Frank's imagination.

He told Frank that he'd seen the suction scars on the backs of sperm whales harvested by South African whalers—huge, the size of saucers. He told how the men had devised a special flencing tool, a blade attached to a long line, with which to make the first cut in the whale's belly.

The blade would be swung in ever-greater arcs until it made the first cut from a safe distance. The whalers had learned the hard way that every once in a while, a sperm whale would have recently eaten a giant squid before being harpooned. The diabolical Jonahs, upon seeing daylight by way of the flencing knife, would reach out and take their revenge.

The creatures play on Frank's mind, and just before I leave him alone on watch in the wheel house, he tells me:

"My idea is to try to catch a giant squid. It's never, ever, been done. They come to the surface so anything 200 to 500 feet deep would be where your best chances are. You'd have to rig up a winch, a level wind on it, more than 10,000 feet of cable, 'cause that's your bottom, 10,000 feet. So you'd have to have three times, you'd have to have 30,000 feet of cussed cable on there. You'd have to have a good braking system.

Hydraulics would be your best; you'd work with reverse hydraulics, one against the other. Otherwise you'd burn them out. You'd have different hydraulic pumps, put the two-sixteenth-of-an inch cable on a reel about three foot wide. All hand made. No rod with that pressure. You'd just have to have a rig where you go through a snatch block and then you go through a gallus frame, like the draggers do, so you're clear of the boat."

"They tangle up with the sperm whales all the time, 15, 20-foot, and jet-propelled. They'd give you a run for your money. To a giant squid, a bonito is like a spearing. They come to the surface at night-ime lookin' for these bonito. You're in the Pacific, that's where your giant squid are, that's where your sperm whales are."

"It's serious. An awful lot of thought would have to go into it, 'cause you get this monster up along side a boat, you got these cussed tentacles that's 30 feet long, each one is a foot round. That's no joke. Big trouble. Once you winch him up to the surface he ain't gonna like what's goin' on. He's gonna start eatin' up that boat. Yeah, you'd have to have a lot of fire power. The boat might take it. It's the humans that's gonna get busted up. That's your problem. All's he's gotta do is haul you in with one of the cussed tentacles, goes around you once, that's it, my friend. Squeeze a little bit, and your eye-balls'll pop out 30 yards.

"The deep is the most unexplored part of the world," Frank declares. "There's bound to be other things. You can go down there with all your fancy cameras, your small submarines, and all this kinda happy horseshit. If one of dem things sees you comin', he's just gonna step aside far enough so you ain't even gonna see him, whatever it is."

Maybe they've all just stepped aside, *Tyrannosaurus rex,* the saber-tooth tigers, waiting their turn to be reincarnated. Perhaps some of them have been. Frank is one of those among us who senses a continuing and vengeful presence.

Even the living-room couch in Frank's Montauk house is a dangerous place. It sits beside a small desk from which the slick of public relations schemes has circled the globe. Jenny began to correspond with Frank on the subject of sharks after viewing the movie *Jaws* 23 times, and after making a pilgrimage to the home of Robert Shaw, the actor who played Quint, the irascible Mundus clone. "She knows every move and muscle-flick in the movie," Frank said.

In my mind, she will always be where I spoke to her one day, at her predestined place on Frank's couch, directly beneath the gaping and razor-sharp-teeth-studded jaws of a huge white shark mount.

She talked excitedly about her latest read, *Fatal Voyage,* a book about the sinking in the South Pacific of the battleship Indianapolis by a Japanese submarine. The cruiser had just delivered the atomic bomb to the island of Tinian. A few days later it was dropped on Hiroshima. Much of the crew was devoured by sharks. Jenny noted how the survivors of the Indianapolis reunite every five years, and how in 1975, the reunion coincided with the release of *Jaws.*

Strange how a girl from Manchester, England, who disavowed

meat after seeing her mother kill a chicken, should have been attracted so profoundly by our aging Monster Man. Maybe not so strange.

As I say, I've detected a frenetic preoccupation with the ocean and its waves spreading among us—the price of ocean views a clear example. It's as though having crawled out, lost our gills, adapted feet, and laid our eggs, we've begun the dangerous crawl seaward, except we're not crawling back as much as the sea is creeping up to claim our salt. As a result, there's a hunger to know those who already live in our ancient stomping ground, who speak fluently the language of its waves and who know at least some of the ancient windless tongues from below. The sea—its rules, its creatures, and its monstrous appetites—is in us. It's why some, like Frank, become fishermen—because they love the pull offshore. They re-enact the teasing which, each time the boat leaves port, goes something like; I know I am an escaped part of you. I smell it and love your breathless tongues and chosen children, but you can't have me; you can rock me, but you can't have me, and your not having me with just boards between us makes me laugh at a pitch beyond hearing to landsmen, a high whistle like air escaping, sssssssssssssss.

Frank's father was a chief petty officer on the Langley, America's first aircraft carrier, built shortly after World War I. Frank tells how the old man was standing bow-watch one stormy night near England, long before the days of radar, when a wave licked him from the deck and into the sea. A second wave picked him up and threw him back onto the ship's transom. Frank said when he was growing up, his father would remind him on occasion that "the man who's meant to hang will never die by drowning."

In an upper bunk, my eyes stare sleeplessly, inches from the ceiling of the Cricket's deckhouse, and I recall all at once, so my stomach turns, the meaning of the phrase 'between the devil and the deep blue sea.' The devil was the caulking along the keelsons of old wooden boats. It separated sailors from certain death by drowning. The creaking of Frank's wooden boat in the rolling sea awakes in me the thought that only the Cricket's planking, about the same thickness as the distance between my nose and the ceiling, separates us from ground zero—the source, as far as hundreds of sharks are concerned, of a miles-long slick of delicious putrefaction, the most dangerous place in the world. This is my panic view.

At the same time, there's little question, as I watch him lurch naked from his bunk—the one with a sign on the wall above it, reading, 'This is Frank's bunk, when he wants in, you get out'—to the head, his gold earring reflecting a deck light on this black rolling night, there's little question Frank's inherited the old man's buoyancy.

Suddenly I feel safe enough, despite the Cricket's creaking planks and the oily path of death rolled out in welcome, to sleep. I reach for the time sharess. I want the girl with red hair and long white legs and a way to make money to get away from it all, and I sleep again.

"I was chummin' people
with a twist of a woyd."

[FRANK MUNDUS]

7

F I S H A N G R I - L A

FRANK WAS RIDING HIS MOTORCYCLE WILDLY through the streets of

Point Pleasant, New Jersey, one night, as his father chased after him.

It was the same Harley he and his first wife Janet eloped on in 1946,

and the one he sold in order to put a $500 down payment on his first

fishing boat, the Cricket I. He called it the Cricket because people said

he looked, in profile, like the insect of conscience from *Pinocchio.* In

fact, with sloping forehead and Roman nose, he does, and he beams

now while reciting the cricket's advice, to "take the straight and nar-

row path." As I hear the words and see the chum slick stretching out,

nearly straight, before us, I believe in fate. □ "He woulda kilt me, if

he'd known it was me," Frank says, hugging a cup of instant coffee for

warmth. □ The old man had been "all home, *choych,* and *woyk,*" a

hard-headed kraut who never had to tell his kids to do something twice. He worked as a summer cop in the beachfront community where the Mundus family lived for a time. Frank always likens fishing—planning the right bait, the right rig, location, the myriad subtleties—to robbing a bank. If the fish gets away in the end, he says, "the cops showed up." Wonder if deep down he thinks of fate as an old motorcycle cop trying to make ends meet, rather than the enforcement of some inviolable law.

Frank was born in Long Branch, New Jersey. His father was a steam fitter by trade and ran a gas station with his brothers, Frank and Louis. Not long after his young Frank was born, Anthony Mundus took his family to Bedford-Stuyvesant, Brooklyn. He went for the $2 an hour offered by the coal-fired powerhouses supplying electricity to New York City.

"A lot a good it did him," Frank says regretfully. "He took his whole paycheck and put it on the hospital desk each week."

It's generally assumed that Frank's scarred and slightly withered left arm is the result of a vicious shark attack. Howard asked about the attack.

Actually, he said, it came from crashing on roller skates as a boy and from the osteomyelitis that followed a poorly repaired compound fracture. It's shorter than the right by four inches, the amount of bone removed after 13 separate surgeries.

Anthony Mundus worked overtime, 18 hours a day, to pay to save the arm, "and when the docs couldn't figure it out," one recommended saltwater. It was decided the family should go back to New Jersey to be closer to the sea.

In Brooklyn, the ocean was a hot, hour-long subway ride away, to Brighton Beach and Coney Island. During the summer before his accident at age nine, Frank said, his mother would give him train money to go down to Coney Island with its Steeplechase, the Cyclone, and Parachute Jump the greatest amusement park in the world. Frank says he was in the water from the time he got off the subway until they left for home, "a water rat."

In winter, there was a beach fire at the end of the train ride, marshmallows and chocolate. Frank tells Howard and me about uncle Louie, his mother's brother, a man who died an anonymous death on the Bowery because of an unfaithful wife. Louie took Frank and his own twins to Coney Island every Wednesday night in his Model A. They watched the fireworks and stopped at Nathan's on the way home for hotdogs.

Louie's wife left him after the twins were born. Six years after she left, Frank says, Louie was dumb enough to take her back. He was an electrical engineer, an intelligent man who went to ruin when he caught his wife in bed with another man. On the day of his discovery, Louie ran into the street screaming for someone to come and witness the adultery. When no one came, he disappeared forever.

"For years my mother advertised in the papers, lookin' for him. You couldn't mistake him. He had a crippled left arm," says he, looking at his own, "a definite mark."

After 20 years, a message came from a flophouse in the Bowery, saying the long-lost Louie was sick. The message gave the number of the flop house. He wasn't there when his sister came to help. A letter arrived at home soon after, saying, "I want to be left alone. Don't look for me. Don't send money."

When Frank's parents decided to move back to New Jersey, they could not sell the five-story "brown stoop" his father had bought for a song having supplied the plumbing, because the "coloreds" had begun moving into Bed-Stuy. His mother had run the building as a boarding house and did the same with what became known as the "Canary Cottage" on Ocean Avenue in Point Pleasant.

Frank was never sure where he was going to sleep at Canary Cottage —"where tonight, Mom?"— because the boarders came first.

But his arm got better in the ocean, with just enough scarring to enhance in the minds of men—those who would soon begin escaping in the same basic direction as Uncle Louie, but perhaps not as far—the myth of the Montauk Monster Man.

Frank likes to give the mates the first night of a double-overnighter to sleep. Last night, I guess because I stayed inside the canvas cocoon with him on his watch, he confided this history to me. I got the feeling—even though he was forced to shout over the storm, or perhaps because he had to shout—that some of it had not been hauled up for a while.

He told me his father died under an oxygen tent after suffering a mild heart attack while on the summer-cop duty of his retirement. "See you tomorrow," Frank told him, but the man died in the night. "His lungs couldn't take it," Frank said. "He smoked so heavy."

As he told me this, and I watched his profile in the light of the radar screen, I remembered how, in the original story, Pinocchio's father was swallowed by a shark as he tried to save his naughty wooden son, he loved him so.

Disney watered it down to make it more saleable, making the shark into a whale. Apparently Disney was not the first to sweeten a tale by removing the ocean's most successful carnivore from it. Scholars say it's likely Jonah did his penance in the belly of a great white, presuming the story had its basis in fact. The gullets of even big-toothed whales are too small to accommodate *Homo sapien.*

When the wooden son realized what had happened, he went back to school and was good. Searching for his father, he fell into the sea, and as luck would have it, was swallowed by the same shark. He found Gippetto, his father, deep in the shark's stomach, reading by lamplight, weak, and about to give up. Pinocchio led him out of the sleeping shark's stomach, into the light of its gaping maw. They jumped off into the sea and made it to shore with the help of a tuna

Pinocchio had befriended. Pinocchio became a real boy.

Frank, like every other kid worth his salt, had seen his parent swallowed by life, reading with weakened eyes, about to give up. Few are lucky enough to bring them forth. Most remain wooden. I am wooden.

Frank's mother died much later, alone in a Florida nursing home. It happened during the first winter he had not gone to visit her. He spoke to one of his brothers only once more after his mom's death. Frank, who had migrated to Montauk by this time, blamed his brother for refusing to let their mother stay at his house. He said it was what she wanted to do after surfacing from a 30-day, stroke-induced coma. "I didn't go to her funeral," Frank said, "because I would have killed him."

Years later, Frank was near his brother's home in New Jersey, at a fishing-tackle trade show of the kind attracting the growing number of sportfishing lemmings— the ones Frank says these days "fish for hope instead of meat"— the shows he would come to star in. Even after he announced his intention to sell the Cricket last year, the Mundus magic was still in demand at the trades.

Like the day last winter he says he was tending his papayas at his Hawaiian retirement home and relishing terra firma, if not denta firma. His jaws were in the midst of reconstruction and were throbbing with pain. The phone rang. The voice on the other end summoned the master to Texas, where a sales campaign for a new pistol called the Shark included in its budget $1,000 a day for the Monster Man, plus airfare. "It'll pay for my teeth," Frank reasoned, and besides, the Double D, the fishing platform from which his Hawaiian disciples would have him ply the depths for monsters, had snapped its anchor line and was temporarily beached.

It was at trade shows, sitting behind the card-table exhibit of a tackle manufacturing sponsor, bush hat on, with his left arm withered from a vicious shark attack—an understandable assumption with no purpose served by correction— his sapphire-and-gold-bejeweled white shark tooth on a neck chain, and his steely predator's gaze, where Frank displayed what he calls his idiot magnetism.

If the scene were viewed from the top of the New York Coliseum or the like, the anglers of hope, "the ones who really don't care about the fish, fish is secondary, they just gotta get away," radiated from Frank like the pattern of iron filings on a piece of cardboard with a magnet beneath. The way they fall into lines radiating from the magnetic source.

Frank says he was born an "idiot magnet." The pull was felt far beyond the Coliseum walls, eventually stretching away from Montauk, cross-country— to England happily, in Jenny's case— and around the world.

Frank called his brother from the New Jersey show to make amends, asking only that he apologize for the wrong he had done their mother. Tony wouldn't. Frank told him, "This is the last time you will hear my voice," and it was. Frank says he's not sure how his brother died.

When his other brother, Louis, left the Army in 1945, he and Frank became partners on the first Cricket. Frank says his brother's wife soon declared that Louis would be home at four every day, and Louis said, "Yes, dear." Frank decided to go it alone and had a new boat built.

The Cricket II was built by a Chesapeake bayman named Tiffany Cockrell with the low-decked and beamy design of the oyster dredge boats that worked the giant brackish basin. The Chesapeake once spawned the greatest number of oysters and striped bass on the Atlantic Coast. That was before industry despoiled the bay's seven tributary rivers, killing the spawn of the anadromous striped bass in the process.

Ironically, this put in motion a chain of events which helped set the stage for the human assault on sharks and, as you'll see, prepared the ascent of Frank Mundus.

Old Tiffany had never seen the Atlantic Ocean, and out of his imagination's respect for its trechery, Frank says, the old man built the Cricket four times stronger than he need have.

Her keel was made from a length of yellowleaf pine measuring 10 by 12 inches thick and cut from the heart of the tree. Cockrell told the trucker who brought the wood that if there was a knot anywhere in it, not to bother unloading. There was no knot, and the keel was notched into the Cricket's stem piece and transom. Ribs were placed close together for extra strength, as though old Cockrell had foreseen the thousands of monsters that on a day like this would sashay beneath the Cricket, looking up.

Two-inch oak planking went over the ribs, with another two inches on top of that and half-inch plywood as a skin to which Fiberglas roving and mat were later added. Cockrell chose a Superior four-cylinder diesel to power the Cricket. Frank says Cockrell built the Cricket's pace right into her, and probably into him as well. She was re-powered two times over the years, once with a GM six and again with a big eight-cylinder diesel, but the Cricket delivered her same 10 knots and no more. She was completed in 1946.

In the early days, Frank ran the Cricket out of Brielle, New Jersey as a charter boat, chumming up bluefish for the market on off days. He said he was skeptical, at first when Al Sari showed up on the Brielle docks, telling fishermen about the wonders of Fishangri-la at the end of Long Island, in the old fishing village of Montauk.

Fifteen years earlier, the Long Island Rail Road, in collaboration with the *Daily Mirror,* one of the largest dailies in New York City and already into Montauk real estate, invented a means for hungry anglers to escape the city's diluvial claustrophobia. A train called the "fishermen's special" left Jamaica station at 3:30 a.m. on Fridays, Saturdays, and Sundays. It arrived just after dawn at Fort Pond Bay,

Montauk, the end of the line.

The deep bay is where the H.M.S. Culloden, a British ship of the line, ran aground in a storm during the Revolution. It's where Teddy Roosevelt landed his exhausted and disease-ridden troops after San Juan Hill, where torpedos were tested during World War II, and where, it's rumored, white sharks mate.

Fishermen, desperate to get on a boat, often climbed through coach windows before the train came to a stop.

The "head" boats (called this because anglers were charged individually—per head) they boarded at the "news dock" were converted Navy sub-chasers that now chased bluefish and blackfish, Montauk's staple species for the blue-collar tribe. For the happy, oft'-drunken and always-odiferous trip home, the Rail Road provided a separate baggage car filled with ice for the fishermen's catch.

Fishangri-la came later, a variation on the same theme as the 3:30 special. The enterprise, located just to the east on Fort Pond Bay, included a restaurant and tackle shop built into a hangar where torpedoes were stored by the Navy during the war.

Al Sari, Fishangri-la's dockmaster and promotional Dalai Lama, liked the Cricket because of her size. He guaranteed Frank 100 people per weekend at $5 a head, a lot of money at the time.

Sari was hitting all the ports on the coast, desperate to build a fleet large enough to float the rod-and-reel lemmings who arrived on the Special. By all accounts the arriving fishermen resembled a herd of stampeding buffalo as they rushed the 50 yards to the waiting boats, leaving, Frank recalled, at least one heart-attack victim gasping in their wake.

It was 1947 when he traveled to Montauk's Fishangri-la to talk to the captains, he says, picking up the story for Howard at the point I'd left to crawl into my shallow berth last night.

Frank's cutting the jaws from the blue sharks Howard's caught thus far and dipping them in the bleach bucket. It's the first stage of his wintertime jaw-mounting sideline. Howard Chong braces against the waves in the fighting chair.

"They said, "Pleeeease come to Fishangri-la,'" Frank recalls his voice keening high, "for God's sake, come out, we'll show you where the fish are.'

"It seemed like a fairy tale," he's saying, because charter captains showing other charter captains their fishing spots was unheard of, even then when there were more fish. Nevertheless, in the first week of July, 1951, he fueled the Cricket. He loaded his first wife, Janet, and two-year-old daughter, Bobby, on board. The Cricket was off. Frank set a course northeast for Fishangri-la, never to return.

Things were getting frantic in Montauk. Controlling the ardor of city-stricken men became a task of epic proportions. In August of '51, an overloaded party boat called the Pelican rolled over and sank off Montauk Point. Frank says he blames himself for the Pelican's sinking. He blames himself for obeying Al Sari without question.

"I had him hemmed in at the dock," Frank says of Eddy Carrol, the skipper of the Pelican. He recalls the unfettered fishing passion, the stampede:

"There were 325 guys on the train and they ran to get a boat. I had a counter on the dock and called ahead—'30, 31, 32, and shouted, 'Let go the dock lines.' There were people jumpin', bypassin' me. We had 41. Sari wouldn't let me go. I heard Eddy say, 'No no, I got enough.' It was my fault, him bein' so overcrowded. I did what the dockmaster said."

Both boats fished near the Montauk Lighthouse that day. A storm came fast.

"At 9:30, the wind picked up, and the tide picked up." Frank's referring to how, at the tip of Long Island's south shore, a strong wind can stand an opposing tide up like a wall, like the sea is parting.

Frank idled ahead into the tide. "I just wanted to show the customers—get the ones up on the bow wet," he says—otherwise they would have complained, like they always did when he decided to head home early. The Cricket had engine trouble that day, so, Frank says, he kept her close to the lighthouse, on the bay side. "The Pelican kept going around the point." By the time Frank was ready to go home, the wind and sea were wild. A 12-foot wave struck the Pelican. She rolled over and went down. Fifty fishermen and her captain were lost. Their bodies washed onto the glacial rocks and clean white sands of Montauk for days.

Strange, the transition, but now Frank's telling Howard the shark-fishing craze started as a "joke." I've heard him say this before. But his use of the word is not meant to make light of, or simplify, shark fever. For Mundus, "jokes," I find, are firmly rooted in irony, the perception of which, like a shark's nose for chum or helpless wiggling on the surface, is Frank's strongest suit.

"It was a September full moon, and we was chummin' up bluefish outside the Gas Buoy. We hooked a mako, and it was chaos. I remember the charter blowing the leader off with a 12-gauge shotgun. We finally got one and realized what fun it was. It started as a joke at night, but I couldn't build a business at night time, so even when we had a bottom trip for porgies or sea bass, the chum buckets was out, and people didn't know it. We'd put out a line and chum and catch a mako, and people found out how good they was to eat. It took two or three years for people to start charterin' for shahks, and it happened by the twist of a *woyd*."

Frank stands, feet apart, in the center of Cricket's deck, remembering and still, while the endless procession of waves from the southwest rock Cricket, gunwale to gunwale.

"Had the day off, lookin' for a party at the dock. You couldn't say shark fishin'—we needed a fancy name. Three idiots come walkin' down the dock, and I tell 'em we're goin' MONSTER fishin.' They said okay, like that. They was shark fishin' and didn't know it. It worked. The only thing we caught was sharks. The next time, they said, "Let's go shark fishin'." We'd get back and cut up the steaks, because back then, these guys came out to Montauk for meat. I was chummin' people with the twist of a *woyd*, from sportfishin' to monster fishin'."

Chumming bluefish, a practice he brought from Brielle, was not common in Montauk at the time. Frank discovered the chumming raised more than fish off Montauk. Howard's listening intently to the history.

How, beginning in the '30s and continuing after the war, Montauk's sportfishing fleet was composed of well-heeled private boaters, including the likes of Zane Grey, Ernest Hemingway, Kip Farrington, and their disciples. These sports pioneered rod-and-reel fishing for swordfish, marlin, and bluefin tuna. For them, fighting a shark would have been an unthinkable condescension.

A separate fleet of charter and party boats catered to the blue-collared hordes fishing food-fish: blackfish, cod, seabass, from the bottom, and in the case of the plentiful bluefish and striped bass, from the middle and top of what marine scientists call the water column. Frank saw rivers of working men meeting rivers of striped bass as the fish moved down their spawning estuaries in spring—the Susquehanha, the Hudson—to meet the warm, food-filled influence of the Gulf Stream, the greatest river of all.

If Frank knew as many words as he knows fish he might think it significant that the word "column" is used to describe classic supports, as in Doric, as well as the body of text in a newspaper, as well as ocean water. Perhaps I see significance only because I know more words than fish. Could be there's nothing to read from the shared meanings of words. Frank's looking at me funny. He goes on.

"The chamber of commerce was upset. If they coulda tarred and feathered me, they woulda," says Frank, explaining how the Montauk Chamber of Commerce thought shark fishing would chase away the tourists. The opposite happened, beginning slowly around the docks, like at Bob Gosman's.

"If he sold a case a beer, he would consider himself good, maybe three candy bars. Halliday used to hang there, and Chester. Those was the town drunks. 'Frank,' Bob says, 'every time you bring in one of them sharks, I always go and ice another case a beer.' They couldn't see we was bringin' more people to Montauk than we was chasin' away."

Frank uses what sounds like the royal "we," but I'm sure he means himself and Cricket and their shared past. Forty years is a long time.

"If we didn't put a million dollars in Montauk, this ain't coffee," Mundus shouts.

Actually, it's instant with that greasy Cremora in it, but I take his point. He tells Howard about the jealousy of the other charter captains as he began getting into the sports columns in the New York daily papers and magazines. Life did a two-page spread, and so did an Italian girly mag. The other captains accused him of stealing their charters. He's denying it:

"The silly bastards was givin' me their parties," he says. "They would tell the party, point-blank, quote unquote, 'If you want to catch that shit, then Mundus, he'll take you out. I ain't goin' shark fishin'.' Frank says the other captains saw the shark as a lowly creature, "like goin' snake huntin'. It was a garbage fish to them.'

"The people would come over and tell me what they said. When they climbed on the boat, and they found out they not only catch sharks, but we can catch the same stuff as what the others was doin', they wouldn't bother goin' back, and now I'm the one who stole their party."

Frank says the frenzy grew through word of mouth, and then got into the magazines. "The Italian girly book — I couldn't read it, but I got a lotta mail from Italy," he says with a grin, the kind that rises from the starboard side of his mouth. Life had a two-page spread with the archers in it. Sharks fulla aaaaaarows like a pin cushion. Got finger-waved from all the old biddies for that," says the captain glee-fully, waving a middle finger to the horizon.

Frank started chumming with the twist of a *woyd,* and appetites changed. The guys who once could only scrape a few dollars togeth-er for a head boat began to migrate from Queens and the Bronx onto the Island, to Levittown, and better-paying jobs. More and more could afford the relative luxury of a charter boat. Slowly, at first, sharks became the working man's fish, and a monster— the cerebral niceties about honor between species in mortal combat having mutat-ed to accommodate a street-fighter's requirement for vengence.

But vengence for what? Frank tells of blue sharks nailed high on telephone poles like crucifixions along the route back to New York City or stuffed into phone booths, dumped into the swimming pools of suburbia. Frank has Howard in stitches.

"The archers came out of the woodwork. One of the archers got the bright idea of shootin' a shark with an arrow. 'Ya think we can do it Frank, like they hunt fish? Tie a string on an arrow?' I said sure.

"We drilled a hole in the arrowhead, and then took the leader wire through the hole, twisted it, then gave them 15 foot of leader wire. And you would tease the shark up to the boat with a teaser—a teas-er's nothin but a string with a fish on it, no hook.

"So the shark was right underneath their feet. They would shoot and drive the arrow into the blue shark, and then, when the blue shark would take off, we'd have the leader wire attached to the rod-and-reel, so that his buddy could catch him on rod-and-reel. Now, when he got in close, if he stayed up onto the surface, everybody could shoot loose arrows at him.

"One time we'd lost a blue shark — he'd rolled up in the line, rolled up in the 15-foot leader wire, bit it off, and swam away. Now, about a half an hour later, here comes an arrow up the slick, because he's still got this arrow in his back, and it looked funny 'cause it was kinda wobblin' from the water pressure vibratin' it. But it was three-quarters of the way out of the water. The fish was right on the surface, and there was the arrow stickin' up, didn't bother him any. He came back for more bait.

"This was a fad for a while, it caught on real quick. Everybody was talkin' about it. All the archers was talkin' about it. It was in the archers' magazines. Guys standin' alongside of this blue shark he shot with his bow, his 40-pound pull, whatever it was.

"It was a hard shot because when they pull that long bow back and the fish is right there underneath their feet, it's hard to shoot, because the bow would hit the side of the boat.

"We got this one blue shark what's 200 pounds. His back is two foot wide. I tease him right up. The archer's got two foot of target to hit, and he's three feet away from him with the tip of his arrow. He's standin' there, his knees are knockin'. He's shakin', and I say, 'Shoot.' He lets the arrow go and misses.

"'All right—you ready? okay, here we go again,' and I'd tease that big blue shark in, right there. You could step on his back, put a saddle on him and ride him. And his knees is knockin' again; he shoots again and he misses.

"I take a hold of the leader wire and pull the arrow back. I reach down to the water to grab the arrow, and the blue shark makes a fast U-turn, and he's right there. I make believe I'm gonna hit him, like wid an ice pick. I'm gonna jam it right in him, right there.

"He starts hollerin', 'No, no no, gimme another shot.' The other guy says, 'Joe, what the hell's the matter— how could you possibly miss?' His answer was, he says, 'The reason that I missed, 'cause I'm under such terrific pressure.'

"Terrific pressure? I close my eyes and I see a rhino comin' at him, buddabum, buddabum, buddabum. Now, maybe that's pressure— terrific pressure. Eeeeeeeee," Frank screams with joy.

"What happened with the archers was the fact that the photographer and the writer from *Life* magazine wanted to ride along wid us one time and take some pictures. They did. There was one blue shark. He was a natural, he was, a born actor. He just laid on the surface out there when the guy was fightin him with the rod-and-reel. He musta had 50 arrows in 'im. He was still layin' there. He didn't sink, he didn't do nothin'. We had 11 or 12 archers—that was when I could carry over 6 passengers, up to 20 — the arrows are flyin' at him.

"Well, they printed that picture in *Life* magazine, with a story about shootin' sharks with bow and arrows. *Life* magazine goes all over and then people drag it all over, and send it all over. I heard from Scotland and Ireland, a couple other places where people wrote letters 'cause their relatives was in Montauk, and they said what a horrible thing it was.

"One day we're out fishin', and there's a knock at the door. The wife [Janet] goes to the door, and here's a guy standin' there with a blue uniform with shiny chrome-plated badges. She says, 'What can I do for you?' He says, 'Is captain Mundus home?' She says, 'No, I'm his wife, what can I do for you?' He says, 'Maybe you can answer some questions,' he says. 'I'm from the New York district of the A.S.P.C.A., and we've got so many complaint letters— cruelty to sharks—that I was sent out here special to check up on this.'

"She said, 'He doesn't do it, it's the customers.' He says, 'Oh, that don't make no difference, he's still responsible for what goes on on the boat.' There was a few questions about how many archers does he take out, so on and so forth. How many sharks does he slaughter, all this kind a thing. Then he says, the fatal question was, 'How far off does he do this?' and she said, 'Oh, 15 or 20 miles offshore.' And then he smiled, folded up his pad he was writin' on, and says, 'Well,' he says, 'that's out of our jurisdiction, anyway.' He goes away. 'Well, thank you, ma'am, I found out what I wanted to find out.'"

The *Daily News* runs a story about Frank's wife being visited by the A.S.P.C.A. It runs right before the New York Sport, Travel, and Vacation Show that's held each year at the New York Coliseum, where Frank had a booth.

"They make the A.S.P.C.A. look like a paper bag fulla assholes. The letters to the editor start to come and go. 'He's a no-good bastid.' Another letter, 'No he's not,' 'Yes, he is,' 'No, he's not,' 'Yes, he is,' and I just sit back, laughin'. Got about a week's worth of letters, yes-he-is-no-he-ain't, but better to be talked about this way than not talked about at all.

"Durin' those shows, alotta times, they're four-deep in front of the booth. One guy worms his way through all the people what's in front of the booth, and he says, 'Frank Mundus?' I says, 'Yeah.' He says, 'I gotta shake your hand.' So he puts his hand out, and I shake his hand. He says, I gotta shake your hand because I'm from the A.S.P.C.A.,' and he laughs, and he runs through the crowd like I was gonna chase him. Eeeeeeeeee," Frank giggles in the same octave as the growing wind.

As the years went by, the bluefish populations waxed, but also waned in natural cycles of abundance. Foreign fishing fleets working on rich schools off Montauk and all along the coast were harvesting species that had kept the big predators near shore. For a time, the charter boat meat fishery for striped bass, blackfish, cod, and porgies stayed healthy, but the swordfish which had lured the richer "sporties" were becoming scarce close to shore, where the fleet fished at the time. The years of Montauk tuna fishermen trading vodka and cigarettes for barrels of hook-bait butterfish were over. Finally, even striped bass got scarce from the pollution in the Chesapeake.

Chartermen found themselves stuck between the old pride in gladiatorial tests—artful angler versus the fast and powerful swords and tuna—and their need to make a buck. Mundus appeared like the black knight.

"Soon people were stepping over piles of tuna at the dock—stepping over dem dirty swordfish," Frank says in mock irreverence for the ocean gladiator, "to go pet one brown shark. That's how it started. They'd drive out from New York City just to touch a shark—so we took their money." This was still before Frank discovered the bountiful 40-fathom line farther offshore and the white sharks following behind the pilot whales, and long before Peter Benchley discovered Frank.

In answer to a question Howard put to him an hour ago, Frank says the author of *Jaws* never spoke to him, but never had to.

"He took his scissors and cut out every article ever written about me. The first scene in the book [and movie] came from a 3,000-pound white in just 75 feet of water off the bathing beach in Amagansett. There was something in every scene that happened to us right out there. The 4,500-pound white shark was the ending, when we tried to bait a white and had motor trouble. Everything was there, but there was 10 pounds of fiction in every scene. I hate fiction," he says with a quick, pointed glance at me.

"*Jaws*, it shook the nuts from the trees, and they rolled in my direction. People come down with machetes, slingshots—they just had to kill *shahks*. They went berserk."

"All we've got to remember
is a huge pile of
buffalo skins somewhere."

[DICK STONE]

Chapter

B O N E   C L O U D S

SOMETHING BIG BIT THE BLUE-SHARK BAIT in half during the night. I'm

back on the chum ladle. Frank says we're seeing blue sharks because

it's July. They come in with the Gulf Stream, early, usually in June,

and are often followed hard on by big whites. Howard hopes it's the

case this year. Porbeagles, the winter sharks, have left. They are a

cold-water species which summers off Canada and the Scandinavian

countries. □ In spring, off Montauk, the porbeagles stay relatively

close to shore where the cold coastal water descends oceanward into

the depths like a pane of icy glass. The Gulf Stream, with its warm-

core eddies and meanders, pours in over it from the south and east. □

There is little mixing at first. The diagonally descending wall of cold

protects, for a time, the cold-water fish, the schools of herring, and

cod. They are buffeted from the warm-water predators charging north within their protective stream, searching its warm extended fingers until they're within striking distance of the food they've come for.

The Stream is one of the planetary currents which gets its speed and direction from the rotation of the earth. The prevailing east-to-west trades at the equator pile water against Central American land masses. Ocean waters move by virtue of their differing densities as well as by prevailing weather patterns. The warm and saltier (and thus denser) waters of the equatorial current move into the Gulf of Mexico and the Caribbean Sea, flowing "downhill," as the scientists say, from areas of high atmospheric pressure to areas of lower pressure and lower salinity. In the case of the Gulf Stream, the direction is northward and with a constant push to the west caused by the earth's rotation, the Coriolis Effect.

In spring, the Stream water pours from the Gulf of Mexico, the spawning ground of the bluefin tuna. It moves past the Bahamas, out through the Florida Straits, carrying with it the spawn of a thousand species and the microscopic life that gives the Stream its perfume and distinctive deep-blue hue, a fecund invasion of the colder, emerald-green northwest Atlantic.

By now, July, the Stream has already made a sharp right-hand turn south of Long Island. At the bend, the shards of cold continental shelf water carve giant whirlpools of warm water like a knife peeling an apple, spinning them southwest, in the opposite direction of the Stream.

Depending on the year, these "eddies," which serve as the predators' exploratory cocoons, spin closer or at a greater distance from Montauk. They are many miles across, huge cyclones of water that reach thousands of feet to the tilefish and red crabs on the ocean bottom. As the eddies move southwest, they're visible to satellites in outer space. Today, the infrared view from space is available almost instantaneously to fishing boats with the right electronics. Fishermen have learned that tuna prefer the leading edge of eddies; swordfish, the trailing edge — the eye from outer space telling the greatest predator of all time where he's most likely to find what he's after.

This year the Gulf Stream has "spilled over," as Frank says. Experience, year after year visiting the same fishing spots, has given him the picture others require NASA for. Whether the Gulf Stream is overflowing its cold-water banks, as Frank sees it, or an eddy has moved into the Dumping Ground, as in the moon-view, it amounts to the same thing: the ocean is deep blue and smells like a big, beautiful woman, an angry one today.

The waves are still proffering Cricket skyward and then seaward, as if deciding which should claim her. Shearwaters and gannets soar on invisable cushions. The petrals dance, and Frank's blue dogs circle with my ladling. I sense something (as big as the bright blue hole breaking momentarily through the thinning clouds) is swimming below us unseen, and I ladle another silky portion. I think about a similar ritual at the stern of my friend Warren Hader's Devilfish, the difference being that Warren made about 50 bucks for each of his ladle-sized offerings.

Warren was one of a few charter captains who didn't look down his nose at shark-fishing. Frank took him under his wing for a time after Warren retired from a lifelong career as an undertaker and moved to Montauk.

Frank's gone below to bed.

I'm recalling Warren's Buddha-like belly stretching a clean white t-shirt to bursting. Just last summer, the suspendered protuberance was showing the way from below decks as the charter captain's six-foot-five-inch frame moved by long graceful strides toward the transom of the Devilfish. Along the way he ducked beneath a rack of massive rods and reels used for big sharks and tuna.

He strode onto the backdeck and past a fish-fighting throne

stacked with small white boxes and plastic garbage bags. The latter bulged like his shirt. Each of the 22 boxes bore a name. Richard Goodman's was scribbled in pencil. Martha Wittke's name was spelled out in plastic ID tape. The boxes were all decorated with canceled postage and were addressed to Burials At Sea, Inc.

Captain Hader crouched at the transom, tucking his knees under the stern rail for support, as he would when wielding a gaff. Big hands making the small cardboard casket of one Charles Bligh seem smaller yet, worked patiently at the shipping tape and flaps with a fillet knife retrieved from below.

"There's no rush," he noted with a beneficent smile, while his big methodical hams removed the twist-tie on Mr. Bligh's clear plastic bag.

"There's no rush now," the captain repeated, as the mouth of Mr. Bligh's final containment was made to yawn, first heavenward, then to the sea. I knew about Warren's sideline, which I never figured was my business. I'd jumped on the Devilfish that day only to ask about tuna.

The annual international tuna management meeting was coming up again, and again there was revolution in the air—this time over swordfish as well as bluefin.

It was June, late for Warren to be catching up on the winter's buildup of boxes. Nevertheless, the morning he'd squeezed randomly between fishing trips and extended journeys to cities like Miami and Gloucester on fisheries business was sepulchral.

The waters of Block Island Sound were flat calm, unlike today. The molten facets of its surface reflected silver, graphite, and purple from a high-vaulted sky. There was no discernible horizon, except to the west, where a line of puffy white clouds billowed whiter for the bruise of storms surrounding Montauk's bubble of peaceful high pressure.

Billowing whiter, for what Hader called a "proper burn," was the bone ash of Charles Bligh, descending like a perfect replication of the low clouds to the west. "That's what they should be," the captain said, going on to explain how the retorts in crematoria used gas-fired blowers to bring the temperature up. If the fire's not hot enough, and if bone ash is not sifted properly, the white cremains are mixed with wood ash from the casket, making them gray. The flesh goes up in smoke, said he.

"That's casket," the charter fisherman said, pointing to a patch of dust mixing on the surface with an oil slick from the exhaust of the Devilfish. Beneath the slick, the cloud of Victor W. Cabot billowed bottomward. I asked him if he'd ever seen fish respond to the billowing ash. He smiled and, feigning conspiracy, said, "I'm building my own artificial reef."

We both laughed. Artificial reefs—sunken boats, tires, bricks, and the like, are meant to attract fish for sport fishermen just as they are meant to earn grants for young scientists fending off unemployment. I have, deep down, suspected they are nothing more than an expedient and politically safe way to dispose of human detritus. Artificial reefs had become interesting political formations, which was why Warren and I were sharing a laugh.

Seems we've inherited a time when the dearth of space in which to throw society's waste corresponds with the not-unrelated mass urge to leave the land and go fishing. From a politician's furtive point of view, providing out-of-sight reefs for the pleasure of the voting and fishing herds kills two birds with a single stone, or in this case (with the aid of science) sludge block.

The state university on Long Island, at the time of this writing, remains a safe harbor from which the politician can scientifically justify, with the help of the unquestioning coverage of Long Island's largest daily paper, any manner of tax-saturated projects. One is a plan to create offshore cinderblock atolls from the ash of incinerated garbage and sewage sludge. One day INDUSTRY would be placed out there on the cinder atolls, according to the professor in charge of atoll research and development, presumably so New Yorkers will again roam free across Long Island like caribou.

Seems to me the artificial reef pitch is not unlike selling time-shares. To the recreating public, the word "reef" overshadows the word "artificial" and hints of pink coral, rather than the blacker truth. Instead of car tires worn thin on the Long Island Expressway and dumped into piles below the waves, the mind's eye sees undulating sea fans.

On the frozen decks of party boats in January, out from their slimy clam baits, cigar smoke, and heated hand-railings, the palm trees of delirious escape sway in the wind like hula dancers. Cod and blackfish are caught, hauled from the reef of artificiality proving its fecundity, a good idea, a cornucopia, in the minds of thousands.

The reefs are popular in that they are out-of-sight, unapproachable, infinitely researchable, which means they are something a politician can sink his teeth into without risking epidermus.

Warren babbled happily while he worked. He told me how he bought the Devilfish in 1972 and began chartering out of Montauk in the same year, with Frank's guidance, after retiring from a lifetime in the funeral business. He kept his hand in by moonlighting burials at sea.

As empty boxes began piling on the deck, he told how he worked directly with crematoria — a growing business, he said — and funeral homes.

"I don't want to be bothered with the families. Sometimes they want to come out. This way I can do it at my convenience, and I don't charge too much." He said he sent the families the longitude and latitude, "like a diploma."

Captain Hader was a fisherman who watched the charter business dwindle due to overfishing, as well as to the regulations designed to prevent overfishing. He rose to the political surface of a few fishing organizations on the East End of Long Island and made himself into a civilian fisheries manager, a species peculiar to the United States. The business of managing marine resources is done almost entirely by government decree in other nations. Warren was appointed to the Mid-Atlantic Fishery Management Council, one of eight regional councils in the country.

These were created by Congress in 1976 by the Magnuson Fishery Conservation and Management Act, the so-called 200-mile-limit law. The councils are peopled by federal civil servants and industry representatives, like Warren, of diverse backgrounds. Both the commercial and recreational industries were meant to be represented equally, but they came not to be.

At first I thought of the councils as longhouses built on stilts, two legs in the sea, where council members would come to talk to fishermen about their problems as they returned from a day's fishing. Simple societies would do it this way, because taking fish from the sea is fundamentally a simple industry.

But perhaps because of sea-level rise and the resultant anxiety, the professional resource managers decided to repair the council headquarters to the hills, spiritually speaking. They lost contact.

What I mean is: over population is a relative thing. The more land there is relative to numbers of us, the less restive we are as a species. Threaten us with less land, however, while at the same time we're happily increasing our numbers factorially, and we become nervous and mean on an instinctual level, the way seals do when there are too many of them on a rock. Anxiety over sea-level rise is actually the fear of overpopulation. It takes subtle forms, as Frank knows better than most. Overfishing is a function of too many people—"and some of dem ain't human"—not of too few fish.

In this light, there is nothing funny about high tide, and if I were more enterprising, like those studying artificial reefs, or like Frank, who is seeking a federal grant to help him find monsters off the

Hawaiian Islands, I would propose a study to prove that the general state of anxiety increases as the tide rises, and vice versa. Sadly, making more room by building atolls out of sewage sludge won't keep pace with our procreative urge. It ain't Frank Mundus that's Jacques Cousteau's worst nightmare.

In any case, the councils became increasingly political and unwieldy throughout the decade of the 1980s, with seagoing men given less and less of a role, as though somehow they had become conspiratorial with the sea.

Captain Hader eventually found himself appointed to the International Commission for the Conservation of Atlantic Tunas. ICCAT, as it's called, is an important organization, but one, I found, that functions, in the age of computers and satellites, more like the Catholic Church of the Middle Ages. The U.S. is one of 22 nations, including Cote D'Ivoire, Cyprus, Equatorial Guinea, Trinidad and Tobago, Spain, and the former Soviet Union, that dwell on the smaller, and somehow older, ICCAT globe.

I asked what the scoop on tuna was.

"Abrams is in Tokyo. He's had it up to here with McHugh," Captain Hader said, bringing the edge of a free hand to his eyebrows. By this time I had been pressed into service and was passing along the boxes containing those gone before.

James McHugh, at the time, was the chairman of the Mid-Atlantic Council of high fisheries priests, and an old acquaintance of Frank. For a few years, he had been urging that regulation of bluefin tuna be brought under U.S. fisheries law, while remaining under the aegis of the international commission as well. Until 1991, no species of tuna was managed by the U.S., as a result of pressure brought to bear by West Coast canneries at the time the Magnuson Act was being written.

McHugh, a retired fire-extinguisher salesman, went to bat for the magnificent and heavily-fished bluefins. He saw their extinction being optioned by the grotesquely high price paid in Tokyo for prime sushi meat, by inaction in this country, and by what he felt were political tradeoffs within the international tuna commission.

McHugh was considered naive and heretical by people like Gerry Abrams. Abrams was a tuna buyer and fellow delegate to the international commission. Commercial types like Abrams and even some in the federal fisheries service came to see McHugh as either mesmerized himself, or influenced by those mesmerized, by what was known in government circles as the "Flipper Phenomenon." The affliction was named for the cuddly dolphin star of the television series. Veteran fisheries managers recognized this Flippercosis first by a behavioral aberration; the projection of a mystical innocence, a martyrdom, on the fishes of the sea.

It was the Flipper phenomenon that was responsible, in part, for having slowed the last vestiges of whaling. But beginning in about 1988, the sorrow spread to the lowly fish, a major source of protein to half the world. Thus began a strange and zealous time.

It began in the United States, where, for one thing, fish as food to be hankered after has always been a relatively foreign concept, except on the coasts. A ranking member of the National Marine Fisheries Service once tried to explain the Flipper Phenomenon by theorizing that all peoples live with, in fact need, a shared guilt that defines their culture. Former empires like Spain, Germany, and Japan have a history of conquest, genocide, and conquest-lost to look back upon. For them, fish come guilt-free.

Americans, according to his view, have never lost an empire per se, but spend their regret on the loss of their once-rich natural resources. "All we've got to remember is a huge pile of buffalo skins somewhere" is the way he put it. What he meant, I think, is we've killed more buffalo than Sioux so our guilt naturally flows toward animals.

In any case, Flipperholics appear to be created when ordinary persons catch a glimpse of the huge and growing human appetite and the abatoir of corresponding size, through a crack in their society's homey kitchen door. That is, when they sense there are too many of us. Ultimately they begin bleeding comisery for sacrificed fish, and that's hard to hide, as Mr. McHugh found out. Blood from the stigmata gets on memoranda.

Right now, blood from a bullet hole in a blue shark Howard's just landed washes the deck pink with each roll of the Cricket. Better, I suppose, than the bloodless dust on the deck of the Devilfish. I could hardly hear the shot over the wind in the shrouds. The gunpowder smelled good. Now it's blown away.

As it turned out, McHugh was a prophet of sorts. With little hard evidence, something fisheries science is by its nature shy of, and influenced by those representing the increasingly powerful sportfishing industry, McHugh set about to dismantle the East Coast longline swordfishing fleet. He was frustrated by nearly 10 years of discussion, but no real progress, on swordfish conservation.

In a weak moment—strong to some—McHugh misrepresented, in writing, the position of the Mid-Atlantic Council, saying its members supported a plan cooked up by federal scientists in Florida to cut swordfish production by as many as 30,000 fish.

If adopted, the plan would have put U.S. swordfishermen out of business. Captain Hader realized that if the U.S. took such a unilateral action on swords, a highly migratory fish, it would have resulted in a doubling of efforts by unrestricted foreign fleets to catch them as they migrated out of U.S. waters. Hader and others on the council opposed McHugh on the issue and confronted him with the incriminating document. McHugh resigned his chairmanship.

The defenestration was a watershed event and was accompanied by a minor revolution in the commercial fishing industry. Fishermen whose detractors counted on them to be forever offshore and politically out of touch realized, with Captain Hader's help, how close they, if not the swordfish, had come to commercial extinction.

The worm turned for a time. Market fishermen were able to organize and keep the debate over the fate of the delicious fish the Spanish call *El Emperador,* an international one. But it was a new game, with the environmental community leaping, often before looking, into the fray. The struggle had become one in which, for the first time, it was suggested that swords, other types of tuna, striped bass, even the sharks—that no one caught, let alone ate, when Mundus started monster fishing—would be better off not swallowed. A good concept from the fish's point of view, but, like abstinence of any kind, impractical on a large scale.

One of the top fish feds in the country, who was committed to achieving the conservation of the migratory predators internationally, told me that people like McHugh were too far in front of the power curve with their ideas. That is, relatively few people in the world felt sorry for fish.

Duke Kahanamoku would have understood the power curve, I think, because he understood waves. If you ride waves, especially big ones, you must stay in the hook, the curl, the green room, like the one just breaking aft of Cricket. If not, you lose speed, stall, and eventually eat your lunch, like McHugh.

Captain Hader and others believed the real danger was from the increasingly powerful sporfishing lobbies, who, with the help— sometimes the unknowing help— of groups like Greenpeace and the Audubon Society, were peddling the Flippercotic in order to legislate commercial fishermen out of existence, to make the sea something it had never been to man.

One tuna buyer cynically accused Audubon of shifting its interest from birds to fish, focusing first on the majestic bluefin tuna because "who's gonna send them a check for flounder?" In fact, Audubon's new director of fisheries matters had circulated to other environmental groups his recommendation that in blufin tuna they would find their next "megafauna" worthy of focus. A Flipper with gills, as he put it, that was perhaps not as in need of protection as sharks but would attract more sympathy because the terror of *Jaws* was sure to enjoy a lengthy half-life.

The point is: these giant concepts—what are fish for? and how many are there?—would have seemed totally absurd only a short while before. A deep fear—or is it fear of the deep?—has changed us.

Perhaps on an intuitive level, the tens of thousands in the U.S. who take up the rod-and-reel each year include in their definition of "recreation" the sense that to catch a fish is to play provider, to ignore for short precious moments that they have become domesticated animals who really prefer to eat other domesticated animals or no animals at all. After the fantasy, the fish is freed. Catching and releasing has become an esoteric coitus interruptus for sportsmen who think of themselves as the environmentally pure.

First they followed Frank offshore to the 40-fathom line. Now they've gone beyond the Cricket's range in order, it would appear, to strike a friendly claim there: catching and releasing and making an ostentatious display of harmlessness, just in case the sea rises as high as predicted.

Believing you've evolved out of the food chain is a rather luxurious reach for immortality, in a way, and it's depressing to think there are those, in growing numbers, who believe the mere possibility of the big ocean wanderers, the mere knowledge of their existence, without tasting their rich red flesh, will suffice. Don't get me wrong; it would be nice if it did suffice, but it doesn't.

Deep down we want it both ways; we want to know it and taste it because that's how it was meant to be. It's why Frank is bothering to have his jaws tapped and fitted with handrailings for midgets. I trust there are worms hankering for us, or sea lice, in the case of those broadcast by captain Hader. They, too, have their sport. It's natural. "Then the worms shall try that long preserved virginity," as Andrew Marvell warned his coy mistress.

Frank says he's watched his charters evolve from food fishermen to sport fishermen to fishers of hope. Not just hope they'll find fish, but hope they can attach themselves to a world with teeth, a world that literally bites back, just once before they die.

Like he says, "Nothin' on this oyth is increasin', the only thing there's more of is humans, and some of dem ain't human."

If there are too many of us for the original design, the design will change — has begun to change, if people like poor Tom Luby are any indication—to allow for fewer of us and more swordfish and bluefins. But this won't be done by Puritans who deny basic appetites. The Luby in me says, someday, it will be done willingly by us all.

We're approaching a preview of the final showdown right here on the Cricket. This is no longer just sport, not just fishing. Starting with Mr. Banks, the evolution to the world's present happy panic occured on the Cricket's backdeck. It happened, I'm growing convinced, BECAUSE of the Cricket's backdeck and her master.

I remember the shafts of sunlight illuminating the bone clouds of Romero K. Wingate and Rose Canter as they met and were united in the emerald-green water of Block Island Sound. A fine dust hung in the still air above. Warren said he was sometimes haunted, in a practical sense, by the boxes that collected during the winter months when the Devilfish was still hauled out.

"I mean, in the back of my mind, I know it's sumpin' I gotta do."

The Devilfish had rocked in gentle contrast to this heaving today.

Captain Hader pried the top off a can. Some of the boxes held coffee-sized cans, some fancier urns. "This ain't a whole body, I'll tell you that," he said, committing someone's only half to the deep.

Warren struggled with a knot at the top of a plastic garbage bag. "These are mixed," he said, hefting 40 pounds of cremains to the rail. "I didn't used to get a lot of Catholics, but now I'm getting more and more—Jews, too. They're supposed to be buried in the earth in order to go back to the elements. But everything is economics now." Cremation was becoming much more popular because the cost of graves had become astronomical.

"It's supply and demand. Yards that have ground are expensive. It's real estate, and it's health laws—I mean concern for drinking water. You just can't open a cemetery where you want to—see the way it's going down?"

The big charter captain pointed to a fan of descending particles with one hand and shook out the lawn-size plastic bag with the other. A beautiful plume of perhaps 20 persons expanded weightlessly through a jade-colored sea toward a nebulus of small irridescent fish and an eternity of sand.

"I knew Davy from Fishangri-la," Frank says, breaking my chum-summoned reverie.

Frank had come back on deck, and I heard him telling Howard Chong about Davy Crockett, the mate he considered his best ... "Davy Crockett could outfish, outthink, out bait, out wire, out every-thing anybody. He was with me three or four years, then he left. He was in some kind of alcoholics unanimous, in a hospital, then he come back and started all over again. Then he was with me for two more years.

"Davy was just a kid when I first met him, and he was matin' for George McTurk on the Frieda M., the one he turned over at the light-house. Then he went into the service.

"He was one of the original frogmen. He said when they was on a practice or a real run you had to be on the surface, perfectly lined up in a row, and a fast little boat would come by with a hook on it. You put your arm up and swung on up. If you missed, they'd keep right on goin'. That's it; you're gone.

"When they had demolition work to do and they blew up a boat, you had to keep your head out of the water so the concussion wouldn't killya, and then take your finger and run it up your ass, because you hadda close all the vents in your body. That's what killsya— one stick a dynamite, one mile, will killya—blow you from asshole to appetite. In the water, that's the range, unless you got your head out of the water and you plug up the other end.

"When he come back from that he was in bad shape. I mean, he was at least a quart, quart and-a-half, sometimes two quarts of Seagrams 7 a day. He kept a bottle under the bed when we worked together on the dragger Ranger. He'd wake up in the middle of the night, he'd puke a little, then grab the bottle and have two or three slugs.

"We fished together on the Ranger a few years in the winter. Davy was the only man who could scramble an egg inside the shell before he broke it. I mean, we'd be out there four or five days, come ashore. Davy would hit the gin mill right away, and he'd stay on the sauce for whatever we was in for, three days, four days, he'd stay on the sauce 24 hours a day.

"When we got ready to go back out again, Davy was rumsick bad the first day. He couldn't keep nothin' on his stomach, but you couldn't stop him, he was still doin' his job. He was hurtin', you could see that he was hurtin', but he would still do his job. That was the first day."

"The second day, you could just about get him to eat an egg sandwich, maybe. He couldn't hit the side of the fryin' pan, he was shakin' so much. Second day, he'd get an egg sandwich down. The third day, he'd start to eat normal, the fourth day, he was in good shape, the fifth day he'd be back to normal, the sixth day we'd be in, and he'd be back in the ginmill again. It was the cycle he worked.

"We was out there on the edge, where it drops off to 100 fathoms. I remember we was on the dragger out there in January and February. It's warm there when you get that far, because you're out in warm water. If you don't have any wind, you can walk around in your t-shirt and bare feet. One day it was flat calm, and I'm walkin' around in my bare feet. Davy comes out and says, 'Boy, it's nice weather. I guess I'll take my boots off,' he says, 'My feet sure do sweat.'

"I says, 'Davy, your feet sure do stink. I got the top bunk—I'm right over the top of you—you pull them boots offa you, it drives my nostrils up into my head. Do somethin' about it.' I was waitin' for a chance to say somethin' about it, and there it was.

"He says, Okay, and reaches over and gets powdered Ajax. He goes cachunk, cachunk, cachunk. He used powdered Ajax, so help me God, as foot powder.

"I says, 'Davy, that's grindin' powder, you're gonna grind your feet." He says"—Frank lowers his voice to match that of his former mate's—"'Fuckummmmmm.'"

"When he first started fishin' with me, we was catchin' them big blue sharks. He wouldn't let go a that leader wire. I said, 'Davy, it's no disgrace to let the wire go; we'll get the fish back again.' I says, 'Davy, you're gonna get yourself hurt.'

"'Fuckummmmmm, it's only a blue shark,' he'd say. 'I can still hear him talk.'

"Well, he'd grab a hold of that wire with a double pair of canvas gloves. He'd take a double wrap on each hand, and them blue sharks would roll up that wire. He almost got it one day. The blue shark rolled up the wire, and it was like gettin' your tie caught in a lathe— his hand was underneath the blue shark side, and he couldn't get out. I've got my pliers, I'm standin' behind him, I can't reach. The only thing I can do is hold on to Davy.

"He finally got his hand out. He tore three fingers out of the glove, tore his skin bad on the three fingers. I said, 'Davy, you're gonna get yourself killed, but not on this boat.'

"I finally hadda let him go. It wasn't the fact that, physically, he couldn't handle himself; it was that he lied to me."

Absently, I sign the surface with chum and watch it go down.

"We used to keep a key hangin' on a nail inside one of the cabinets for the cabin. On a day trip, if I got down before Davy, why, I'd have to open the cabin and start to get the rods and reels out. One mornin', I reached for the key in the cupboard. It wasn't there. I thought maybe it fell down, I searched all over for this key; it wasn't there. I said, 'Davy's got it.'

"In a half hour or so, Davy comes down with a six-pack, ready to go. He always had a six-pack widdim, and he would bury it in the bait box, so the customers wouldn't find it underneath the bait. Nobody would look for beer there. Then he'd drink the customers'. If the customers had any, he'd have a six-pack before we got to Shagwong Point, and that's only 10 or 12 minutes.

"Anyhow, he comes down the dock, he has on a life jacket. I says, 'Davy, where's the key?' He says, 'It's hangin' on the nail.' I says, 'No, it's not.

"He puts his hands in his pocket, pulls his hands out, and he's got his hands in a fist. Then he takes and puts his fist in the cabinet and pulls out the key. You don't have to be a magician for this. I mean, this was no magical trick that he done. I said, 'Davy, why didn't you tell me you had the key in your pocket?'

"'I didn't have it in my pocket. It was hangin' on the nail.' Well, I don't know how many times I looked for it there in that half an hour. I wanted to be perfectly sure. When I blame somebody, I want to be perfectly sure.

"We got into an argument, back and forth, back and forth. He was at the point now when he was gonna start lyin', and I just hadda let him go. As good as what he was, I just couldn't trust him, because if he was gonna lie about a stupid key, he's gonna lie about somethin' important.

"Even the fact that he fell asleep at the wheel and coulda put the boat on the rocks at the lighthouse.

"We had a customer called Rotten Ronald on that day. We was on our way home, and we was drinkin' freely. I was makin' up some tail ropes, sittin' on the bait box underneath the cabin. The wind was blowin' hard out of the sou'west. It was the only thing that saved us. The wind kept us off."

"Davy would set by that wheel 24 hours a day and steer. Well, I didn't like it. I liked to get away from it, I would do anything, so I'm down below makin' up tail ropes, and Davy jumps down and says to me, 'Did the motor miss?'

"I said, 'Davy, if that motor missed a beat, I would tell you about it.'

"'Well,' he said, 'long as I'm here, I'll pour myself one.' It was just an excuse to come down and get himself some vodka. So he pours himself a double, triple, shot of vodka real quick and was up on the bridge again, aaaargh? and I was sittin' there makin' up tail ropes, and 15, 20 minutes goes by and somethin', the feel about the boat wasn't just right. I got up, and I look, and holy shit. We were aimin' in toward the lighthouse.

"I back out of the cockpit, and I look, and there he is, layin' across the steerin wheel. I jumped up, put my back to the mast, spread-eagled my feet, so I could balance myself there, and I watched.

"We had two plastic windshields, one in the front and one on the side. Now, the one on the side, it was a comical thing. If you had somebody else at the wheel it would scare them half to death. The wind would catch a hold of it and flip it up. Most of the time, you'd have your hand up there, and it would pinch your fingers or bang you in the elbow.

"That thing was continually comin' up and hittin' his elbow, bang, bang, bang, bang. Aaaaargh?

"I studied the situation. We still had another couple hundred yards to go, but we was aimin' at the lighthouse. I watched that plastic thing hit him in the elbow, physically move his body when it hit him, bang, bang, bang. It wasn't botherin' him at all.

"I got so pissed off, I reached over and grabbed him by both shoulders, and I threw him. When I threw him, I didn't care if he went overboard. Davy you couldn't bother if you threw him overboard. It woulda been better. He went flyin' across the bridge, and he landed in a ball on the other side of the bridge with his big eyes.

"I screamed at him, I said, 'You son-of-a-bitch, you're gonna put a boat on the rocks, but it ain't gonna be this one.' He says, 'Well, I guess I'm fired.'

"I said, 'No Davy, you ain't fired; you're flagged. I don't give a shit if you're steppin' on your tongue. You ain't gonna get a drop to drink, not on the boat.'

"Well, I knew what was gonna happen. He was gonna drink harder, have himself five, six, seven more shots and some beer before he climbs on the boat. Then he was gonna start sneakin', and I was gonna find beer cans down in the shithouse. So then I caught him in the lie.

"But Davy was the best man I ever went to sea with, because Davy would never worry about Davy, he always worried about the other guy. If you was at the wheel for any length of time, he would always pop his head up and say, 'Can I get you anything? Is there anything I can do? Can I help you.' He continually worried about the other guy.

"They found him right in front of the Montauk Marine Basin in the middle of the winter, doin' the dead man's float. Never had an autopsy to find out if there was foul play or not.

"Shit, you couldn't kill Davy by throwin' him in the water. He was like a rat, a water rat. Somebody hadda bust him over the head. I don't know why. Even when he was stone drunk, he was likeable, never got nasty, always funny, real funny. When he'd tell a customer a story about catchin' a fish, his eyes would get big, his hands would be goin'—why anybody would bop him on the head ... but that was the end of Davy."

I'm back on the Devilfish with Warren. "Ah, how many—did we just, er, dump?" I recall asking Captain Hader.

"About 150," he said and noted that crematoria were cropping up all over. He said the sales pitch that accounted for their success—and, consequently, the success of his moonlighting—was something to the effect that cremation also returned the loved ones to the elements, "only faster and cheaper."

There it was again, timesharing in favor of space-sharing. It had occurred to me, even then, that Armegeddon would likely be accomplished voluntarily.

Warren was shaking out the last plastic bag when he lost his grip, and it floated beyond his reach. The party boat Wilhelric, its rails crowded with dozens of eager anglers peering through a forest of rods, turned, in the distance, toward the Devilfish. "Ah, shit, I think he wants to fish here," said Captain Hader.

He gaffed the floating bag and washed the ash from the deck with a little green hose. We slipped back into the safety of Long Island's eastern most harbor. That cruise of the Devilfish took place only a few months before Warren himself died.

"The fish was all cut up.
Its belly flaps, folded back,
were the size of a
double bed."

[NANCY BANGERT]

Chapter

B I O L U M I N E S C E N C E

ROLLING SWELLS, SLIGHT BREEZE, FIVE BLUESHARKS HANGING, a rifle

blast puts a hunk of shark on my upper lip. Frank is cooking eggs and

ham, taking orders. Slammed, rolled, and free-fell in the night. Slept

well. Storm petrels walking on water. Jim stirs the monster mash. □

"My whole cussed body's beat up," Frank says, expessing what we all

feel after the beating the sea's given us. But he's talking mostly about

his teeth. His jaws hurt. "I gotta get rid of the brontosaurus and ele-

phant off my back," he says of the pain. In four months the new teeth

will be permanent, at a $1,000 a pop. I recall Captain Hader won-

dering why Frank, instead of going for normal, removable false teeth,

is bothering to have the new choppers and their "handrailing for

midgets" anchored to his jaws. Today, I don't wonder. It seems per-

fectly natural Frank would want strong teeth, teeth that continually replace themselves, like sharks have.

The teeth of the white shark are triangular, with serrations enabling them to tackle thick-skinned marine mammals. Its jaws close with tons of pressure per square inch, the whole package designed to deliver crippling wounds with the first bite. After the big one, the animal waits for its prey to bleed to death. It then bites again, holding meat, blubber, and sinew in place with the lower teeth, and sawing back and forth with the larger uppers.

Frank's paying out line and a styrofoam float from one of the smaller rods and telling Howard how people look at a fighting chair these days, and assume it grew there, in the middle of the cockpit. In the pioneering days of big-game fishing, rods were laminated ash, he says, and the reels held linen line. Frank watches the water and begins to talk about Red Stuart and Tommy Cifford, two of a handful of fishing guides who, says he, could handle decent-size fish in the early 1950s.

Tommy Gifford was known as "Twee Twed," a familiarization of "Three Thread," for his preference to fish lighter line. Linen line was actually constructed of braided threads, Frank explains—the more threads the stronger the line. Three-thread was about the lightest.

Frank's saying Red Stuart was sent down to pioneer sportfishing in Peru by Michael Lerner, heir to the Lerner Dress shops fortune and founder of the International Game Fish Association. He came back with photographs that showed how Mr. Lerner had rented a small coastal freighter, on which the newfangled fighting chair was bolted. They used a double-ended dory to bait the fish, and when it was hooked, the rod would be passed up to the big boat where the fight would take place from the new fangled throne. The method was used in the early days of hunting bluefins off Montauk and "Rosie's Ledge," near Watch Hill, Rhode Island.

Red came back from Peru with tales of fighting 50-pound squid.

"Spooky at nighttime," Frank is saying, "how hard those bastids pulled with their jet. If you gaffed the squid in the head, it would squirt a quart of ink at the idiot in the chair." There were so many marlin off Peru, Frank continues, Red wouldn't even bother to bait them unless they were 500 or 600 pounds.

I dip the ladle and make another offering. The tiny chunks descend like the ash of people. There is no talk, no engine, no radio. Just the wind and the banging of the head door because the clothespin that keeps it latched has sprung free, like a butterfly of anxiety.

She might have got scared in a traffic jam on the Sunrise Highway, just west of Babylon. The radio broadcaster giving the hourly news update might have sounded like this to her, as the meaning of his words wrestled past her habitual checklist of trivial pursuits: hair lengths to be considered, new this, new that, nail colors ...

"... fin rot, fish kills," the broadcaster says, finally breaking through.

"Six million gallons of sewage sludge dumped each day at the 106-mile offshore ocean site," he continues, "all from metropolitan New York." Maybe those words, or the year's murder tallies, or new H.I.V. infections, or sea-level rise, sink in, and she's suddenly afraid of people.

She drives out of Babylon to the peaceful East End of Long Island, like others before her, drawn by a magnetism.

I know now I was taken by the salesgirl of future comfort, in part, because she has the same sad eyes as a friend, a pretty dock girl and fish-cutter whose obituary is now neatly folded and yellowing in the *Star* morgue.

I interviewed Nancy Bangert for the *Star* only a month before she took a shotgun to herself. She'd served me warm slices from a loaf of bread she'd made with bananas and walnuts and recalled the day after Frank brought his big white shark back to Montauk. She was working on the dragger Lady Irma at the time. Nancy had told me:

"We were going fishing early but decided to go over to the marine basin to see the shark first. I remember looking at the sun and saying to myself, 'What a lurid sun.' It was the kind of light you couldn't trust. The fish was all cut up. Its belly flaps, folded back, were the size of a double bed. Then we went fishing and the sky got leaden, oppressive. I was gutting bluefish on the deck when the lightning came. Rain and hail. The wind and hail were holding the chop down. Then all the electronics blew. I went to the wheelhouse and put my rain gear over my head because I was worried the wheelhouse window was going to blow out. There was five or six inches of nickel-sized hail on the deck. The lightning was phenomenal. The wind pushed the boat way over on her side."

Howard's fighting a small blue shark now, and Frank is telling him to keep the rodtip up. He begins the story about the time he fished with Red Stuart for blue marlin in Barbados.

Red would sew up a bonefish so it would swim when trolled. Sometimes the marlin would attack it, sometimes they wouldn't. It took 10 to 15 minutes to rig one of the baits, and Red eventually saw the light and shared it with Frank:

"'That's the trouble,' he said. They're too perfect. The blue would never make a pass at the perfect ones. You can have a bait that's too good. It's like snappers with live shrimp. They strike when the shrimp are a little crippled, aaarungh?"

Again fishing with Red Stuart—1952, it was. This time in Bimini for the same Michael Lerner who had a big tank outside his house with local species in it, Frank says. "There's all kinds of fish in there," he's saying of the tank. "That's when I discovered why nobody was botherin' nobody. It never ocurred to me until I caught a grunt and put it in the pool. Oh, hot-diggity-dog, is there goin' to be a massacre in there," Frank recalls, relishing the thought. But nothing happened.

Then he saw the logic: "If this one spends his energy gettin' the grunt, the 'cuda will know he's tired. Fish know how much energy they can waste and still get away. They know they're food. They may be dumb, but they ain't stupid. It's a lot worse in the ocean than in the jungle," says he. "In the jungle, they can make a mistake and get away. In the ocean, the first mistake is your last."

Frank raises his whiny voice in song to illustrate the conceptual breakthrough Red Stuart and he had made in the art of rigging successful baits:

"You've got to ACCEN-tuate the positive, ELIM-inate the negative, LATCH on to the affirmitive, but don't mess with Mr. IN-BETWEEN."

I'm wondering if the brilliant colors that fade upon a fish, that burn bright when they're fighting for their lives, are lighted, under normal circumstances, to signal vitality, to mask weakness and loss of strength from the hungry in the sea of constant and life-preserving anxiety. Brilliant armor. This is what Frank sees that others don't.

But who's Mr. In-between? I think I'm beginning to see. It's the one who dwells in the sea of God-given trouble fearing nothing, requiring no color, no bioluminescence—what, me worry?—like us. We have forgotten we're food.

Howard's in the chair again, getting ready for a fight. Frank's painting fingernail polish on the knot that holds the leader to the Jap hook, as he calls the type used by Japanese longline fishermen. It's designed to snag in a fish's jaw, rather than fleshy parts. Frank demonstrates the design by dragging it across the lip of a plastic bucket. It catches on the lip, as advertised.

The polish adds "tinsel" strength, he says—"seizes" the ends of knot. "Nail polish, rubber bands, and clothes pins—can't run a boat without them." He talks under his breath to the bait made of half a blue shark. He pays it out into the current on its ball float, the big bobber, and tells Howard what might happen, with any luck.

"You sit in the chair. I'll mash on the starter. The advantage of the ball is it keeps the line tight. The point [of the hook] just hangs on his lip for the first half hour. When he runs, just relax. In the meantime, we'll get the harness out and get the seat adjusted. Push against the foot rest, forget about your hands and arms. Otherwise, with heavy tackle, we'll have to put you in a basket and take you home. I've worn out football players just off the field. It should take about an hour on top. If he goes to the bottom, nobody is gettin' him up. It's like robbin' a bank—you plan the whole thing. Then again, the cops might show up."

He points above, to the Cricket's mast and boom, with its tackle custom-rigged for controlling huge animals. There are two shackles, he explains, one that fits into a ring on the fishing line's double-ended leader. "We lower the shackle. One guy snaps it on. The boat's in gear, doing a half circle, the shark inside the circle. A wire lasso is slipped around the leader."

"Soon as you see the dorsal go by, pull on the lasso. The shark still doesn't know what's goin' on," says Frank.

I'm chumming. The image of Howard's white hope, shackled fore and aft, hangs like a grail against the monotony of boundless sea and sky.

"You let go," Frank instructs Mr. Chong. "I start up and go home. We got a white shark. We'll rob the bank, if the cops don't come."

The ball is out. Frank dumps a box of butterfish into a cage he's made from the kind of white wire mesh one might encircle a rose bush with. The giant teabag goes overboard to soak. Butters drift through the mesh like silver dollars descending through the deep green.

"We might as well start a small riot," Frank says, now slipping a blueshark liver over the side before returning to the carcass to carve off long slabs of fillet for hook baits. "We're in 180 feet of water," Frank says, "if you go all the way to the bottom."

Nobody gets his joke. Too subtle for the conditons. The Cricket's still freefalling about every fourth swell, although the surface of the waves is now smooth. "That's right, boidies, break it up into little pieces," he says, watching petrels attack the riper butters that float to the surface.

Howard, antsy in the chair, asks how far away the chum attracts sharks. "How far can you smell smoke?" Frank answers. "Someone's cookin' steak on an outside grill. If you wanted, you could follow it right up to the steak. If you smell an incinerator, you just keep right on walkin', rrrrrrright? Pig's blood or human blood—they don't know what it is. But porpoise blood, whale blood, basking shark blood, is a pleasant smell, their steak. I had state troopers who had access to a morgue. Brought out five gallons of human blood. Didn't woyk."

July Third is beginning to warm. The swells begin to subside, although Cricket continues to rock, rail to rail.

"A tisket, a tasket, there goes my little white basket. Anything they can't catch naturally, like butterfish, squid, they like," Frank says. "I'm gonna go put on the coffee pot, now that we've shitted up the neighborhood."

I crawl into my bunk for a nap, then wake to watch deep-green 10-foot swells passing under us, one after the other, after the other, after the other.

Petrels and shearwaters hover and worry the slick. Mr. Chong is out of the chair and just washed his feet with fresh water and put on a pair of rubber sandals. Hope he doesn't have to fight a fish thus shod. He looks like Big Minh in camouflage jacket and Marine Corps cap. An hour passes under our feet.

Frank's below, asleep with earphones and the kerosene stove on.

Can't be much oxygen down there. Frank called Jenny while I was napping, and she said Michael Potts caught a 700-pound mako today 50 miles to the west of us, and Greg Beecher on the Dawn landed a 600-pound bluefin. We're one big fish so far, the one we never saw, the mystery fish that cut the wires clean and straight across in the night. The wind has increased, more south than west now. It's supposed to turn northwest later. Another hour—or was it a month?—passes beneath us.

Frank is up again and telling how sharks travel at night, when they're more aggressive. "They'll chew on the cage tonight," he predicts, going on for a long time about the migratory paths of sharks, the sinuous herds of them he's found and mined over the years. Like the Caribbean fishermen, he says, who set their pots in the path of the single-file march of migrating lobsters.

Frank speaks of the ocean's clock. His annual reunion with fish is how he hears its ticking. "Used to be the second week in May," he says of the porbeagle sharks. "They like cold water. Norwegians followed them all the way down past Montauk.

He's staring toward the horizon, with his feet planted wide near the middle of the Cricket's backdeck. She's a work boat, deep of draft, and, like all such boats, has a peaceful center. His memories of seas past and the fish that showed themselves to distinguish a day here, a day there, from all the indistinguishable days on this same expanse, these memories he delivers in a voice that is slow and high-pitched, appreciable over the wind, like an ocean bird's. His voice rises, "Arrrruh?" at the end of a thought, wanting to know if you understand because it's important that you do—a kind of chant.

Makes me think of the chanting overheard by fishermen off Montauk on foggy summer days early in the decade, the chants emanating from the small open boats manned and womanned by disciples of the Reverend Sun Myong Moon as they hand-lined for tuna. In addition to the cheap and enraptured fishing labor, Reverend Moon's Happy World company was among the export buyers of bluefin tuna competing on the Montauk docks. Those chants were fundamentally different from Frank's.

"The blue shark comes in from offshore, from your Stream," he's instructing now. "Porbeagles stay close with the cold water. When the stream makes the turn, we get the overflow. Arrruh?

"The Stream follows the continental shelf all the way up. Veers off in the New York area. Overflow comes in by us. Later it's stronger and like a bathtub. The Gulf Stream don't move in, it's runnin' harder, has to go someplace. Arrruh?

"We'd first hear about the blue sharks from the draggers. First hear about the porbeagles from the tilefishermen workin' farther offshore.

"The bluefin you can watch from the Bahamas [as they begin to move with the Gulf Stream in early spring.] They go past Florida, past Jersey, until they catch 'em in the pound nets in Canada. In spring, they're travelin', not eatin'. Swim with their mouths open, plankton's all they need to keep goin'. A 300-pound fish will fatten up to a twice that later in the summer.

"Dolphin [mahi mahi] are long and skinny down in the Caribbean, not enough to eat in that clear water. Up here, they can hide more in the murky water, can find food, sneak up on baitfish. There's more plankton here." He begins cutting out another jaw for the bleach bucket.

"One year there's a whole pile a manta rays and no baskin' sharks. The boys, when they're lookin' for swordfish from the towers, they seen ten mantas a day. This year just one. But—arruh?—if there was one, there was more than one. Arrruh?

"The blackfish whale we'd grind up and use for shark fishin' until 1972, when they *banded* whalin'. Then we shifted to baskin' sharks. Found out the oil in a baskin' shark is in the meat itself. During the

War, they longlined sharks for vitamins. Then they found synthetics for the vitamins they got from sharks—for every one but the baskin' sharks. In Scotland, they used to net 'em."

He emits a low moan for the pain in his jaw—"The more I think about it, the more I think it's him," says he, still dwelling on what it was cut the bluefish bait and wire leaders straight across nearly 12 hours ago. "There's more whites here than people think. I'll go out on a limb and say there are more whites here than in Australia."

He says he found the whites because he first found the pods of blackfish (pilot) whales. Experience taught him the whites slipped in behind the whales to stalk the young and infirm. Where the whites come from, he says, neither he nor anyone else knew.

Chum made from ground-up blackfish whales attracted sharks. This he knew for sure. Frank learned this after a charter, bored with slow fishing, harpooned one so he could say he did. Frank had to tow it back to Montauk, where there was nothing to be done with it, so it became mash. Before that, in the early years, Frank would meet the bunker seiners and buy the mixed "trash," the so-called "underutilized" species which the Promised Land plant just west of Montauk squashed for oil and meal.

"They'd put five-dollars-worth in a six-by-six box," Frank recalls, "loaded on board by niggers with coal shovels." Frank remembers Sam Stanley, an old man from out of the past, the father of a charter from Virginia, who knew of a mink farm with a meat grinder for sale. Frank brought the grinder to Duryea's ice house in Montauk, where the first mash was rendered. It was mash made from blackfish whale that produced the first white. It was the first monster mash.

"I believe white sharks follow any big group of fish. That's why the double-overnighters to the dumps. I know we have more white sharks here than in Australia. Scientists know nothing. One thing's always bothered me," Frank is saying.

Talk of white sharks rouses a sleepy Mr. Chong. He's rapt.

"Alf Deen struggled with a big white shark once, over 3,000 pounds, in Australia. Had it to the boat two or three times. Lost it every time. It had a scar the size a harpoon would make near the gill plate, toward the back, near the last gill plate. My 4,500 pound fish had the same mark. It could'a been a different fish," Frank says, intimating that it could as easily have been the same fish, that white sharks could circumnavigate the earth on their migrations.

"They done a lot of white shark fishin' in Australia," he says, "used to fish with seal. Just wait for the shark to come and chew on it. Better chance down there—shallow water."

I ask him if white sharks go into Montauk's Fort Pond Bay, home of Fishangri-la. It's an old rumor, an old fear. "They talk the same way about Treasure Island," Frank says, "or 'Washington slept here,' or Atlantis.'

"They don't know about sharks," he repeats. "They only started messin' wid'm. Now they cut 'em in half and count the rings like a tree," he says, referring to how marine biologists had learned to count rings in fish vertebrae to determine age. "For years, when people asked me how old a big shark was, I would say, 'Let's cut it half and count the rings.' It was our favorite joke."

Joke, he calls it, but again, it's an observation. He means the rings of a shark are evidence of an intuitive connection he has to the sea. He drifts into the story of a girl who chartered the Cricket as a birthday present for her dad.

"It was a single overnighter. Fishing was slow, only a couple of fish around midnight. I tell her I'm gonna move. She says, How far?' 'About an hour, I say. She says, 'I'll break out dad's present.' Then," Frank says, "up ahead, from out of nowhere, I see a pile of balloons pushed offshore by the wind, lying on the water, all blowed up, so I pulled back on the throttle and told the mate to pick them up as they slide past the bow."

"Everyone's singing 'happy birfday,'" Frank says, recalling how at the exact moment when voices were raised in celebration, he'd exclaimed, "What's that we got?," producing the balloons from the sea.

Just another sign he and the sea are in synch, and HOLY SHIT, just as he's finishing the tale, what looks like a huge dorsal fin rises to the surface off the starboard side.

For a moment, adrenalin drives us to the brink of ecstatic chaos. The monster has come, and on Frank's cue. There's mad scrambling on the backdeck. The fin turns out to be that of the harmless ocean sunfish, a mola mola.

"Here, sunfish, sunnyfish, you bastard, you about gave me failure," Frank moans after a crestfallen moment. There follows a round of cursing brought on by the sunfish's counterfeit thrill. Frank talks disparagingly of the pretender, as its large stubby body flops drunkenly on the surface behind us. "They're slimy, like eels. Their skin is thin and like number-36 sandpaper. Meat looks like coconut meat. Sharks won't eat it. They have regular guts. Sharks will eat the guts, not the coconut meat and skin."

Frank says he knows only one man who eats them, a barber named Tony with a standing order. Tony claims the intestines of the mola mola make fine sausage, and he trades Frank a haircut now and then for the entrails. Frank says he's known Tony for years, but only after the man heard he was to retire did he tell him his story. Seems he was in the Italian army during the war, says Mundus, and watched a German soldier who'd fallen off a transport ship get attacked by a shark. He died on the deck with one last cigarette in his mouth, Frank says, and it was Tony gave it to him.

Suddenly Howard has a fish on. We hadn't seen a fin in the slick for some time. By the way it's pulling, it's a big one. Frank tells Howard, "Time yourself, give yourself five, 10, 20 minutes, whatever you want. You've got a decent fish here. Watch the reel. If it slips, stop reeling—you're just wasting energy. Still don't know what the hell you've got."

The fish makes two good runs. "The way the line's cutting through the water, it's not a blue shark," Frank says calmly, but with passion building. "Stay there, Howard, he's comin' your way. His head's turnin'..."

It breaks off. Two thrilling disappointments back-to-back. Silence. The sound of wind. Jim puts the 30/30 back in its scabbard.

The captain finally speaks. "Even toward the end, he gave us head motion, wasn't s'posed to." He means the shark was of a more aggressive species than the blues we'd been landing. And big. He reminds Jim to get a good backbone shot when a big one is brought to bay. A big one other than the white, of course, which must be taken by the book—Frank's book. "Even if it's only on the tail. Take the shot," he tells Jim, "that'll straighten him out."

"Why do these fish continually make assholes out of us humans?" Frank demands of the wind.

Howard's all limp, like he's lost his life. You pursue meaning, happiness. Suddenly its there. Its dorsal fin is cutting through the water right beside you, all danger and exhilaration, but it's an impostor; coconut meat, sausage, a free haircut. Then, just as you think all is lost, you tie into the real thing, a powerful life. You have it, and it has you. You're moving all over. You're tight, hard, sweating, laughing, ecstatic. Then your fish is gone, and you die all at once. Howard's having a smoke, slouched in his throne, flicking an ash, sightless.

It's hot now. Jim pries the top off another bucket of mash. We smell like chum. We are chum, I fear. Hours pass transparently. Blue sharks slither through the Cricket's descending offering. Cricket heels way over. The bucket of jaws skates across the deck; a hanging blue swings and hits Howard in the back. Frank spreads his stance but takes no notice, remembering:

"Tommy Gifford perfected kite fishin' in our area, but it was an old Chinese trick. They been doin' it for centuries. He was the one who talked me into usin' it. He had a different kite for every wind condition what you got. It has a regular kite string, and a snap like on an outrigger that the fishing line goes through and you lower the bait to the water. It works like a giant outrigger.

When you rigged a bait up on a kite, three-quarters of the fish is under the water. The head is outa the water, most of the time. Now picture, when you're swimmin' by lookin' up, if you're the fish, the only thing you see is what resembles a crippled fish wigglin' his tail. They can't pass it up. Everything will jump on it. You can put the kite out as far as what you wanta. And you can rig two baits three baits on the same kite. You can troll with it. If you have a school a fish what's figity, they don't like to come close to the boat, you can go back and forth with the kite baits.

"That's when we was first shark fishin'. Tommy was comin' back and forth from the Bahamas with his Stormy Petral. I had met him when I went down there with Red Stuart on the Sandona. He told me, 'You're a natural because you're sharkin'. You're the only boat that's driftin' out there. While you're driftin', he says, 'You can put the kite on the other side.'

"I says, 'Tommy, get off my case with this kite business. We got more fish than what we know what to do with. Why should we mess with a kite?' Well, he sent his mate down with a double box kite. You rig two box kites together. That's actually the best kite, but unless you unrig it, where you gonna put it on the boat? Some fat lady will sit on it, aaaargh? Some drunk will smash it, or some stumble-footed guy will step on it. Anyway, he draws a diagram on how to use it with two fishin' poles.

"So we're out there kite fishin', and I put the kite up and stuck some kinda bait on it. Then we get a mako on the regular rod, and he's sizzlin' line out. Well, naturally, we forget all about the kite. I mash on the starter, and we start chasin' down this mako. The mako's hippity-hoppin' around, here and there puttin' on a nice little performance. Somebody looks on the other side and sees the kite bait, and there's a blue shark chasin' it. He can't catch it because we keep movin'. Every time we'd stop, the bait would go up in the air because we didn't have it adjusted right. Blue shark would get pissed off and go around in circles waitin' for it to come back down."

"Well, we had more fun watchin' the blue shark goin' after the bait than we did watchin' the mako we'd hooked, so I figured this was a good sellin' point, so we used it after that. When a giant tuna hit that kite bait it sounds like you just threw a hand grenade out there. It's just one explosion, babooom, and on your way turnin' around, you know what you're gonna see: a 15-foot hole where the tuna come up. Everything would go after it: white marlin, sharks, the whole works."

Frank's daughter, Patti, is a first mate in the merchant marine now. Frank tells us how, when she was on a training cruise that he knew was scheduled to pass by the Montauk fishing grounds, he flew his daughter a package of spending money, via kite, up onto the deck of the Empire State, the training ship. The officer of the deck was not amused.

The mates are sleeping again because they'll be up all night unless we get a big shark in the interim.

I'm back on the chum box ladling. Our oily slick spreads before me, a shining path to the waking dreams that flow apace from the quiet Cricket. The long legs of the red-haired time-sharess are before me, intermittently, while I catch Frank's musical history of Red Stuart —"don't mess with Mr. InBetween," he croons.

If Luby'd lived, he might have found her, like a drowning man who makes a landfall on a small island of flotsam, like Mr. Banks found the

Cricket. She might have stopped him on the street, like she had me, and tried to sell him a shared unit of unreal estate. One thing could have led to another. "I fish on the Deliverance," he could have told her, something I could not have. She might have confided a fear, he a misgiving. He might have had her and she him, for a time, if he'd lived.

Frank's singing in the chum stench is macabre. I'm thinking how, after the empty hearse left Tom Luby in the sea of tombstones outside Manhattan just before Christmas, it headed back on its familiar trip east. Hearses are migratory too, ever following with their black jaws and portable claustrophobia.

On the outskirts of Patchogue, yet another village of extinct indians, Sunrise Highway no longer parts a seemingly endless expanse of auto supply stores and mini-malls. The last buildings on the right, before the highway presses on through beige-colored fields and scrub pines, are the long low coops of a duck ranch, a camp full of doomed fowl who smell to high heaven and inexplicably raise one's spirits.

Then it's all scrub pines and khaki grasslands, but for the occasional sign advertising the sale of 400 acres or so. The same highway parts the beautifully treed and long-settled Hamptons, passes by the office of the *East Hampton Star,* in its 110th year, going by Promised Land on Gardiner's Bay, where the old Smith Meal plant once squeezed fine oil from the tons of small menhaden then standing in for the spent oceans of spermaceti. Whales, including Frank's blackfish whales, were first hunted by white men from these very shores.

It was in the net loft at the Promised Land plant where Tom Lester, a bayman I met on my beat, worked as a boy. He recalled one of the southern blacks laying for another with a two-by-four and popping an eye out with a blow to the head—punishment for having taken liberties with his woman. The local doctor put the eye back using a teaspoon. He said they lived happily ever after, as far as he knew.

Tommy Lester was a lifelong fisherman and an East Hampton

town trustee. Big, with few teeth, he had a fondness for jellybeans, which he consumed by the fistful during monthly trustee meetings. His voice was *basso profundo*, gravelly besides, and mixed with the remnant accents of his English forebears.

As a Star reporter I'd seen Tommy's low sounds materialize as stone fences to the lawyers in fancy suits representing wealthy second-home owners from "away." In the eyes of the UpIsland lawyers seeking building or dock permits required by Tommy Lester and the eight other trustees, you would first see humor, like it was a gag with the jellybeans and with Dave Talmage, the blind clerk, the way he spat tobacco juice into a coke bottle. Then their looks turned to disbelief and resignation because, in the few remaining years of the 20th century, East Hampton's valuable lowlands were still ruled by authority of a patent bestowed by James II of England — brilliant armor against Mr. In-between, like this trip with Frank, like Davy Crockett's "fuckummmm," like my courtship of the beautiful salesgirl of time.

"Happy horseshit," I hear Frank saying, and I look up from the ladle to see he's peering through me.

"Find me a nice, big, fat whale,
and I'll show you some white shahks.
But there again, you can't go
up to that dead whale and expect
to catch a white shahk.
You have to spend time."

[FRANK MUNDUS]

10

HERE COMES YOUR IMAGINATION

FRANK HAD CAUGHT SEVERAL BIG WHITE SHARKS between the time he

discovered the wonders wrought by whale meat when sprinkled

from the altar of the chum box and June 6, 1964, the day he caught

his first monster. The first of the species was off Amagansett in

1961. The second one was the same year but a little bigger, near a

dead whale off of Block Island. □ "Then we had another one that

tried to bite a plank outa the boat, just like the movie 'Jaws.' If it had

been another boat, it woulda bit the plank out and gone right to the

bottom, but because the Cricket's got too much plankin', it didn't

bother us none. He come up alongside the boat when we was in the

process of takin' him, and he didn't like what was goin' on so he just

rolled around and grabbed the side where the side meets the bottom.

He went RUFF and hung on, twisting his body, and you could hear the teeth breakin' off like rifle shots.

"Then we get a gaff in him and a tailrope on and dragged him home. Then we started diggin' the teeth out. They was in that longleaf yellow pine three-quarters of an inch. Now, that pine is hard stuff. I made a statement to the press that if that was an average, ordinary charter boat—they only have three-quarters of an inch to play with— he woulda tore that plank out. That's a bad plank to lose where the side meets the bottom. I said the boat woulda sunk immediately. It caused a stir."

On June 6, Mundus caught one that made front-page news. He was fishing south of Montauk Point. His mate was a jockey from Florida who'd lost his mount somehow and found himself dribbling chum into the Atlantic in order to make ends meet. Late in the afternoon, his arm, right down to the little fingers holding a ladleful of reddish-brown whale gruel, went stiff. Rigor mortis had instantly set in when he saw what he did rise up from the fishing spot called the Butterfish Hole, a productive depression 10 miles south of Montauk Point.

"If I'm down in the cabin lookin' up to the cockpit, I can tell you a white shark has showed up," Frank says. "Most of the time, if a guy's chummin', his arm gets stuck." Frank recalls the same great white paralysis on another trip, when Robert Boggs, yet another writer, on night-chumming watch in the Dumping Ground suddenly yelled, "FRANK, FRANK."

"I look out, and he's stuck. He's towards the middle of the deck, away from the edge of the boat. If he'd had chum in that ladle and dumped it, it would have gone in the boat. 'He's here, he's here,' says Boggs. Two or three minutes went by, and he's still stuck, and he says, 'Ah, maybe, ah, maybe it's my imagination.' I says, 'Boggsy, old boy, Cecil B. DeMille couldn't a taught you any better.' I said, 'He's there. I'll be there in a minute.'

"I look over, and Dicky the mate is sound asleep. I give him a shot with my foot in the ribs, bango, and I give Gordon Rynders [the photographer from the *Daily News*] a shake with my arm almost the same time, and I holler, 'let's go—we got a white shark in the slick.' I headed for the door. Those two—I look over my shoulder, and they were runnin' into one another. I was out on deck and threw a few ladles-full of chum into the water. Had to take a wreckin' bar and take the ladle out of Boggsy's hand."

"I throw a few more ladles of chum, and then, pretty soon ..." Frank lowers his voice until it's slow soft-Brooklyn, full of danger and describing a birth of some kind:

"... there it is, Old Faithful, little spot, little smudge out there, smudge gets bigger, bigger, now starts makin' color, it's an amber-brown smudge, nowwww it's a head, now here it comes, now you can see it full view. I say, 'Boggsy, old boy, here comes your imagination.'"

Interesting Frank should describe it thus, like a birth. I boned up on whites before coming aboard—"boned up" is not fitting, of course, as whites and their brethren are elasmobranches of cartilaginous construction, which gives them their characteristic sashay. White sharks give birth to their young alive and big. The males fertilize their mates using either one of their two large penile projections called "claspers." It's possible the lucky bastards can switch tools in mid-stream.

Whites are oophagy, which means *Carcharodon carcharias* are among a small number of species whose stronger young do battle with and eat their weaker siblings while still in the womb. In this way, the strongest survive to meet the world full of purpose and with malice aforethought.

Being top dog of the carnivorous apex predators, whites are built to feed on large animals. They prefer warm-blooded types: marine mammals and penguins. They are known to inhabit every ocean in the world, concentrating in areas like northern California, South Africa, South America, and Australia, where seals congregate. Whales and porpoises, too, are on the menu when they are old or infirm. Or dead. In the New York Bight, Frank's theater of operation, dead whales or those sick and slow enough to catch, are a staple.

Like some other sharks, whites have a sixth sense. In addition to sight, they find their prey by sound: they have the ability to feel pressure waves the length of their body, along lines on both flanks called *acoustico laterolis.* They have a keen sense of smell, and they can sense electrical impulses. Above the smile, that spectral smirk that fades to a deathly gape, the prey sensors are concentrated on the shark's blunt snout.

Two nostrils allow water to flow past with the shark's side-to-side gait, past olfactory cells. The numerous dark pores located on the white's nose cone—looking, as the writer Richard Ellis correctly described them—like a five o'clock shadow, are called *"ampullae* of Lorenzini," named for their Italian discoverer. They are jelly-filled receivers, able to detect minute electrical charges of the kind generated by the hearts and other muscles of fish, marine mammals, and, on ever-more-frequent occasions, Homo lemmus of the surfing kind.

It is theorized the *ampullae* of whites and other sharks not only sense what's living and how well, but also serve as compasses by which the animals navigate through the earth's magnetic fields. It's clear something similar guides Frank's idiots to him. The jockey and others froze at the approach of a white shark like the birth of their own worst fears—a birth they are drawn to as surely as if they had ampules of Lorenzini for fillings.

Frank says they saw no pilot whales the day the first real big one found the Cricket in June of '64. The jaws of the 4,500-pound monster continue to amaze the patrons at Salivar's bar in Montauk.

"We had two porbeagles hangin' and a third porbeagle on. We had him on light tackle. He was takin' out too much line, and I had to start the motor to chase him down just to put the line back on the reel again. I was fairly sure I wouldn't have to go that far, just one run, enough to fill up the reel and that was goin' to be it.

"Now, when you have a wet exhaust goin out the transom, and when you don't have any water goin' through it, it will talk to you, it'll bark at you. So Cricket barked at me when I started the engine. I hollered down to that dopey mate that I had who was a jockey before I got him — this was the first time he decided to go fishin' — I hollered down to him to take a look to see if there was any water comin' out. He said, 'Yeah, there's water comin' out.'

"I said, 'Nah, there can't be,' so, anyhow, I just went ahead a little bit, told the angler to put line back on the reel. He did, so I stopped, knocked it out of gear, and went down below and looked. There wasn't water coming out the transom— it was just blowin' the sea water. The impeller on the saltwater pump had broke when we was runnin'. I have a spare pump, and I figure I'll change that after we catch the fish.

"So the guy was fightin' the fish, and I told him, 'After we get this one, we'll change the pump.' By that time it will be late enough to start back home. As he was catchin' the fish, I was clearin' all the garbage off the motor box so that I can lift it and start with the pump. I look over and my idiot mate is chummin' again. We was chummin' with blackfish whale. I was gonna tell him, 'Don't chum anymore,' but it looked like he was havin' fun, so I wasn't worried about losing a few ladles-full of chum— leave him alone, I think, I got other things to worry about.

"All of a sudden, the ladle stops, arm stretched out tight like a fiddle string. Then he can't talk. Well, I knew what he seen. I got up and ran over to the side, and when I did, I seen this big white shark come right up, and he was lookin on board. The jockey'd sucked him up with this whale meat, aaaargh?

"Nnnnnow, he starts swimmin' around the boat. Whenever this happens, you have organized panic, six people runnin' around in circles hollerin' and screamin'. There was four runnin' around—one guy had a fish on; he still had that porbeagle on—and the mate."

"Then I hollered the worst possible thing over my shoulder as I ran down to the cabin to get the rod-and-reel.

"I hollered, 'Throw him some mackerel'—WRONG—because then everybody grabs mackerel and throws 'em, so now it's rainin' mackerel. I had about 600 pounds of Boston mackerel. So when I come out of the cabin with the rod-and-reel, he's swimmin' around, suckin' up these mackerel, havin' a good ole time. I thought this was good, he's a real hungry fish; won't have any trouble hookin' him. I got the special wire rig out, put a couple mackerel on, threw it over the side, and when I did, he came along and sucked it up."

"When he sucked it up—aaaaaaaaah, I felt like a little kid who just got caught with his hands in the cookie jar. I knew I'd done wrong. How the hell am I gonna catch this fish on rod-and-reel when I don't have any water goin' through my motor, and it's goin' to overheat in 10 minutes? It's goin' to burn up," Frank says. Cricket would not be able to maneuver to help the angler.

"I holler to the mate, 'Don't set the hook. Let him swim around. Don't let him feel anything. Take the rod and follow him around, give him plenty of free spool, don't give him any drag.

"Okay, so now I dived down into the bilge. By this time, I've got about 15 thumbs on each hand, cerebral palsy like you've never seen before. I pick up a wrench off the hatch that's 150 degrees from the sun. Five guys hollerin' and screamin':

"'HERE HE COMES AGAIN LOOK OUT LOOK AT THE SIZE OF HIM..HHHHHOLY SHIT.'

"I'm supposed to concentrate on takin' six or seven bolts out of the motor that held the pump on. I've got about one turn on the first bolt when the mate hollers, 'HE'S SPIT IT OUT.'

"I says, 'Good—wind it in, don't put it in the water, let me get this pump changed.' Soooo—

"I started to take off the bolts, he made three or four more passes, got the bolts off, got the new pump, and tried to put the new pump on. You had to line up the gears, small gears, just had to get 'em right, or the holes for the bolts wouldn't line up. Back at the dock, in flat calm water, it would probably take 15 or 20 minutes. Out here, with all this excitement, you'd be lucky if you got it in three-quarters of an hour. He'll be gone, I think, he ain't gonna stay that long, anyhow.

"But the party's screamin' GET 'IM, GET 'IM. I says, 'I can't on rod-and-reel cause I gotta do this.' 'We don't care how you get him—harpoon him, anyway you can, GET 'IM.' Okay, we'll harpoon him. So I told the jockey to bring the harpoon from the pulpit. He brings it down and gets everything ready.

"The shark comes sssstraight up the cockpit, straight to the middle of the cockpit, and I was standin' there like Ahab with the stick in my hand, and I drew back and was gonna pop him right stright between the eyes. No, wait, I think. He should turn, you'll have a backbone shot right in the middle. He got close to the boat, made his turn, *poyfect,* I took the stick and almost scratched it down from his dorsal, down about halfway, and then I come back on it and hit him with both shoulders, the weight of my body, everything, and drove it right home.

"Woooo, he didn't like that one bit, took off towards the bow, the direction he was goin' in. He made half a breach, came half out the water, then headed for the bottom, took off and there went the barrel."

"'Okay, now,'I holler to these guys, 'keep your eyes on the barrel [attached to the harpoon dart], let me know when it starts to disappear. I'll work on the pump, get it straightened out, and then we'll go out there.

"I get two turns on a bolt, and they say the barrel's almost out of sight. I mash on the starter button. We could run a short distance. I ran up to the barrel and shut the engine off real quick and had everybody standin' over the top of the engine fannin' on it and blowin' on it and everything else.

"Okay, back down to the bilge. Again, I tell the guy, 'Let me know when its almost out a sight. In five minutes, it is. I hardly got anything done."

"All right, we run up to it, and on the way up there, I say look, 'We're gonna have to put some more pressure on him; we have to slow him down, or I'm never gonna get that pump changed.' I said, 'There's another harpoon with the barrel and everything, just bring it out, and we'll attach it to that one. We'll have another 400 feet of line, two barrels with 800 feet of line.' We get up to the barrel, and I say, 'Grab the barrel, tie on the other. All right now, here we go' and the one idiot customer takes the box with the line in it and turns the box upside down and makes one giant *boydie's* nest. We've got 25 feet between the two barrels and all the line tangled.

"All right that was our first booboo. Had to shut off the engine and let the barrels go. Holy Gees, I hardly got another bolt done. Out a sight again. All right, start again and take after him. I say, 'Okay take the rod-and-reel and attach the leader to the last barrel and hang on. Maybe that'll slow him down.' I put two guys up on the bow, one to hold the pole, the other guy to hold him and the pole. I say, 'Let me know when you get low on line.' In three minutes, I get one more bolt. He hollers, 'We're almost out of line.' I mash on the starter and come out on the flyin' bridge. I look at the spool. There's still a half a spool of line. I look up, and the barrels are still right there. I call 'em everything I could think of, including dopey bastids. I figure, as long as I got the motor started, I might as well run up on him. I put it in gear, tell 'em to wind up the slack. I put the barrels under the pulpit, come to a stop, shut it off and tell 'em, 'Don't you dare holler unless you're almost out of line. That thing's gonna overheat, and one time it ain't gonna start.

"All right, I go down, get one more bolt on. They holler and scream, 'We're outa line.' I mash on the starter button, and I'm mad, go up on the flying bridge and look, and they're completely outa line, and one guy is draggin' the other guy toward the bow. They're both tryin' to hold back on the 130-pound test. Before it breaks, I put it in gear— otherwise, we've lost the whole spool a line. Now I'm mad because they waited too long, aaaaargh? They almost cost me a spool a line.

"All right, we done that one or two more times. I got the pump changed and now start up the motor— can't get water. New pump, changed, still no water, the barrels goin' away, come on, we gotta go. Four more times we primed it; finally, we got water. Now we can con- centrate on the barrels.

"We picked up the first barrel from the bow. Now we disconnect the other one, put it in the cockpit all tangled up, and I say, 'Untangle it, 'cause we're gonna need it when we get him up.'

"'Pull, you bastids.' Yeah, the party's pullin' like this," Frank says, demonstrating the weakest effort imaginable.

"'C'mon, pull,' I'm screamin'. I almost got the black whip out— bang. The dopey little mate's pullin' the same way, 'Oh, my hands hurt.' Holy shit, so I've got some cussed crew: one guy in the whole batch and he got wore out. 'All right, give me the cussed line. You, ya dumb little bastid, get up on the bridge and run the boat.' 'I never run a boat before,' he says. 'Well, run it now— do it, do what I say, fol- low the line.'

"Now I pull as hard as I can. I'm gettin' him up as I'm tellin' the jockey how to run the boat and I'm tellin' one of the guys to get the other stick ready 'cause when I get 'im up, I'm gonna have to hesi- tate a minute, take that other stick and put the second one in him.

"Okay. When I get him up, my arms are comin' out of the sockets.

I still gotta throw the stick—bang, I got a good shot. He goes all the way to the bottom. Now there's two lines, two barrels. We have a coffee break, and then we go back. We pick up the barrels—'pull, you bastids'—it took another hour to get him back up. I get the other harpoon ready—hit him with the third one. Down he goes, down with three barrels, three lines.

"I say, 'Grab ahold of the barrels now, and watch what you're doin' 'cause somebody's goin' to get killed.

"'Look out now!' I put the fourth harpoon in him, and down he goes with everything again. I mean, it's really turning into a shithouse mess. Now there's four rigs out, startin' to get tangled up.

"'Okay we're gonna get him next time. I don't care what you guys do—hang on to everything. Take a turn on everything, your neighbor's leg, anything you want, take a turn on something because we're not gonna let him go.' I hit him with the fifth one and scream, 'Everybody hang on.' They're all slidin' around. We got him to the point where, after five hours, he was fairly much tired. When they can't run away any more, they roll. Well, he started to roll, which was in our favor because it was like the Jolly Green Giant. He was all wrapped up in his work, and after we get the tail rope on, we started untyin' all the other stuff."

The sun was sinking low on the afternoon of June 6, 1964, its bloody light throwing into silhoutte the morbidly curious who swarmed around Frank's first monster. It was too big to tow into the harbor, so it was dropped off near the mouth. A man named Alex Joyce put a half-hitch around one of the cement guardposts marking the edge of the Gosman's restaurant parking lot, down where the Montauk Harbor jetty tapers to a small beach.

Alex had come with a bulldozer, Frank's recalling, "and pulls a post out with his dozer blade, pops it out of the sand, so he could get down to the beach with his machine. He puts the bucket down, puts the short rope on the tail, and then picks the tail up. Now he moves the 'dozer back 'cause he's got a lot of the shark's weight in the air, aaargh?

"So he pulls him up, and while this was going on, the fish was half out of the water, half in. There was a bunch of kids and elderly people standing there lookin' at him, gawkin' at him, and they wandered out in the water, up to their knees, and I'm hollerin', 'LOOK OUT, GET AWAY FROM HIM, DON'T MESS WITH HIM, HE'S STILL ALIVE.'

"We'd towed him home for three hours, but an animal like that, you're not botherin' him, nothing to worry about. So now he's laying there, restin'. He's liable to come back alive. Just about this time it happened.

"WOARRRUNNGHHH," Frank says, mimicking a huge wounded animal coming to life. "Then he made a half a turn, and lucky he turned toward where the younger people were. They were agile and jumped out of the way, but if he'd pinned them down, he would have drownded them in three foot of water.

"That was it. I went down to the boat and grabbed my carbine. I put a full clip in there, 15 shots, and I come marchin' down the street like Matt Dillon. By this time, there's 50 people there. Now I wormed my way through the whole bunch of them with the barrel of the chrome-plated carbine *pernt'n* toward the *boidies*, and I says,'Scuse me, can I get through, scuse me can I get through, GET OUT OF THE WAY, LET ME COME THROUGH, WILL YA?!' And when I got through the crowd—no sense tellin' them to step back—I put the barrel right down to about eight inches or 10 inches from the back of his head and started pouring the lead to him.

"BANG, BANG, BANG, BANG, BANG, BANG, that carbine was throwin' hot fire out the barrel. It was just startin' to get dark. Uh huh, there was a lot said right there. I didn't have any trouble gettin' any room after that. The whole place just cleared right out."

Frank slows his telling here, as though the effort of transporting himself back to June of '64 has tired him out.

"The people'd come from all over, out of the *woodwoyk,* like cockaroaches, when you bring a decent fish like that. By this time, it's just about dark, and I could see all a them teeth and them souvenir seekers, and I said there was only one thing we could do. We didn't have a camera with a flash. There was one little old lady there that had a Polaroid, and she got one or two of the little jockey mate posing at the front of the fish.

"I went down and got my big knife from the boat. I brought my carbine back to the boat and went after the big knife to cut the jaw out because I knew somebody was goin' to attack that. I cut the jaw out, and then I was satisfied, locked it down in the cabin on the boat. I was goin' to get the tail, have the tail mounted. During the night someone stole the tail, yessss, a NICE, CLEAN, NEAT, CUT—stole it.

"The rest of the fish was there next morning. I mean, it was cut, beat, pinched, scratched, and walked on, all the things the tourists do. It was loaded with tourists, but we grabbed a hold of the carcass and dragged it back to the sea."

"Two sides and a backdrop, 10-feet square"

[FRANK MUNDUS]

Chapter

11

C I R C U S   M I N I M U S

WHEN THE TOURISTS SCAVENGED Frank's 4,500-pounder on the beach at Gosman's, swarming it like maggots that June, it was an event which, like the moon landing five years later, signaled the world was changing in a fundamental way. □ Luby, in one of his hallucinatory moments, surely would have seen the two events as related, as I do today at sea with Mundus. That one small step was just flat-footed enough to have jogged the spheres out of alignment. It's not only hairspray eating our ozone that's causing the seas to rise, but an angry moon swirling her vengeful veil of tides. □ Over the years, Frank witnessed the rise and fall of different species of fish on the Montauk docks, in a complex weaving of marine biology and economics. □ Sport fishermen changed too, slowly, as though by the laws of natural selection. They evolved from the elite broadbill connoisseurs and their knuckle-dragging, food-gathering counterparts to the desperate types fleeing the flood of humanity, Noah-like, in the expensive plastic boats oldtime fishermen call Clorox bottles.

By the time of Frank's retirement, millions of Everymen were bobbing offshore with affordable mass-produced Japanese sonar and an imaginary mission to guide them. These were the ones prepared on land, the mini-Munduses, instant Ahabs, the ones with freeze-dried lives to which you just add water.

Something big, terrifying in its implications, had been born, a late-20th-century human thing, virtual, unnatural. Now, after three days on this heaving expanse, watching the Cricket's oily slick of a tongue gesturing obscenely toward shore, I'm sure of it.

The birth began slowly. "There it is," like Frank said, "little spot, little smudge," with a few newspapermen taking license with one of the grand themes: the beast brought low. "Little smudge gets bigger, bigger, now starts makin' color, it's an amber-brown smudge, nowww it's a head, now here it comes, now you can see it full view." First sharks, then white sharks, then white sharks like the one caught a month after the 4,500-pounder in August of '64. That one was left unweighed, Frank said, left unreported for fear of panicking the vacationing public, but the unreporting succeeded only in doubling, tripling, and quadrupling its fearsomeness—"Old Faithful."

"It had a throat on it like that," Frank's saying of the garbage-can-sized chum grinder he had at the time, the only one around in the early days.

"With five guys movin' as fast as you can, you could grind 60 cans in 10 minutes. I picked it up from a meat packin' plant. It had a roller conveyor. We'd have the fish all set up in milk crates. One milk crate was one bushel, exactly. We'd have 'em all filled and stacked to go, and the empty cans stacked and ready. One guy would do nuthin' except take the full one out and put the empty in, take the full one out, put the empty in. Another guy would do noth'n but pick up the full one and run around the corner and just drop it, and the other guy would take it from there out of the way. I would take the bushel and put it on the rollers, go up the roller in one motion, dump, and throw the empty. As soon as I did it, the grinder wanted more. Sixty cans in 10 minutes."

"Wow," says Howard.

Do you see? Frank was chumming people as well as sharks. It was as though the billowing clouds of brown fish and whale essence that drifted shoreward from off Montauk came ashore in perfect waves, broke, and then reached up the white thigh of Long Island beaches. It took to the air and blew west past where the last glacier's terminal moraine of granite and clay plays in the surf like spiky moon mountains, past the last stands of white oak on the East End, brown clouds hugging the rolling hills to where they flatten toward Babylon, and on into the Big Apple, there to mix with the dense ether of confinement to become a rich mixture, a drawing salve.

Saint George had become Saint Frank to the shot-and-a-beer crowd. Then another surprise. Tales of the beached beast traveled beyond the narrow fishing columns, a phenomenon akin to when the Gulf Stream floods its meandering banks bringing the big ones closer, as Frank describes it. The stories swelled and spread, a second slick beckoning to something deep in the collective humdrum.

Peter Benchley recognized it, albeit without giving the devil his due, Frank reminds us again. The *Jaws*-inspired shark fishing craze that took place, almost 20 years after Mundus began pissing off the Montauk Chamber of Commerce with his disgraceful "snake hunts," was responsible for launching an armada of private fishing boats onto the unsuspecting sea.

If the genesis is seen, as Frank sees it, as a chum-and-newspaper-driven beast, it's one which began, fellow Romans, in a coliseum—the New York Coliseum in this case.

For years, Abercrombie and Fitch, the aristocratic supplier to sports of all kinds, held court at the annual Sportsman's Show at the Coliseum. It was the finest of its kind in the world. If you could afford a sporting life—your birthright after all—you went to the Coliseum.

Frank remembers it in the old, uncorrupted times, before the pursuit of happiness became a rout—"before they let all those so-called humans in," as Frank puts it. Lester Eisner ran the show then. His son Don, the next generation, would one day rule Disneyland. Jim Hurley, outdoor writer for the *Daily Mirror,* usurped the Coliseum.

"Up until the time the *Daily Mirror* took over, I was getting my booth free. Used to be the sportsman's show. That was when it was a lot of fun, and we used to raise some hell. That was the real McCoy. I mean, that was a circus. Everybody there was real. There wasn't any phonies. They had the real canoe tilters, real log rollers, real outdoorsmen, real horses, all that kind of stuff ... everthing was real."

Frank says he came to the original Coliseum show with Gerry Ruschmeyer, a Montauk bar and hotel owner.

"He had a big booth in there. A Montauk booth. He would allow a half a dozen guys, the charter boat captains, the privilege of standin' there, handin' out our business cards. That's all you could do. Everything was advertising for Ruschmeyer's Luxury Hotel. But for the privilege of standin' there holdin' out your card, we had to paint the whole booth, crate each fish. Aaaargh?

"That's a pain in the ass. He had a 20-foot booth, then he had a 30-foot booth, and you figure every kinda fish that was caught in Montauk was mounted on that rackboard. Every fish had to be crated from here, so you had to make crates, aaaargh? And handle all the stuff. So it was a lot of work.

"Once a year, Rushchmeyer would invite all the newspaper reporters and wine and dine 'em the night before. Get 'em drunk out of their minds, all for nothin', so they would give him a good plug, and then there was a choice few of us who had the high privilege of takin' the reporters out and tryin' to catch em a fish for nothin'.

"First you had to drag 'em out of bed with hangovers, aaargh?

"Then you had to try to catch 'em a fish in the short time you had, hopin' that they would give you a good plug."

Frank looks at me and gives the word "plug" extra bluntness, revealing his healthy animosity toward my species.

"You know who never got off my case, to this day, was Jerry Kenney [*Daily News*]"

I recall the Kenney column which expressed skepticism of Frank's claim that Big Guy, his last great white, was caught according to the rules of the International Game Fish Association.

"You talk about slander, you talk about bad-mouthin'. I sat at a lawyer's desk in New York. Another lawyer, a friend of mine, took me in for a consultation. It didn't cost nothin' to listen to this guy who handled nothin' but slander cases.

"We gave him the article about catchin' a white shark. He read it. He went on to say, 'you would have to start somewhere around $50,000, if you got $50,000 to play with, and could go to $100,000 in this case, and when you won, if you won, then what you would get in return: one little piece, a small little retraction.

"There was only one real bad one," Frank says of the messengers. The rest of 'em wasn't as bad as him. There was a lot of good ones: Frank Keating, Russ Krandal, and ah .... the guy who was writin' for the *Mirror* at the time?" Frank asks of the horizon. "It slides past me now, but they was all on my side."

It was the *Daily Mirror,* which owned the dock at Fort Pond Bay from which the Montauk charter boats were leaving, its outdoor column having chummed up the fishermen. Frank says it was after the *Mirror* took over the sportsman's show, that it changed.

"The union got so bad. The union was responsible for breakin' up the show. I remember a guy used to come in with a log cabin," Frank says, all rheumy, like it might have been Abe Lincoln himself. Frank, Howard, and I are sitting below decks, on the bunks, where Cricket can't throw us around so badly. Frank has the tea-water on. Our oilers smell of shark juice, our clothes like old sweat.

"He had to have union guys put the thing together. Everything was A and B, easy. He figured out what it was costin' him to have the union guys put it up and take it down, and says no, I'm not gonna bother. It costs more than the log cabin was worth. I'm gonna leave it. They said he couldn't.

"Watch me, he said. You ain't gonna stop me from walkin' out the door. The log cabin's yours, a present. He walked out the door. They sold it to some guy who had a truck, aaargh? There was some finagling done where the union guys made a little bit on it, and the guy with the truck sold it, you know. I seen this.

"I would set my display all up here," Frank says, meaning Montauk. "Nut for nut, bolt for bolt, all wing nuts on, paint it, pull it apart, mark it, so I could put it together blindfolded in 15 minutes, two sides and a backdrop, 10 feet square.

"Every year, the union comes up with new ideas. First, they said you have to have a carpenter and helper for one hour, minimum, to help you erect the booth, or you won't get in. I didn't need 'em, but I hadda have 'em, so I was constantly bein' chewed out by the head union guy. He had his eye on me all the time. The stuff comes into the show wrapped in paper, so it don't get scatched. It's got maskin' tape on and when they bring it from the truck up into the Coliseum, I follow it because they stole me blind. And then they put it here, against the wall, where the booth is gonna be.

"While I'm waitin', I take this finger and pop the tape. The boss man comes along and hollers at me, 'You can't do that, Mundus. You again—you can't do that.'

"'What can I do?'

"'You gotta have a helper for that job.'

"'I gotta have a helper for that finger? To pop the maskin' tape?'

"'If you don't get a helper for that job, I'll shut the whole show down.'

"'All right, I'll put this finger [his third] where you won't see it.' He goes away.

"All this builds up over the course of the years, and I seen that guy with the log cabin, so I knew what I was gonna do.

"Later, you not only had a carpenter and a laborer for one hour to set the booth up—now, with the new rules, you had to have a carpenter and laborer for an hour to help take the booth down. Takin' it down was nothin' because you let it fall. You don't care if it scatches; you're gonna repaint it, anyway, when you get home. I started to take it apart. Sure enough, here he comes.

"'Hey Mundus, hold it, hold it, hold it.' You can hear him holler all over the place. He says, 'You can't do that. Did you put in your order for your carpenter and helper to take the booth down?' I said, 'Nope, and I don't need 'em.'

"'Yes, you do,' he says. 'If you don't have a carpenter and helper, you won't get that out the door.'

"I says, 'Okay, smartass, see that pile in the middle of the room where all the garbage is? See all that garbage out in the middle of the floor?'

"He says, 'Yeah.'

"'Well,' I says, 'take this booth and either put it out there in the gaaaabage, or shove it up your ass, because I'm goin' out the door.'

"I never went back again with my own booth. No, after that, I started goin' back with Penn Reels. I was standin' in their booth. I could stand in anybody's booth. All's I needed was my little briefcase with my *paperwoyk*." We're back on deck.

His paperwork? I chortle to myself, as I cast an especially molten dollop of oily mash upon the waters. He means the little black book he keeps his charter schedule in. And, if that little black, chum-stained Rosetta Stone of idiots could talk, it would tell a tale of the television-numbed pioneers who rushed seaward during Frank's tenure, no less ecstatically than the shiftless wackos who rushed westward for land a century before. Who could blame them, once the Circus Maximus went union?

"Look, look,
he's bleedin', he's bleedin'! "

[RAYMOND GREENBLATT]

12

M A R V E L O U S
A C H I E V E M E N T

THE SPORTFISHING INDUSTRY was built out of plastics, Fiberglass, and technology meant for outer space. It was already well on its way, but soared into the stratosphere of profitability as the delirium of shark fever spread. What started on the backdeck of the Cricket infected fishermen and others nationwide. The hole in the bloated suburban dream opened by *Jaws* was the catalyst that would spill a multitude onto the sea in a blind escape for which most were unprepared. □ Today, just as Frank's about to hang it up, ignorance of the deep is no longer an obstacle. It's virgin territory for endless sales of gadgets aimed at making the sea a comfortable place. At the same time, millions of shoreside condos and marina slips have superannuated beaches and wetlands in the dash for an affordable Sea of Tranquility. □ "There's a few different reasons that people go fishin' on the

Cricket II," Frank's telling Howard, who, by this time must be wondering why he's so far from the blue of the Pacific, here instead, being toyed with by the angry green jaws of the New York Bight.

"One is for the fun of it, and the other is for the serious sport of catchin' a fish. Sometimes that's a little confusing, because sometimes you got people who are what I call idiots, who don't really care about the fish, as long as they have fun. Fish is secondary.

"Fish is secondary to a fair amount of the customers. They wanta come on the boat, they wanta have fun. They want to try and aggravate me and aggravate the other guy. It's a mental challenge as to who wins this nonsense."

Frank begins telling about Allen Germain, a demanding little department store owner from Brooklyn who was of the first category of Idiot. For him, the backdeck of the Cricket was theater. He loved it so much, Frank is saying, he tried to monopolize the Cricket's weekends for a time.

Frank says Allen Germain was always accompanied by Miss Reich, his "secretary." He adds a second meaning to the word, "SEEEECRETARY," by drawing it out. These two were usually joined by Raymond Greenblatt, who owned a private detective agency and always came aboard the Cricket packing a snub-nosed .38.

In a breeze and lovingly, Frank brings his idiots back to life on the backdeck stage — a stage, for sure, by virtue of its location: the only place for miles of green-rolling miles where those trodding its boards won't drown or be eaten. There's a tendency to appreciate everything that goes on here, or went on. By default, every story told seems spellbinding, like *Treasure Island,* every movement with the sea's uplifting, like "Swan Lake."

Howard has a shark on.

Blue sharks hang by their tails from the gin pole on my left and from the stern bits on my right. They are blue-and-white, reeking curtains drawn to reveal the stage. The play is Frank's Coliseum. Luby the younger, visible only to me, dances to the Fifth Symphony. Mr. Banks, standing beside the giggling A.S.P.C.A. cop, is there watching from the flying bridge, high over the streets of Harlem, to see how this test between men and beasts will end.

What would Mr. Banks have thought about the South African government having turned Robbens Island into a tourist attraction? For most of the last century, the island was a leper colony and an insane asylum. It also was the place where Nelson Mandela broke rocks for 18 of his 22 years as a political prisoner. The South Africans claim the largest white shark ever was caught just off Robbens Island. I'm sure Mr. Banks would have liked that, although the South African government recently made it illegal to catch whites for sport.

"You watch," Frank recalls telling a charter captain he shared a Coliseum booth with one year, "when they open the doors and let all them so-called humans in like cattle, within the first half hour, this short fat guy with a bald head will show up, and that's goin' to be Allen Germain, and he's goin to holler— before he gets 50 feet from the booth, he's goin to holler—'MUNDUS.'"

"He had a Russian hat on at the time," Frank's saying. "I was prepared for him. Here he comes." Frank squints his eyes, looking back at Allen Germain walking through the door of the Coliseum on his quest to monopolize Cricket's time offshore.

"He was wide as what he was short. He says, 'Mundus 'Come on, we gotta go to dinner.'

"'Alan, wait, gimme two minutes. I just got set up here.'

"'Mundus, come on.'

"He was a bastid to go to dinner with," says Frank, explaining that he'd doctored his black book in anticipation of Germain's demands.

"Hadda go to a fancy restaurant, and hadda sit right in the middle. This was a dummy book I was handin' him. I wasn't goin' to give him all my Saturdays and Sundays, so what I did was make two books, one book was in the booth, and this book had all dummies in it, names, addresses, and deposits.

"He takes the book and starts turnin' the pages slow. Now he's turnin' the pages faster, and all of sudden he screams out loud, 'MUNDUS, you're a son-of-a-bitch.'

"Miss Reich says, 'What's the matter, Allen?'

"Allen says to Miss Reich, 'The son of a bitch has got most of the Saturdays and Sundays booked.

"She was sharp. She says, 'Well, maybe they're just phonies.' Allen says, "No, look, they got deposits on them. What am I gonna do?

"Miss Reich says, 'Well, you're just gonna have to fish on another boat sometimes.'

"He says, 'There's no other son-of-a-bitch that'll have me.'

" 'Bout this time, the waiter comes along—we was makin a lot of noise. The waiter says, 'Can I help you?' Allen looks up at the waiter and says, 'Yeah, give me a gun, I'm gonna shoot the son-of-a-bitch. Ha, ha, haaaaa," Frank keens at the memory.

"He hadda take the days that I gave him," Frank says. "That was the only way I could control him."

Frank says the only reason Germain and Greenblatt went fishing together was to aggravate one another. "The only reason they went fishin' with me," he says, "was so the two could aggravate me."

Frank says that of the three species of idiots he's had through the years—the food fishermen, the trophy fishermen, and those like Allan Germain—it was the latter type that kept returning, year after year, until they died. For them, the Cricket was a fortress, like the Monitor or the Merrimack, or a shrink.

"Raymond Greenblatt set up his own detective agency, had 11 detectives workin' for him, and he was makin' money, too. Raymond didn't know his ass from a hole in the ground as far as who stole what, but he says the other guys did. He just walks around with that stupid .38 on his hip all the time;—you know, he's a big shot." Sherlock Holmes he wasn't, Frank says, but he liked Greenblatt. I can tell.

"Greenblatt wouldn't shoot anything alive. He wouldn't hurt nothin'. One time, the two of them was fishin', and he threw all the live bait over the side because he couldn't stand the idea of Allen puttin' them on the hook and hurtin' 'em.

"But you hadda be there to see him shoot the mako," Frank says, and goes ahead and brings me and Howard Chong, who's fighting another small blue shark, and Jim, rifle at the ready, back in time on the same deck we're on today.

"There was Allen, sittin' in his favorite spot, the fightin' chair, sound asleep, like he always is, and snorin'. You could hear him all over the boat. All of a sudden, I'm watchin' Raymond, and I see him walk over to the dead mako hangin' and I see him pull out the .38, and I says to myself, 'What the hell's he gonna do?' It was about a 150-pound fish hangin'. He goes BANG, BANG, BANG. Allen jumps. Raymond looks around at Allen and says, 'LOOK, LOOK, he's bleedin,' he's bleedin'.'

"Allen, before he started snorin' again, he says, real slow, 'Marvelous achievement.' He just gets 'achievement' out, and he's back sleepin'." BANG, Jim dispatches Howard's blue shark. My last oblation mixes with the blue shark's blood adding urgency to the Cricket's beck and call.

Shooting a dead shark with a handgun is not a great achievement, it's true, but what's a great achievement—writing obituaries? Same sorta thing, says the Luby in me. Who is the more interesting, he asks, the one who spends the day shooting predeceased fish or the one who beats a dead horse? Be honest.

Frank says Bruce Jenner brought his javelin out on the Cricket, despite his Olympian achievements, to spear sharks, like Ajax at Troy. Some things just need to be done, not for any logical reason, but for the sake of myth. Greenblatt's adventure needn't be preserved in a freize, but I agree with him that the story of our gumshoe, savior of baitfish, tailer of adulterous spouses, and slayer of already slain monsters, speaks to our time.

Mr. Banks nods in agreement from on high. I cast a ladle-full. Frank says, "Happy horseshit," and I'm relieved he's talking about someone else.

"Now, the other guy, who's a good fisherman. He wants to go out there and have fun, but he also wants to put his back and his talent into the sport of landing a big fish on light tackle. Aaaargh?

"We didn't have that many good fishermen. We had some fishermen that wanted to be good, some that would never be good. Some was potential anglers, and a very few of them were good—that I could turn my back on, that I didn't have to worry about them makin' a mistake in the middle of the fight.

"Experience still is not the best teacher, for a lot of anglers, because they'll keep makin' the same mistake over and over. Unless you can turn your back on an angler and not have nothin' to worry about, you wouldn't call 'em good.

"I know this is gonna sound funny, but the best potential angler, to catch on the fastest, is the slowest. You get a guy that, when you say, 'Hey Joe, you gotta fish on,' he gets up, he yawns, says, 'Okay,' walks over, calmly puts his belt on, calmly picks up the pole. This is the guy who's gonna learn to fish the fastest.

"But you say, 'Hey, Mike, you got a fish on,' and he goes, 'Holyshitwhere'smybeltwhere'smysneakers—he's the fastest, but the slowest. So it's just reversed. You have more who are excitable than you do what are calm—very few are calm—very few who will take their time.

"That's why the woman makes the better fisherman; because they're calm, most of them are calm. They might be excited because they got a fish on, but they're not panicking because they got a fish on. They're not running in circles, screaming, so's you can't get a word in edgewise. Even your kids. Take a kid that's big enough to hold a fishin' pole, and he'll wind up to be a better fisherman faster than the guy who's done a lot of fishin' but is still excitable.

"When you tell somethin' to somebody who's excitable, it goes in one ear and out the other, or it doesn't even enter into that ear. He'll look up towards the sky, he'll be spinning his handle, riding his clutch as hard as he can, and you look at the spool, and it's sittin' still, and he's not gainin' line, and he's turnin' that handle and he's lookin' right straight through you, and you tell him, 'Stop, stop windin', you're not gainin' line,' and he says, 'I know, I know, I know.'

"'Well, if you know, stop toynin' the handle.'

"'Okay, okay,' he says, so you take two hands and grab a hold of his wrist, and you stop him, and you say, 'You're not gainin' line — look at the spool.' The eyes still see nothing."

Frank says one of the few women who panicked, but had reason to, was poor Bea, who usually accompanied Rotten Ronald on trips aboard the Cricket.

"When a wise man,
established well in virtue,
develops consciousness
and understanding,
then as bhikkhu ardent
and sagacious, he
succeeds in disentangling
his tangle."

[SIDDHARTHA GAUTAMA, BUDDHA]

Chapter

13

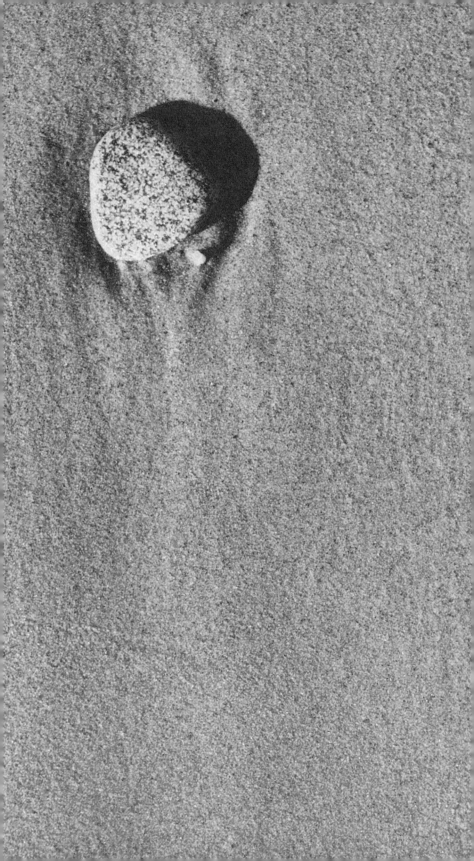

L I K E   B U D D H A

RONALD 'PARRY WAS A BANK EXECUTIVE from the city who led two

lives, one of them drunk. He was in charge of loans, big loans," says

Frank. "But he was like Dr. Jeckyl and Mr. Hyde. By the time I seen

him, he was stoned. □ "Bea was a retired prostitute he called his wife,

or a friend, or whatever he felt like sayin', if he felt like sayin' any-

thing at all. □ "He got her outa *Screw* magazine. Said he put an ad in

Screw magazine that read: 'Wanted, retired hooker.' He said he had I

don't know how many come knockin' on his apartment door for

interviews, yeah, INTERVIEWS. □ "One day the two of them climb

on the boat. He heads for the booze. She comes up on the flyin'

bridge. Got on sunglasses. I could see behind the glasses was all

black and blue. I says. 'Good mornin'— how are you, Bea? She was

one of them that had a lot of mileage. She tried to make herself look like something, but you could tell, one look would tell you she was an old model. Her fenders were bent, and everything was busted.

"'So,' I says, 'how you feelin'?'

"'Yeah, I guess you can see,' she says, pickin' up her glasses. I said, 'Holy shit, what happened?' she said 'That son-of-a-bitch beat me up again. He's always beatin' me.' I says, 'Why don't you leave him.' She says, 'The bastid knows I got no place to go.' It was the truth. She didn't know how to do anything. She'd a wound up down the Bowery if he left her.

"When she was catchin' her giant tuna, she was one of the very few females that did not listen to what I said. She took a hold of the handle on the big reel, put her head down and constantly wound, wound, against that drag, whether she was gettin' line in or not, and I stopped her. I talked and talked and talked. She said, 'Okay,' but just stared straight ahead. Finally, I put my hand on her hand, took her hand off the reel. I said, 'Look—this is the way you do it,' I showed her how to do it.'

"Now, she would calm down. She was calm. Get back in the chair again and away she went. I'd grab ahold of her hand, and she'd look at me like I wasn't there, look right straight through me, glassy-eyed, aaaaaargh, like I gotta get the fish.'

"While she was catchin' the fish, with all these problems—my God, she was light, didn't weigh nothin', and for giant tuna you gotta have somebody that's heavy—she was doin' everything wrong. It's a good thing the fish was cooperative. He was a slow fish, 500-something."

"Now Ronald gets in my way, and starts complainin' about the mate's gloves. 'The least he can do is wear new gloves for his charter. he says, because he don't like old gloves, half worn out, smelly ...

"'GET OUT MY WAY,' I yells at him. He's standin' right between me and her. 'Holy shit. GET OUTA THE WAY.' Then he wants to take a picture —'GET OUTA THE WAY.' Don't ask me how. She caught the fish. She was physically exhausted, beat up. She fell down on the cussed motor box. Her hands was solid blisters from friction, from just twistin' that handle as hard as she could.

"He says to me, 'Put another line out.' I says, 'You gonna catch the next fish?' He says, 'No, put another line out—we got time; I want to see her catch another fish.' I says, 'You're nuts. Look at her—she's got blisters on her hands. She's out of it, and you expect her to catch another fish?'

"'Well,' he says, 'it's my charter, and I'm payin' for it, and I want you to put another line out. 'All right,' I says, 'what kind of tackle?' He says, 'Put out 30-pound test. Maybe she'll catch a record.' Aaaaargh?

"I says, 'Ronald, that's nuts, she ain't gonna be able to get off the box.' I put the line out, but before it hit the water, I took the bait off. I put it out just to kill time.

"A few times she had yellow jaundice so bad when she climbed on the boat, she looked like a Chinaman. I never seen anyone turn yellow like that."

Howard's down below in the head and didn't catch Frank's gaffe.

"She decides she's gonna quit drinkin'. Goes to the doctor. The doctor gives her pills. I was down in St. Maarten for the winter. He comes down with her. He finds the pills. Comes out of the cockpit, and he hollers up at me, says, 'Hey Frank, lookahere.' He's got a whole handful of loose pills. Says, 'We got a junkie on our hands,' aaaaaarhump—he throws them all overboard.

"The only fish Ronald ever caught was when they cut his pants off. Bea wasn't with him on that trip. He's in a bar, so he invites Annie Houseknecht, and she invites this big, fat colored lady who was a parole officer. Now here's a pair. Annie's on the bridge. Dicky, the mate, was with me. Ronald says, 'Put a bait out.'

"I says, 'Well, Ronald, we're trying to see what we're goin' to catch, what kinda tackle we're goin' to use. 'Put the bait out,' he says.

"'Okay, we'll put one out blind.' That was in the days when you had a lot of fish, and sometimes it was better to wait and see how big the fish were that was around, to see what kind of tackle you was gonna put in the water.

"Okay, so we threw one over the side, 50-pound test, and we get a pickup, a big blue shahk. Annie goes first, says to the colored lady, 'You're gonna catch the next one.' Annie's pullin'. It doesn't want to come up, so she says, 'You know what you can do with this pole.'

"So the colored girl says, 'I'll try it.' So she grabs a hold of it, says 'This ain't a fish. This is a elephant.' She hangs on five minutes. 'I can't hold this no more — you take it.'

. "Ronald says, 'I ain't gonna take it.' He says, 'Dicky, you take it.' Dicky says, 'I ain't gettin' paid for pullin' your fish in.' He says to me, 'Frank, you take it.' I says, 'You know better'n that. Your fish — you catch it.'

"He was stuck. Hadda put a belt on. He starts catchin' this fish, the one and only fish he ever fought the whole time he was on. It's flat calm. The sun's up. He's wanderin' around, tryin' to catch this fish, doin' everything wrong. Dicky's tryin' to tell him what to do."

"His pants drop. He had on long pants. Down they go, right to his ankles. He says, 'Help me.'

"Dicky says, 'Help yourself. You got yourself into this mess; Aaaaarg?' Dicky looks up at me, and I go like this—'Don't help him.'

"He's shufflin' around with his feet, his pants wrapped up around his ankles. He's got on a pair of white boxer shorts. He finally kicks, kicks, and kicks — he's tryin' to catch this fish. He finally kicks the pants off. Now he's wanderin' around with a pair of shorts; the belt was bitin' into his shorts. He was complainin' about his shorts.

"I hollered down to Dicky. I said, 'Dicky, you heard him, he says his shorts is botherin' him. Cut 'em off.' Okay, Dicky pulls out his knife and goes zzzzzip.

"Now he's balls-ass naked, fightin' the fish. This is what he wanted. He wanted this, with the two girls on board. Eventually, he catches the fish. He's walkin' around the cockpit, nothin' on from his belly button to his toenails. And what are the girls doin'? They're very busy bakin' a cake or somethin'.

"They're not even talkin' to him, never mind lookin' at him. So he got insulted."

"Annie finally got some pictures but was laughin' so cussed hard, the pictures come out all fuzzy. He looked like Buddha, with his belly. He hadn't seen his penis for I don't know how long. He hadda look over the mountain, like Buddha."

"But the old fellows say
we must read to gain knowledge,
and gain knowledge to
make us happy and admired.
Mere Jargon!
Is there any such thing
as happiness in this world?
No."

[THOMAS JEFFERSON]

Chapter

14

LIFE, LIBERTY AND THE PURSUIT . . .

"HERE, YOU TAKE THIS ONE," Howard says as he helps strap me into the stand-up fighting belt with its distinctively female and groin-level stainless steel receptacle for taking on the rod. Frank's grinning as Jim hands it to me. It's already bent double by a big creature somewhere below, fighting for its life. □ The clouds are higher now, but a sickly yellow. Howard's lounging on the throne he's paid $5,000 for. Suddenly, I feel like the jester. True, I've yet to ask Captain Mundus a question, but I'm clearly on board in a reportorial capacity. □ I've caught big fish before, it's not that—"ungh, you bastard," grunt I as the big fish starts a bottom-bound run, and the reel sings its discouraging song. □ Frank predicts it's a brown or a dusky and says this fits with his theory that we have a cold thermoclime below us—the reason the fishing has been slow today, despite the long drift and miles-long meandering river of chum.

He recalls that when Peter Gimbel was out with his cage during a week-long trip with very little sign of sharks, a practice dive revealed that the hard, cold edge of the thermocline over which the Gulf Stream pours in early summer was just 30 feet below the surface and only 38 degrees. It was July, and up top the water was over 70.

For a time, Frank had recorded sharks' body temperatures for the government, and learned that blue sharks lacked the circulatory plumbing that allowed others to dally in cold water. Blues were the first to leave an area of cold water. The others—makos, whites, and, to a lesser extent, browns had an ability to raise their body temperatures above that of the water around them, as bluefin tuna do.

Taking into account the way my line is cutting through the water and the possibility of the thermocline, Frank sees a brown.

"This is what I could never figure out," he says: "how could we catch fish before man made this so-called temperature gauge, and before the marine hardware stores sold these temperature gauges.

"Today you listen to these would-be hotshots on the radio; you listen to them, and they're chirpin' away, talkin' about water temperatures like it was carved in stone—that they had to have a certain degree to catch fish. This is an advancement, to them. 'Well,' I feel like askin' them, 'what did you do before that, before the temperature gauge was put on the market? It was only 10 years ago.'

"How can you be an instant expert, in 10 years, on water temperature? And you're only reading what's on the very top. So what the hell good is the temperature gauge?

"There's the different drop-offs, there's the shape of your bottom, baitfish is a big factor. Yeah, anytime you got bait, you got other fish. It stands to reason, the book tells you. One fish eats the other fish. YOU'RE DRIVIN' DOWN THE HIGHWAY, YOU DON'T STOP AT A DINER THAT SAYS 'CLOSED.' Aaaaargh?" Frank bellows.

"Same with fish. When they're movin' from spot to spot they don't stop on the sandy bottom when there's no fish—they keep on goin'. There's a lot more to it than what us dumb humans will figure out. We've only tried to scratch the surface in the last 25 years or so."

"My God, when we first started shark fishin', in 1951, you couldn't buy a book that had sketches in it that showed what kinds of sharks there were. In '51, if you was goin' shark fishin' forget it. Nobody knew nothing. The old wives' tales that a shark has to roll over to bite, or that a splash will chase a shark away—just the opposite.

"There was no studies on sharks and very little on marine life."

The marine life on the other end of this goddamned rod wants to live with a passion. Frank chooses this time for a history lesson I should be writing down—removed

from

   this

      fight

        to

          the

            death and he knows it. Oh, how tutorial he's become, with the lounging Howard rapt, his Asian eyes nearly closed like a tiki god's. I see Rotten Ronald laughing in lotus position, his penis hidden, thank Buddha, below his mountainous belly.

"At first, the other charter boats wouldn't do it," he's teaching. "They didn't want to handle chum. There was no chum in Montauk. We hadda go out to the bunker boats, and they'd shovel down the bunker to the cockpit, and we'd take 'em down to East Hampton. There was that mink farm down there with a big grinder. Then we'd bring the chum back to Duryea's ice house. It was the only place to keep it."

Oh, great, I'm thinking, the granola-nazis would love that: Skin the pelts off the shiny little rodents for expensive coats, then grind their bodies to call sharks to slaughter.

"Merchants finally realized it was a payin' business; if they bought chum and put it in their freezers, they could get double their money back by just turnin' it over to the boats. If you gave the chum to fishermen to go shark fishin', you knew that when they come back, they was goin' into the tackle department and buy more tackle."

Howard asks him about tackle, types of rods and reels, etc. The Socratic dialogue continues while the vertebrae in my back are about to buckle into a dorsal fin—or plates, like a stegasaurus's.

"Sportfishin' is not that old from its very beginnings," says Frank.

"I can remember when I was goin to school," he says. "You go down the docks and see a guy what was goin' for giant tuna—why, he walked down the dock, and his knuckles was makin' noise draggin' along the planks. You hadda be an ape, hadda be in good physical shape," he says, looking right at my spine and grinning, like he's watching ontogeny recapitulating right here on the backdeck.

"People don't think," he says, still watching me like I'm a frog in a noose, "but there was no such a thing as a fightin' chair. We never had a fightin' chair. We never had outriggers. We had old linen line that was twisted." Frank gives the word "twisted" a little extra, in honor of my back.

"Nylon was the first thing to come out. Surplus. That drove the fishermen crazy. It was poppin' reels, blowin' reels sideways. It was supposed to be 125-pound test, but I swear you could move a building with it. And STRETCH—it would stretch a mile before it would tear an inch."

I wish this reel would blow out sideways. I have the bastard up. Frank deigns to peer over the side to declare the beast a brown shark, "200 pounds." As though commanded, the animal takes off again like a locomotive. My reel sings again, a mocking whine.

"They were forced into building better reels. I was fishin' when the glass rod come out. Before that we used to go down to the hardware store to buy a male calcutta [bamboo] pole — female calcutta was solid, wouldn't work. Cut it off on the tip to fit the hardware, cut it off on the butt to fit the other hardware that went into the chair.

"You had an old office chair with a gimbal and two pieces of pipe and a deck flange, so it would turn. If the pipes didn't fit right, you'd have wobblization.

"So, if we've come so far, why am I standing here like a human yardarm, wobblization incarnate? The Hawaiian dangles a foot regally off its modern rest.

"You put your reel on your pole with two hose clamps, put your 12.0 on there. You put two more guides on there, so you could turn the pole around, turn the hose clamps around, let the reel go around on the other side, because once you caught one fish on there, the pole stayed that way. Turn the pole over, and let it bend the other way. That pole would cost you $5.

"Now, if you was real fancy, if you was a rich charter boat, you would have split-bamboo poles, laminated, sanded down by hand, taped by hand. This is a lost art. Even those you hadda baby. When you were finished usin' those you hadda hang 'em straight off a nail in your garage, so they would pull down straight. You couldn't stand it in the corner. The guides were put on with heavy button thread. You wind them on yourself. One guy would turn, the other would hold, and then, when you was done, you used fingernail polish to finish it off."

I wonder if King Chong knows that in his heyday, Captain Mundus painted the big toe of each foot: green on the right, red on the left, for port and starboard. Talk about happy horseshit. I catch a glimpse of a dark shadow and a flash of white about 12 feet down. Paul takes the 30/30 out of its scabbard. The Cricket pitches and the thought occurs that this mother could pull me overboard. Jim keeps up a steady ladling in hopes of something muscular beyond belief. Frank's relaxed.

"It was funny to watch the salesman come down the dock and say, 'Hey fellas, I want to show this fishin' pole made a glass.' Everybody laughed. We all went up to heckle this guy, only it didn't work. He'd say, 'Okay, if you don't like these poles, take this one and break it.' Well, a solid glass pole was about physically impossible to break. The salesman would just sit by and smile until we would run outa ways to try and break 'em, and we was standin' there with our chins hangin down in wonderment. Whoever had the money bought the glass rod."

Wonderful, what about a Fiberglas backbone? We're headed in that direction any way: I can see the fish again, heading under the boat. He's forcing me to the edge of the Cricket; my body's cantilevered over the rail. I'm praying for traction on the slippery deck. I'm going to get you and your advanced circulatory system. I'll have you in steaks on a grill, your jaw in Frank's bleach bucket.

"All this stuff added up to catchin' bigger fish on lighter tackle. Go back to 1952, when I went down south with Red Stuart on the Sandona."

I don't want to go south. I just want to be released from this beast on my own recognizance.

"At the time, Red was one of the nation's best sport fishin' guides. I went with him one winter from Montauk to learn a few tricks, and I did. Not that he would teach you. Just watchin' him do this and do that, imitating his ways," says Frank, looking off into the past, oblivious to my struggle.

"When we was down fishin with him was when mono first hit the market. We was catchin 100-pound tarpon on 30-pound test plastic line. They thought this was crazy. This was considered ultra sports. And every year, it's been brought down and down and down, so now they're catchin' 'em on fly rods."

The shark is on the surface. Paul's going for the wire. POW—the rifle speaks. I'm showered with a cooling mixture of seawater and shark blood. The gunpowder smells like opium. The line goes slack.

"Ahh, that's what I call light tackle—light, as in infantry," say I.

Frank goes on as though nothing has happened. "The boats back then were nothin'. Look at your electronics. The first 10 years I was out of Montauk, I used nothin' but the clock and compass." I slump against the motor box.

"The hard part about goin' without anything, like the old radio direction finder or the fathometer was, you go straight offshore, tuna fishin', you hadda do everything close to even numbers so you knew where you was, one-hour, hour-an-a-half, two-hours offshore. Then, when you got there, you hadda start watchin' your clock and your compass. As you were trollin', you'd make your squares— east, west, north, south. Now, when you was ready to go home, you knew roughly you'd come out of this or that area."But the hard part about it was figuring out tide and current. In the thick fog, I can show you on the map where you're gonna go to the west, where you're gonna set still, a dead area, and where you're gonna drift to the east.

"For instance, if you go southeast off Montauk for 20 miles and stop, you will come directly back toward the lighthouse. But you go 25 miles southeast, and you'll drift directly to Nantucket. The current splits, and if you go past, you get sucked to the east. It's like openin' up a door. You go into another room."

I'm still panting. Another room, for sure. He's right. We are not in a room of space—there's too much of it out here—but one of time, with a window facing yesterday, another looking eagerly toward tomorrow. The ceiling in this room is black with storm clouds, the heaving rug is red from my bleeding shark. Hawaii is here, in Howard the condo-builder and in Frank's fruit-filled retirement, but not in warmth, though we're in the Fourth of July room, drifting east.

I'm getting that feeling again: like Frank and Howard have a mysterious symbiosis going, like this trip is fated for something.

"If you're in the thick fog," Frank continues, "and you got a sou'west wind, a fairly good breeze, and you're five to eight miles offshore due south, you think you're goin' to the northeast. You're not: you're standin' still.

"Now, how do you know you're standin' still? Somebody says, okay, you drop a sinker to the bottom. That sinker goes straight upwind so fast you can't hold on to it. You figure you are drifting to the northeast. You are not. The wind has got you against that current, and that's all current, forget the wind.

"A piece of newspaper helps a lot. Take a piece of newspaper and throw it in the water when you're driftin. Newspaper's got hardly no windage to it because it's flat to the water. Now, if that current is stronger than what the wind is, that newspaper is gonna leave you and go straight upwind. As far as I'm concerned, that's about all newspapers are good for."

Frank gives me the Mundus smile, the one with gritted teeth. I hope it hurts his pegs.

"Now you got all kinds of stuff. Man, now you got supersonic fishfinders and all this kinda happy jazz."

I chime in and tell Frank, speaking of happy jazz, how two years ago Darryl Loranz, president of the Loranz electronics company, put together a promotional junket to Scotland for outdoor writers. They linked the gunwales of sport boats together and swept the length and breadth of Loch Ness in search of Nessie, the inedible last of her species, with the latest in the company's computerized fish-finding televisions. Frank looks sad, or resigned. Cricket's drifting toward a new room. Frank knows she's nearing the atolls made of sewage bricks, out beyond his retirement, beyond the death of the last monster.

He saw it coming, the Loran navigational system showing the way like an invisible extension of the Long Island Expressway. The Loran uses radio signals to fix a boat's position on an electronic grid. To the great majority of instant Ahabs, the gadget has supplanted a full understanding of tides, winds, and currents. Depth finders, the little electronic boxes that grew from submarine sonar technology and then evolved into other little boxes televising once-private schools of fish, have replaced a fundamental knowledge of fishing seasons and cycles of abundance.

Mundus knows that boats today can receive infrared satellite photos showing the location, in real time, of Gulf Stream eddies and meanders, allowing fishermen to pinpoint the big ocean predators.

As happened earlier in the American whaling industry, finfish fishermen, including Frank, first worked close to shore and moved off as stocks dwindled and demand grew.

In the late 1960s and early '70s, foreign fishing and factory vessels, including Russian ones, worked the bountiful fishing grounds here off the Northeast coast. They hit hard the near-shore species that had kept the big ocean predators close. Bunker, or menhaden, was one of these species. Promised Land, just west of Montauk, was home to a rendering plant that squeezed industrial oil from bunkers. By the 1960s, the bunker seiners had worked through their target species and were taking inshore "trash" fish. Unfortunately, the "trash" was also on the diet of tuna, shark, and swordfish. The result was that all U.S. fishermen were forced farther offshore. The 40-fathom contour on the continental shelf—the other side of the world for sport fishermen, prior to this time—had to be staked out.

"What the Russians didn't get, Promised Land got," Frank's telling Howard. "They got what was left over from the Russians. That was the icing on the cake. Actually, Promised Land done more damage than the Russians because their boats covered more territory," he says, sounding blasphemous and unpatriotic all at once.

"Before Promised Land, fishing out of Montauk was like heaven.

Charter fishermen had all the swordfish they wanted, all the school tuna they wanted, all the white marlin they wanted. For God's sakes, you put two feathers in the water and go one hour offshore, one hour, and you had your box full of tuna fish. You pull your feathers in, just leave the outriggers out with your skip baits, ride around lookin' for swordfish—if a marlin jumped on there, fine. Aaaaargh?"

"You'd see six, seven, eight swordfish in one day, just goin' two hours. Nobody would go past two hours. I was the one that started 40 fathoms.

"Where I got it from—I was talkin' to one of the draggers. He suggested I make a trip out there. He showed me where it was on the chart. That's how we started goin' out there. When they'd lift their bag, everything was nibblin' on it. They wanted me to get rid of the sharks, because every once in a while, a shark would grab a hold of a full bag [cod end of the dragger's net] and bite into it, and they'd lose their whole tow.

"I told the silly bastids, 'Look, I know how to get rid of the sharks. If you don't want the sharks anywhere near you, take a negative and a positive wire, and just hang 'em in the water. They can't stand electricity, and it'll drive 'em away."

He's talking about over-amping the sharks. Does he know about the *ampules* of Lorenzini?

I'm thinking this is amazing, as Frank goes on about his discovering 40 fathoms and the electrical trick he learned one day when someone switched the Cricket's battery wires by mistake. Benjamin Franklin, the father of electricity, in his autobiography talked about fishy revelations that came to him here, just off Montauk:

"In my first voyage from Boston to Philadelphia, being becalmed off Block Island, our crew employed themselves in catching cod, and hauled up a great number," old Ben wrote.

"Till then I had stuck to my resolution to eat nothing that had had life; and on this occasion I considered the taking of every fish as a kind of unprovoked murder, since none of them had done or could do us any injury that might justify this massacre. All this seemed very reasonable. But I had been formerly a great lover of fish, and when it came out of the frying pan it smelled admirably well. I balanced some time between principle and inclination, till, recollecting that when fish were opened I saw smaller fish taken out of their stomachs, then, thought I, "if you eat one another I don't see why we may not eat you"; so I dined upon cod very heartily, and have since continued to eat as other people, returning only now and then occasionally to a vegetable diet. So convenient a thing it is to be a reasonable creature, since it enables one to find or make a reason for everything one had a mind to do," wrote Mr. Franklin.

Frank says, "Someday, somebody will come out with a little transisterized damn thing, wear it on your wrist. When you fall overboard, you push this little button, and it will send out a little bit of electricity. The only place you'll feel it—I know from divin' under the boat—you'll feel it, just a tingle, just a little annoying on your very tender skin, mostly your lips. That's a direct shot. Less than that, you wouldn't even feel."

"What will kill a fish will bother a dog. What'll kill a dog will bother a human. That's the way electricity *woyks*," says Frank, reinventing the stuff.

Surely more than coincidence, wouldn't you say? I mean, Frank flew kites around here, too. Wonder if Ben ever got that far—I mean the part about "what will kill a dog will bother a human." If he'd known about the *ampules* of Lorenzini, he'd have seen the flaw in Frank's reasoning: the charge that slows the nearby shark calls others from farther away. After, when your batteries run down, you're in very big trouble.

On second thought, it could be Frank does realize this. Right now he's grinning past his gums, in pain, spitting tobaco juice into the slick. The final showdown will be between man and shark, and it will be on a day like this. People on the last outcropping or ark, or atop a bloated humpback watching fins circle with their wrist-zapper batteries waning, will somehow reason, like old Ben says we're wont to do, that this is a fitting end, after all. The sleek inheriting the earth.

The New York press corps,
still frenzied from the week before,
raced back to Montauk
in time to photograph the kids
riding the huge carcass like
a Brahma bull....

15

SHUT DOWN OR
SHITTED UP

WE'VE EBBED AND FLOWED; west from Europe we rushed. Once set-

tled, the young rushed back east and oceanward again after whales.

Then west again in a gold rush when the yellow metal was discovered

in California. Because of gold fever, East Hampton in 1849 lost 300

able-bodied men who otherwise would have gone whaling out of Sag

Harbor, despite the fact whaling had become a distant-water fishery.

□ The current rush is not for land or resources—they're gone or are

unobtainable. The rush now is for a spot you can pretend you've con-

quered, a place where you can still see the beauty and feel alive, like

on Cricket's backdeck. And when the young have energy for con-

quering, and there's nothing to conquer but sludge and nowhere to

rush to, then the rush alone must do—poor Luby. □ It isn't only plas-

tic fishing boats and pleasure craft making the escape offshore.

Beginning suspiciously close to July 20, 1969, the day Neil blundered onto the moon, all manner of vessels, from surfboards to garbage scows, began heading onto the offshore frontier.

The garbage, sewage sludge, and industrial wastes generated by the City of New York and surrounding municipalities had become too much, by the early 1970s, for the old dump site located just 12 miles outside New York Harbor. Fishermen had seen no life there for years, and I recall how surfers objected to sharing their waves with the schools of "Coney Island whitefish," the name we gave used condoms that drifted east, along Long Island's South Shore, from the city sewer system.

The waves were emerald-green, and friends would sit, straddling their boards, talking waves, acknowledging, on occasion and with appropriate deference, a school of Coney Island Whites swimming by, their toothless mouths agape. The species was prolific, their spawning seasonless. Back then, they were funny to us—small, perhaps, but to be reckoned with. Their tiny jaws consumed future humankind in a way the great white could only dream of, if they had a need to dream, which they don't. For this, the whitefish deserved a respectful distance. The surfers sued the Environmental Protection Agency, and, as a consequence, the deepwater dump was created, 106 miles from New York Harbor. Go east, young man.

The same year, the first federal fishing regulations were being written, primarily as a means of booting foreign fleets from the bountiful grounds off the Northeastern states. The great open plain of the Atlantic was fenced at the 200-mile mark by the Magnuson Fishery Conservation and Management Act.

At first, American fishermen, who'd watched the big Soviet and East German factory ships suck up tons of fish, rejoiced together. Within a decade, however, the battle for fish was being waged inside the fence, between unsophisticated U.S. commercial fishermen and the growing "mosquito fleet" of sportfishing counterparts. I say "unsophisticated" because the demand for seafood in the U.S. is trivial, by world standards. The industry has always been comparatively small and composed of individual boat owner-operators.

By contrast, the demand for escape in all directions had entered its go-for-baroque period a decade after the Magnuson Act.

By the late 1980s, in the land of meat and potatoes, the sportfishing industry, built around the need to escape humanity's rising tide, had economically and politically overpowered the one providing food for the landed consumer. On nearly every coast, it was decided the public resource would be better spent by the rising tide of freedom seekers.

The rod-and-reel, one of the more rapacious of fishing gears when the catch of its millions of practitioners is weighed, nevertheless appeared to be singular and unselfish. Unlike a net, there was no chance the rod-and-reel would catch Flipper. What it did succeed in catching was the approval of the new environmental church. The rod-and-reel was "discriminate," environmentally correct.

Frank realized he and other charter captains had put the instant Ahabs in business—taught them just enough so that when they had money for a boat of their own, they became dangerous.

He saw them evolve on the Cricket's backdeck. First came the hell-raising Greenblatt and Rotten Ronald types. Then there was the occasional true sport and the "head-hunters," as Frank calls them, "what were comin' down strictly for meat and had everything except the bone through their nose." Then, he says, "there was them that started figurin' how much the mako would sell for, so they could make money on the deal, or try to.

"You could hear 'em down the cockpit when we was striped bass fishin'—when we had all the bass out there. One guy says I got 200 pounds sold. The other guy says, 'I got 300 pounds sold.' They had 'em sold before we wet a line, and if we didn't catch 'em 600 pounds, they'd go home mad.

"Take the sport fishermen versus the haulseiners with the strip-ed bass," Frank says, referring to perhaps the most infamous battle between commercial netters and hook-and-line sports, which began in about 1895 and was still going strong 100 years later.

"The sport fisherman would jump up and down and holler and scream, 'the haulseiner is gettin' all the bass,' aaargh?"

By haulseiners, Frank means the descendents of the early English settlers on the east end of Long Island, who used dories to set semi-circles of net in the ocean, to trap bass and haul them to the beach, first with horses and later with truck winches. The East Hampton baymen came to represent evil incarnate to the growing hordes of sport lemmings. When the bayman Tom Lester died a few years ago, his daughter received a letter from a sport fisherman that read: "Your father was punished for killing bass. Good riddance!!! He was a pig to slaughter. Billy Joel should join him in hell." (Billy Joel, the rock musician and Amagansett resident, had taken up the baymen's cause against restrictive state fishing laws the year before.)

"Now, if the truth was known—which they do not want, the truth," Frank is saying, "the truth is, there was only three big haulseine crews on this end of the island. If you talk to them and they could show you their receipts, they will only have three good sets, on the average, in the fall of the year, where they get a hundred boxes of bass. Now, you pile a hundred boxes a bass on the beach, it's a lot, right?"

"Now, they have three, that's 300 boxes, times three for the season, that's 900 boxes, sounds like a lot, right? Now, we'll go to the sport fisherman. How many boats do you think was, at that time, fishing for bass, countin' the little guy, a hundred? How's a hundred sound?

"Wokay. In the morning, each boat, when them bass was in there, when I was fishin' for 'em, if they didn't have 300 pounds [3 boxes] average to the boat, they wasn't fishin'. So, you have 300 boxes in the morning, you have 300 boxes in the afternoon. They don't have to wait for the weather, for the wind, like the haulseiner has to, so it goes on continually. Some days, they'd get 400 pounds. We'd go out there a few times and we'd have 600, 800 pounds. Take all the bass from the sportfishing boats into the parkin' lot, please, and make one pile of them from one half-a-day trip. What do you got? Three hundred boxes? No. Just take your pencil—you don't even have to sharpen it. What do you got in a week's time? The sport fisherman with a hook and line was out-fishin' the haulseiner. No, they wouldn't listen to this, but they was makin' an awful lot of noise about it. Now, that's the truth. Yeah, go ahead, clean up your own backyard first," Frank advises the fishermen he helped invent.

"They was usin' all the charter boat captains. I hate people like this," he says, spitting out the name Otto in his next breath, along with a squirt of Redman.

"One time we had Otto out, there was a dead whale off Block Island. I heard about it off the boys on the Viking. They was bottom-fishin' out there. They was passin' by it, goin' past to Cox's Ledge. The next day we went out there, and we happened to have Otto on as a charter. He had a chain of diners. When we got to the whale, there was one or two of these white sharks, decent size, swimmin' around."

"As we approached the whale, they had already broken off pieces of blubber, which were floatin'. They had pieces of blubber on the surface, but they couldn't catch 'em. It was like a kid tryin' to catch a beach ball. Every time they stuck their head out of the water to go to bite, this piece that musta weighed 30 or 40 pounds of blubber would bounce ahead of 'em, and it would make 'em madder and madder.

"We seen this from a distance. I couldn't figure what the whitewater was, whether it was tuna fish or what it was. As we got closer, I could see what was goin' on. It was couple of white sharks pushin' these pieces of blubber around.

"They had the whole whale. All's they hadda do is go back to the whale, but no, no, they got mad at these pieces 'cause they couldn't catch 'em."

"So we came up on one of the bigger pieces, about half the size of a 50-gallon drum that they had tore off, put the flyin' gaff into it, hung on, and went up close to the whale. We cut off a piece and put it on for bait.

"It didn't take long before the first white shark came up and grabbed a hold of it. We had him hooked and went off chasin' him towards the horizon. As he went away from us, we hadda stay with him, 'cause we was losin' line. He stayed right on the surface, and he was continually shakin' his head, like he was really mad at it. Then, by puttin' pressure on it, we pulled it outta his face, outta his jaw.

"When we pulled it outta his jaw, the guy in the chair don't realize this, that it's only the bait he has on. He feels somethin' heavy on the other end, and he still thinks he has the fish. He's windin' and the blubber is skippin' along the surface. That white shark was really mad, this time—I mean, really mad that we took it right out of his mouth.

"He just spun right around on the surface and came chargin' at that piece. I didn't bother hollerin' to stop because I knew the white shark was gonna get it, and he just pounced on it, went under the water about 10 feet.

"He was just shakin' the shit out of that thing. Finally, we hooked him. We had him on for about an hour, I guess, and then he turned around and bit the double line off, so we lost the one we had on rod and reel.

"Now it's gettin' late in the day, and Otto wants to get a fish. He still don't realize it: these things ain't no good eatin'. He figures big fish, lot of food for his diners, sell a lot of fillets, but I don't know what he's thinkin'. So we go back to the whale, and I'm startin' to get another bait ready, and he says, 'What are you messin' around with that? Why don't we harpoon one? It's gettin' late.' He says, 'We can use em.'

"So I don't stop to figure out what he means: 'We can use 'em.' He wants one, and it was in the days when the public wasn't mad when you used a harpoon. So I harpooned one, and we spend a couple hours on it, I guess, and dragged it home.

"About half the way home, he starts talkin' about cuttin' the thing up on the dock. I says, 'What for?'

"He says, 'For the diner, for my diners. I get a lot of servings out of that.'

"'No, no, no,' I says. 'Not when those things are that big; they're no good eatin'. Well, when he found out that they was no good eatin', he was a ravin' maniac." Jim, Paul, and I howl.

Ahab the diner owner was angered by the alleged inedibility, unsalability, of the white monster. For the first time, I'm skeptical of something Frank's saying. His stories have been as the wind before this, steady and true. But there is something revealing in the Otto story that doesn't add up. Appetite for food, Frank understands. The appetite for money, he does not. He likes money, but the reduction of everything to it, as though seeing by an extra sense, defines people Frank considers non-human, the kind driving around rapturous in their Benzes as they buy and sell deeper into the wound.

I mean, Frank was a meat fisherman first, right? His first charters had fished for their larders. He expounded on the virtues of blue shark and mako meat when sharks, by most people, were considered inedible snakes, and now he's telling Otto that white sharks aren't any good? Maybe he's hiding something, even now, on the eve of his retirement. I can see it in his eyes.

Perhaps there's a seafood more delicious than mahi mahi, or bigeye on a mesquite fire. Something that makes toro sushi taste like pork rind. It's juicy, sweet, with a hint of oyster flesh. In Japan and other Asian countries, soup made of shark fins is said to enhance sexual prowess in men. They think it gives them the same endurance as having two big ones. In any case, white shark fins were selling for over $100 a pound last time I looked.

Maybe the Japanese are right. They know how to build cars and electronic things, and it makes sense, if you think about it. Why wouldn't the flesh of the white shark have special powers, especially the ones from around here? Whales passing through the New York Bight are the white shark's favorite diet. It's the same migration of whales that first provided baleen for the corsets which lent the hourglass shape to a century of women. How many of us owe our existence to whales giving up their lives for great grandma's alluring curves? Progress. Nitroglycerine, made from the fat, tore road beds through mountains and made ammunition to keep freedom ringing.

Whale meat even made it into C-rations during World War II. Spermacetti from the heads of sperm whales made smokeless candles. How many ships were kept off the rocks by whale-oil-lit lighthouses? How many minds were fertilized studying by whale-fueled light? Superfine whale oil was even saved in secret barrels to lubricate satellites and space ships, I'm told. In short, what we've become was born of sacrificed whales. Should we be surprised that white sharks here, outside New York Harbor, unlike anywhere else in the world, are attracted by the death of this great provider of our present tense, biting off huge basketsful of rotting pride, 50-gallon drumsfull of overpopulated progress, and with gusto?

It follows like day the night that we would find the flesh of the local white beyond compare — the taste of absolute freedom — and Frank, I think, has vowed not to let this out. Not even Benchley saw this.

If Otto were allowed to turn his catch into 'sea trout' or scrod fillets to sell at his diners, all hell would have broken loose on Sunrise Highway. White shark steaks with sauce of rhino horn. White Castle shark burger. Serving up the last of the fearsome species with fries.

No, Frank has seen into the new room. He's watched the new breed of fisherman enter it. The ones still calling themselves sports and wearing garlands of environmental green as they swagger into a metamorphosed coliseum. This coliseum is still supported by newspaper and magazine columns, but ones in which Frank now rarely appears. He knows that many of these are true sportsmen no longer, having outfitted their plastic boats to catch and sell along the length of the food chain right up to the mighty bluefin tuna.

The once-lowly horse mackerel— plaything to the rich, in the days of linen line, and worth only cat food in death—had sprouted airfreight "wings," as they say on the docks, and was flying to Japan, where the yen for the dark-red belly meat was powerful.

Sportfishing had gone —"thar she blows"— professional. Never mind the sale of a day's catch, even at the high prices paid for bluefins by Japanese export buyers, came nowhere near offsetting the cost of a fuel-guzzling weekend ride offshore. Never mind the Ahab-lawyers and Ahab-construction kings who didn't need fish money in the first place were stripping the resource from the full-time market fishermen. And while their industry leaders worked the halls of Congress to put an end to net and longline fisheries in the name of conservation, the millions of mini-Munduses were tearing through federally set quotas like piranha.

And what of Frank Mundus's sharks? During the same years that foreign fleets were pushed farther offshore, along with the Big Apple's sewage, whaling was banned by international agreement. The herds of oceanic buffalo, harvested a century earlier to near-extinction for their fine lamp oil were put off-limits. Frank was forced to substitute basking sharks for blackfish whales in his monster mash recipe, but too late. The whale mash had already lit the imagination of millions. "Jaws" was released in 1975.

For a time, the appetite for seafood all but disappeared around here. *Jaws* made the sea a place to be eaten, not to eat from. And, as it turned out, the E.P.A. decided to disregard a fisheries service warning that the proposed deep-water dump site 106 miles off New York was in the path of the giant cyclonic eddies peeling off the Gulf Stream each summer. The eddies, which transported swordfish, tuna, whales, and sharks into the area, would likely spread sewage sludge, scientists warned, as far south as Virginia and as far north as Massachusetts.

The summer before Luby's death, a wind blew from the southwest without ceasing. No tuna showed up off Montauk and this interrupted the lucrative export trade in sushi that had been developing. Fishermen who witnessed the caravan of sludge barges pushing seaward through the waves of the New York Bight visualized a curtain of brown descending into the depths, diverting tuna, causing mutations.

Luby's captain made the mistake of telling a reporter from *TIME* magazine that tilefish were coming up on the longlines with deformities. Tilefish prices bottomed out. The evil wind continued to blow, washing red-bag medical wastes ashore the length of Long Island. That summer the masses stayed onshore, despite the heat. It was not the bite of Jaws they feared, but that of AIDS-infected hypodermics, a new species spawned in the city's sewers. A draggerman from Rhode Island called a press conference to show off a fish he'd caught with a hypodermic in its stomach. Dolphins and whales washed up in unprecedented numbers, dead of a mysterious immune disorder.

Dangerously provocative—what the sea had always been to the true seaman—she became for journalists the year of the red-bag wind. The storytellers' urge to awe, the natural inclination to increase the tale, surged like Jack's beanstalk in the presence of mystery. For the word "mystery," you may substitute the likelihood that no one had contrary facts enough to write a letter to the editor. Like gas, unbridled reporting will fill any vacuum. In this respect, outer space contains less grist for hyperbole than the sea, where even the most sophisticated among us has only a superficial perception of the boundless volume, and where even the hardest facts are better imagined than seen. In such a medium, a strong and juicy image — schooling hypodermics or billowing sewage, for instance — when planted in only a few grains of fact, will thrive, thrusting its tendrils upward and seeking the general level of ignorance to become truth enough.

Still and all, you have to admit it's curious how our collective diaper runneth over at the same time the sea level's rising. Seems like a major trend to me. "And the second angel poured out his vial upon the sea; and it became as the blood of a dead man: and every living soul died in the sea."— Revelations.

The appetite for seafood all but disappeared. Coincidentally — and I don't believe in coincidence anymore — it was the same time the phenomenon known as the shark tournament came into full flower. "Dem bastids," Frank's fellow charter captains had followed his lead. "After Jaws, everybody who owned a boat cashed in on it because they had run outa bonito, swordfish, and marlin," he says. What the charter captains learned from Frank, their customers learned from them.

No longer did the crowds gather at the docks to watch the awesome spectacle of one red and green-toenailed fishing captain with scarred arm and bush hat haul monsters from still-secret depths. Now the crowd itself was fishing—not very well, but fishing. Marinas had figured out how to put their summer fleets of weekend fishermen to work, drawing yet more crowds to the new frontier. The tournaments were suburban-medieval. One-sided jousts in three acts.

In Act I, a hundred plastic boats explode to life, tearing out of Montauk Harbor (and every harbor along the East Coast) before dawn, with enough engine and fuel to get them 30 miles offshore and back by the evening weigh-in. At a $400-per-boat entry fee, it's *Jaws*-glory and big cash prizes that drives them on, not so much the hand of the princess with the glue-on talons by the pool side.

On board, the beer's on ice. Transdermal scopalamine discs numb inner ears against the heave. Skin is ready for burning, hearts for attack. Gold-chained, like conquistadors.

Act II: In the afternoon. Flags and pennants fly. Blues, threshers, makos, hammerheads are raised on gin poles for the triumphant harbor entry. Hoisted again to the scales, in turn, to the ooohs and aaaahs of hundreds of onlookers wearing t-shirts advertising sharks, advertising marinas, ad infinitum. Ooooohs and aaaaahs. The marina barker barks weights and the names of boats like Mako My Day ... Daddy's Toy ... Four Play.

Yeeeuk! squeals, as fisheries scientists, performing necropsies on already weighed beasts, turn the dock into a giant pizza with the works.

Act III: Nightfall. The rotting juice of the competitors' tons of discarded sharks drips from the marina's 20-yard dumpsters. Next day, in the landfill, small mountains of sharks, still graceful in their piles, are claimed by seagulls and flies.

The golden age of tournaments did not last long. The federal scientists, who at the same time were writing the nation's first conservation plan for sharks, grew uneasy under the crush of unabating shark lust. And while charter captains were often hired for these two-day massacres, few were comfortable with them. Frank abhorred them — clumsy, beer-soaked, plastic replications of his feats.

The week after Frank and Donny Braddick brought Big Guy back to Montauk, two families out for the day on a private boat named the Violator, of all things, found the still-floating whale Frank had fed cookies from. There was nothing left to stand on. They harpooned another white weighing over a ton. The New York press corps, still frenzied from the week before, raced back to Montauk in time to photograph the kids riding the huge carcass like a Brahma bull, its jaws staked open with a two-by-four. When the shark was first raised, tail-first, onto the scales, bushel-basket-sized chunks of rotten and reeking whale meat fell from its maw onto the dock. Their kids, the Violators told reporters pridefully, had passed the rifle around after the harpooning. Family fun run amok, flooding offshore, and just one week after Frank's triumph.

The next season, tournament organizers acted to stem the carnage, to make the spectacles environmentally correct. With the encouragement of the fisheries service, only the largest, competitive sharks were brought to the scales, enough to festoon the gibbet. The meat was bagged and frozen for the needy. Let them eat sharks. The rest were tagged at the boat and released for science; future recaptures meant to reveal the animals' growth and migratory secrets.

"Happy horseshit," says Frank. Without the Jap hooks he used—the ones designed by Japanese longline fishermen to stick in the jaws of fish, feeling good about tagging and releasing sharks was folly. The cheaper hooks bought by the weekend warriors were more often than not swallowed by the sharks, which then fought their last battle gut-hooked. After being released, most sank to the bottom—dead.

"Maybe two out of 12 are hooked in the mouth. Add it up along the coast. I don't need no crystal ball. I'm goin' to Hawaii."

The year of the red-bag wind, Frank decided to give it a few more years and then pack it in. The weird fascination with sharks was still there, but there were fewer of them. The cost had become prohibitively high for the boatless to take an overnight charter far offshore to where the sharks could be found—except, that is, for the occasional monster lured closer by something bloated and putrescent.

"The bartender says,
'Yeah, you guys are going shark
fishin'—don't give me this shit.
If you guys get a shark over 100
pounds, bring 'im in here and flop 'im
on the bar. I want to see it.'
Six guys march in like pallbearers
with this shark, the bartender
screams, 'No, no, no'—Flop
on the bar goes this blue shark,
oozin' all over the place."

[FRANK MUNDUS]

16

R E V E N G E

WHY AM I SO RELAXED AND JOYFUL? I'm howling now at the captain's description of the victory-over-blue-shark ritual performed by his early anglers. □ "At first they brought 'em home to dump in somebody's swimmin' pool ..." □ Ah ha ha. □ "... to hang up someone's flagpole. When we first started shark fishin', there were blue sharks that wound up just about any place you could imagine. They put 'em in the phone booth here in Montauk, down by White's liquor store. There was a blue shark in it the next day, standin' up. They had him all propped up, and they had his fin tied, had a hat on him, had a cigarette in his mouth. He was supposed to be makin' a phone call." □ Ha, ha, oh, boy. □ What was it about the brown shark that made me vengeful? □ I caught a giant tuna once, an hour-long trial, but, despite the exertion, I'd felt no animosity toward the animal. The opposite happened. I nearly wept when all was said and done, after the bluefin was sold by the captain to an export buyer who offered me a bite of its heart, as tradition required. When I declined, he dropped the heart in the corner while he loaded the 400-pound carcass, filled with ice, into the wooden air freight boxes they call "coffins."

It was when I left, as my eyes caught sight of that big heart—my body still ached from its desperate power—sitting where the buyer had dropped it, alone, where two cement walls and the floor came together, that I gulped back tears.

"They carried sharks home in every way possible," Frank's telling us. "They didn't care if their brand-new cars would rot."

"A guy with a brand-new Lincoln Continental, we caught him a blue shark; Dicky was with me. We get back to the dock, and he says, 'I'm gonna take it home.' I said, 'Go ahead; I don't know what for.' At that time, we didn't realize you could eat the blue shark. So he backs up this brand-spankin'-new Lincoln Continental.

"I says, 'That's your car?'

He says, "Yeah.""

"I says, 'You're gonna take a 150-pound blue shark home in that? First of all, I don't think you can fit it into the trunk.'

"Ohh, he starts braggin about how big the trunk is. I says, 'Goodbye'—I ain't gonna argue with you. I'm goin', so I went up to the gin mill. I left Dicky with the problem. When I come back, it's gone. I said to Dicky, 'Where, what?'

Dicky said, 'I kept arguin' with him after you left, but he gave me another 20 bucks, he says can't you try a little harder to get him in?'

"Dicky told me he rolled him up in the trunk like a coil a rope but got him in there, and there he went with that Continental. He had to get rid of it."

"The shark?" asks Howard.

"No, the car," says Frank. "You see, the stink gets down in the cracks and keeps on goin', and you can't get to it to wash it out. How you gonna wash underneath there?"

Howard's laughing, too, a deep, hearty laugh, although he must know that sharks are revered as gods on the islands where he lives. What does my brown shark, still twitching, see with its cold hooded eyes?

I think the urge to rejoice at the death of such a beast arises because we find repulsive, yet familiar, the way it was attracted to us. Besides, sharks have shiny suits, sharp, inexhaustable teeth — they bite their females when mating, and the females have developed thick skin to protect themselves. They give birth to their young alive and hungry. They're like us, perhaps meaner, but too simple to know what mean is.

We feel deep down they've earned the coveted ride to the Bronx in the trunk of a Continental, Mafia-style, by virtue of their having swum upstream, against the rich stench that by now, halfway through the Fourth of July trip, has saturated the atmosphere above and below Cricket and her crew. We say we fear you, we appear not to respect you in death, but what else but respect should we call sacrificing a $30,000 car to your juices?

"Last one was with a camper," Frank recalls, "a nice camper, with rugs. They had one mako and two blue sharks they was gonna take home in the camper. I said, 'You're nuts; you can't do it.' I called 'em idiots, told 'em what was gonna happen.

"They got plastic they was gonna put down on the rugs. I said, 'Don't do it. You won't be able to do it.' Away they went. Same sad story — I walk away, come back, and it's done, they're gone.

"Next time they come down to go fishin', the one guy had a funny look on his face. I said, 'Well, what happened — what happened to your camper?'

"He said, 'We got lucky.' I said, 'No way. He says, 'Oh yeah, we got lucky.' I says, 'You couldn't have. Them two blue sharks and a mako hadda mess up that thing bad. You couldn't have got that lucky.' He kept on insisting he did get lucky, becauuuuuse," Frank says, delaying the punchline —" somebody stole the camper."

I'm laughing, Howard's laughing, Jim, with the chum ladle in his hand, is smiling, even Paul, who's been up nearly 24 hours and looks as soggy and beat-up as we all feel, is laughing. The brown shark slides, port to starboard, in a wash of its blood. The blood pours from the scuppers and adds to the trail we hope the big white has, by this time, found.

"A lot of them put the sharks on the roof. The juice runs down the winda and goes in the well behind the winda. You tell them they're gonna have a chrome-plated car by the time they get to East Hampton. The sandpaper skin just eats the paint right off the car. Sure, the cars look chrome-plated, but they don't stay that way very long. I think oxidation starts in two minutes, ha, ha, ha. They just rust."

It's about an hour after dark, and I crawl under my wet and chum-stained sleeping bag for some shuteye. Only about 20 more hours to go, unless we hook into a big fish soon. I search for pleasant stable things to think of: my beautiful young daughter, my constant wife, thoughts of whom faithlessly slide toward the young tart of time. The Cricket's cradling and the vernal, procreative smell of fish lure old intimacies to mind, along with something I'd nearly forgotten.

I once worked as a deckhand on an offshore lobster boat. Its captain happened to be the same Dave Krusa who skippered the Deliverance, on which Tom Luby fished. The first offshore vessel he owned was a swordfishing longliner. He wound up losing his shirt on the deal because of partner problems, and he would bring up the experience from time to time, to remind himself and his crew how easy it was to go broke on the water.

One day—I forgot why, probably because the deck talk had circled 'round to females again (we'd been at sea for three days and the circles were getting tighter) he told us about looking down in the hold on his first boat and finding one of the mates mating with a swordfish caught earlier in the day.

"That's disgusting," I'd said.

"Not really," answered the captain. "It was one of the prettier swordfish in the hold."

At the time, I knew there were reasons why fishermen took to a life at sea. Most I knew functioned poorly in normal society. But the pretty swordfish story was my first inkling of just how different they could be. Now I wonder whether it was perversion, pure and simple, that explained the dalliance in the hold. Or was the deckhand heeding a call he didn't quite understand, to practice making creatures able to survive the final flood?

In a dream I'm Ben Franklin, colonial newspaper man — horny harbinger of revolution, wearing a shiny shark-skin suit. The knickers of the suit have dropped to the deck, exposing claspers two, one for my wife, the other, I'm ashamed to say, for the red-haired salesgirl of eternal resorts, who alternately presents long white legs and an elegant blue-green tail. A rifle shot wakes me, proof in the night another shark has bitten the dust. For a split second, I thought the mermaid had been shot by my wife in a jealous rage. It's possible the dream came from the swimmers within.

Scientists have learned our tiny reproductive fish have an olfactory sense. I'm sure that, after all the sub-atomics have been accounted for, we'll find they also have a magnetic yearning for the right time, the right place, the right victim of love. Is it any wonder we live to feel the warm rush of waves, the pull of bigger fish?

"To the Pernt of No Retoyn"

[FRANK MUNDUS]

Chapter

17

D E S T I N Y

IT'S MORNING. I FEEL I'M IN THE BILGE OF THE ARK, eavesdropping on fresh gospel as told to an Hawaiian trophy hunter, in lieu of procreating beasts. The captain is in pain for having been tapped for new teeth by a god who, this time, means business. I'm hot, woozy, in the stench of chum and the endless foothills of this Fourth of July storm. A reporter with the scoop of all time, am I, but with no one to read it; for the flood now is human, the sea alone articulate, worthy of intercourse. □ Howard wants his fish. We all want our fish, but Mr. Chong has traveled 5,000 miles, sailed into the teeth of a summer nor'easter, a treacherous storm of the kind that sank the Pelican from Fishangri-la. Now he's sprawled in the fighting chair with its dragon crest — falling asleep. □ By now he should have had the last trophy in his stuffed and mounted pantheon well along toward the Fiberglas of immortality. A big fish. A Buick of a fish. A white shark far bigger than the 1,000 pounds Mundus says is the minimum size worth dealing with. Howard wants it to come up from the dark. He rouses himself to spoon another ladle-full — an oily token of his will. Rise beast full of teeth, up from the dark, up from the past.

Ten thousand years have passed since Noah came aground on Mount Ararat. In recent times, God has realized there is no need to go back on the old promise He'd made to Noah. The tiring task of taking every living substance and removing it from the face of the Earth had become necessary once again, but was being handled nicely by the bipedal convenience monster.

Cheeky two-legged bastards. The Lord knew it wouldn't be long before satellites were babbling in one television-homogenized tongue, high up in His, or is it, Her own backyard. Might as well leave the rest of the animals off the ark. The inventory was getting smaller, anyway. This time, let the charter captain handle its manifest.

I see the light! I'm reborn! You will recall the Cricket II's maiden charter trip was made with 16 mackerel fishermen and a Model-A Ford on board, a few million species short of "every creeping thing of the earth."

If you look at that first trip from here on one of Frank's last, the Model-A and the mackerel fishermen were symbolic of a new covenant between God and Monster Nimrod, Noah's great—to the seventh factorial, grandson.

There was no thought of conservation, as we think of it, when Frank began fishing. And if he ever did consider his killing, it would not have been considered excessive, because he and the Cricket were only one boat. One boat sailing upon an untapped vein of sharks.

The earth had not turned so many times beneath Cricket. She was yet to come around into the crowded sun on the day he realized the sharks, the happy animus of his soul, were disappearing too. And what a boat he and Cricket turned out to be. How could he have known the Cricket would become a subcultural modus, and people would become so eager to catch a glimpse of the razor-sharp-toothed and balanced earth of bygone revolutions, of spent dinosaur days? Piles and piles of dusks.

"I hadda have transportation down to the boat," Frank says, recalling how the Model-A had come to be on the backdeck.

"Amen," I whisper involuntarily at the captain's feet, leaning against the engine box. He's just "mashed" on the starter to move Cricket, the growlrowlrowlrowl of her engine tickling me the way the time-sharess might have if this were an earlier version of the ark saga, in which the animals came two by two.

"Comin' back, I had the boat, right?" Frank asks nobody in particular.

"Amen," I mutter. In the absence of his monster, Howard is all ears, too.

"The boat was built in Virginia, so how was I gonna carry the nuts and bolts and all the extra garbage that I wanted down there?

"Somebody woulda had to take me down and bring the car back. So I figured, well, it's a Model-A. It'll fit in the cockpit. Shouldn't have that much trouble.

"So I run the car down. When we got ready, I backed the boat up to a steep embankment. Wasn't a bulkhead, just a steep embankment. I got it close as I could and tied it to the trees by the stern bits and pulled it in tight."

Frank says he made a ramp out of planking from Cockrell's boat-yard and drove the Model-A up to the stern. He took more planks and laid enough of them port and starboard to get the front wheels over the Cricket's cockpit.

"Then, when I got it over the top where I want it, I put a jack on it, jacked it up, took the planks out, dropped the ass-end down, got the front end down, gave the planks back to the boatyard, took the air out of the tires, and away we went.

"We got back to Brielle about two weeks late. We got back the night before we had our first charter—mackerel fishin' in the spring of the year. The guys come down the docks and I said, 'Fellas, I'm sorry, I'm not ready.'

"They say, 'What's the matter?'

"'I said, 'You can see what's the matter—I got the Model-A Ford in the cockpit.' One guy says, 'Look, you was out in rough weather wid it, wasn't you?'

"I says, 'Yeah, that's no problem.' He says, 'There's only 16 of us —we can fish all around it.' So I says, 'Okay, let's go.'"

In those days, there weren't many boats that had radios. The fleet of charter boats—it wasn't much of a fleet, only a dozen boats—was anchored. Frank says he approached them from downwind and worked his way through the anchored boats.

"It was funny to see the guys sittin' there in the wheelhouse, bull-shittin', then you'd see 'em yellin' and screamin' as we passed by.

"When we anchored up and started fishin', why, my guys was sittin' on the fenders, on the hood. They was all over, throwin' mackerel all over the place."

Amen. It's like listening to the Word. Can't help but think the scene Frank's recalling with such a genuine burst of humor foretells a distant and bleaker future, when the last of the providers are fishing for mackerel from the tops of cars stranded far above the Long Island Expressway, somewhere in a Colorado mountain pass, perhaps, bumper-to-bumper in the final traffic jam. Water rising, fins circling. I want more from the Book of Mundus. At the same time, I hope my little daughter is sleeping peacefully with the birds singing just outside her window, with no sound of water, no incessant diesel, no scary monsters.

Frank, who loves trusty machinery like others love dogs, is saying he was not about to leave the car in Virginia. It cost him a whole $25, after all.

"It was 24 horsepower, and you could go down the highway just as fast as anybody else. I took the bubble seat out so I could put fish boxes on the back. After that season, it got a cracked head, so you couldn't keep water in it. It got so hot that when you got two miles from my house, across the Mattisquan River Bridge, to where the boat was, even with coastin' and everything else, when you got there, you hadda put it up against the oak tree and put it in gear. The back wheels would just spin because the motor still wanted to go.

"So eventually, goin' back and forth like that, why, the head broke. Pieces of the head fell down into the piston. The piston came up and broke the rod. But it would still run. You could watch that piston settin' still with the motor runnin' on three cylinders, with half gasoline, half kerosene.

"Then I got two flat tires—the two back tires went to the *pernt of no retoyn*—but it still had steel rims, so I had the bright idea of ridin' back and forth on the steel rims. Well, I eventually got caught by a cop 'cause he seen the sparks. He says I couldn't do that 'cause I was chewin' up the highway.

"Eventually I had to run it into the junky. It was a runnin' piece of, machinery. He gave me $10 for it."

The wind whistles its approval; stainless steel monster shackles applaud against Cricket's mast.

I'm sure the reason the Almighty decided to entrust Frank with His latest offer of salvation is that Captain Mundus appeared to feel the same tenderness, patience, and respect for gas and diesel engines as Adam had been encouraged to feel for his missing rib. By 1947, the Lord realized nothing very good was coming out of the original liaison, only more people, and it was clear the male and female of the species didn't much like each other.

Engines, on the other hand, were more trustworthy. Men liked them better. What's more, there were enough of them to help the flood along by adding carbon dioxide to the hairspray and refrigerant in the atmosphere. Internal combustion engines also consumed the black gooey remnant of long extinct creatures, and this must have appealed to the Prime Mover's fastidious nature.

Now Frank's talking engines. Amen. About the Cricket's first one, the four cylinder, 150-horsepower aluminum Superior. The Cricket's always sounded the same, he's saying, whether her heart was four-cylinder, six-cylinder, or eight.

It's true. She growls unlike newer boats with better-baffled engines. Growl, growl,

　　　　　rowl-rowl-rowl-rowl,

a predator's purring — she stalks the white monster of the moment by burning the black essence of the past, growl-rowl,

forests of ferns,

monsters and meek,

eons of slithering, procreating, small, medium, and large jaws snapping—a mammoth hunger since reduced to black crude. The goo, refined, burns in the engine's chambers of combustion, reverberating now through the Cricket's oak planks in rhythmic explosions, quick life and exhaustion, the final sooty extinction of dinosauric growl-rowlrowlrowlrowl...

Cricket's growling takes me back to a trip I once took to Washington with a busload of Montauk fishermen who were attempting to subject sharks to democracy.

On the way, I listened to stories about a lone man on a small boat fighting two giant tunas off the Canadian Maritimes by himself. And, as the industrial stench of northern Jersey seeped through the bus windows at dawn, the story of a single seine filled with 360 giant bluefin, two of them weighing 1,500 pounds each. They had turned the shallows of Cape Cod Bay bloody with their frantic thrashing. It was the same year Frank and Donny Braddick fed melon and cookies to Big Guy on their decaying island of whale flesh.

The meeting was held at the headquarters of the National Wildlife Federation in the northwest section of D.C. where the national headquarters of everything are interspersed with fine old townhouses and upscale theme-saloons. I remember a showdown of sorts among those attending the meeting. Three separate sapiens—fisherman, scientist, and bureaucrat, all bloated with coffee and slimy Cremora— faced off on a plain of perfect rugs and folding chairs and in THE LIGHT: the Ektachrome slide-light of indecipherable fish charts.

In the decade of the 1980s, in the course of more fish management meetings than I can count, I watched that light play eerily on the faces of commercial striped bass, swordfish, tuna, and, eventually, shark fishermen, their hard, fuel-stained hands cupping cigarettes in the dark for support.

In every meeting, the light of science reflected off the silver screens as though from above, as though the fishermen were deep in ignorance, an endangered species looking up like Frank says migrating predators always do, looking for recognizable shapes silhouetted against the deep-penetrating sun.

Howard's looking over the side. Frank's deep in engines past.

"I picked up the four-cylinder aluminum Superior, not thinkin' that the aluminum was gonna give me all kinds of trouble, and it went for a while. Sure, it was a hard-pullin' little engine, four-cylinder, four-cycle. I got 10 knots out of that thing.

"That's when Uncle Bud come into the picture. That was the first year I was runnin' an open boat. He came out from Preferred Oil Company, from the city, with a bunch of guys, and they jumped on the boat. One thing led to another 'cause he was such a good mechanic. He was the kind of mechanic that started out with a Model-A Ford. He was so good he could just listen to the motor and tell you what was wrong wid it.

"I worked a couple of winters with him in there, myself and Bill White where we got grocery money from. We was starvin' to death. Bud says, 'Come on in; you can be a mechanic.'

"I said, 'I ain't no mechanic.' He said, 'Well, you can turn a wrench. I seen you work on that motor, and,' he says, 'You're good enough for a mechanic. I'll just show you what to do.' I says, 'Okay.'

"He started workin' on the Superior. One thing had let go, then another was ready to. He took a radiator out of a Mack truck and put it on the coolin' system that was outside the motor box, big radiator. He put on a different startin' system. He had it startin' on 24 volts, runnin' on 12 volts, all kinds of gadgets and gimmicks, put in a different steerin' system.

"Well, the operation was a success, but the patient died. Because what happened was it didn't have enough power on high-compression. I mean, we had trouble gettin' it started. In those days, we used raw ether in the can. Got a quarter-pound can of ether, pour it right in the top, in the breather. Well, I got it started. Wide open I only got 900 r.p.m.s out of it, idlin', five. Aaaaaagh?

"I was so cussed pissed off I took that whole can of ether and poured it right in there. "I says, 'Die, you bastid.' And that thing went up to about 5,000 r.p.m., and I threw the can over the side, and I looked, and she went right back idlin' just like nothin'. Turn around and everybody's off the boat, they all jumped off the boat, thought it was gonna blow up. So Bud says, 'Well, that's all we can do. I can't think of anything else. I'll give you a call tomorrow.'

"Next day, me and one-eyed Gerald Stanley and a couple of guys, we took it down to Three Mile Harbor, and we yanked the Superior out in about three or four hours. We yanked it out and I took a sledge-hammer and drove it through the block. Now, I go home for lunch, and Bud calls up. He says, 'I got the answer, I got the answer.'

"I says, 'What answer?'

"He says, 'How to fix the motor.'

"I says, 'Well, you better take the sledgehammer out of the block, then.'

"He says, 'What did you do?' I told him we hauled it out. I can't mess around — it's the middle of July; we gotta put another motor in. I says, 'How, how, how could you have fixed it?' I felt like a guy that just committed murder and thought I had the perfect murder and Sherlock Holmes comes along and figures out the answer. I says, 'Why? How?'

"He says, 'We coulda took another piston and cut wafers off the topada piston to bring the compression up, screw dem wafers on topada other piston, and' he says, 'it woulda brought your compression up again.'

The jury rigging sounds like my life. Cut a wafer of this and screw it to that. Borrow from Peter to pay Paul. Take the redhead's legs to bed with my wife.

"Ahh, forget it, forget it, it's out," says Frank of the old Superior.

"The funny part was: when she finally blew her head gaskets, she had that outside radiator system on her — we was pourin' saltwater in it every 15 minutes, couldn't keep water in it with a blown head gas-ket. It was turnin' the water into steam, so about every 15 minutes, I'd say, 'Dicky it's your turn.' You could see the steam comin' up the mast — we looked like Old Faithful, so Dicky would go down, take a bucket of saltwater, and just pour it right in. It would last another 15 minutes. Every 15 minutes, we'd turn into a dry cleaner's. The steam would come up the mast," Frank says, spreading his arms like Old Faithful in mid-spout.

This Uncle Bud sounds like a seat-of-the-pants inventor. Sounds like he made Cricket look, with her external cooling system and clouds of steam, like a kind of evolutionarily confused animal, a lungfish or platypus, caught between prototype and archetype. This is why Frank liked him, I suppose. Bud was a kindred spirit, a Dr. Watson to his own Sherlock Holmes, out to solve the mystery of how to catch big fish and earn a living at it. The poetry of deduction was as much fun as hoisting maneaters on the dock galluses. It was Bud who rerigged an old Model-T magneto to tickle the *ampullae* of Lorenzini, then give the sharks the full charge to stun them. Even in death, Bud proved his mettle, convincing Frank he had indeed been one of the chosen to share in his Idiot Covenant.

Frank says Bud was on the Cricket when Frank spread the ashes of an old Scandinavian carpenter friend named Eric Seeden upon the waters in front of the Montauk Lighthouse. The ashes went whoosh, and with my own experience with Captain Hader, I can picture the particles descending. Then a wreath was thrown as the priest added his words, and, as a finishing and fitting touch, Frank says, he pulled the pin on a carbide flare and tossed it near the wreath. It didn't go off, so he tossed a second, which ignited underwater, making the sea glow emerald as the old carpenter's bone clouds merged with Mother Atlantic.

The sun had nearly set. The Cricket and a few others from the cortege of boats were well on their way back to the harbor when the first flare finally ignited and glowed in the distance. Bud was moved, and told Frank that when his time came, he wanted to be buried in exactly the same way. A few years later, he was — Frank caught him a white shark in the interim — right down to the delinquent carbide flare.

Bud's day, Frank says, was exactly the same as when Eric's remains were entrusted to the deep — slick calm and quiet. A second flare waited until Frank headed back, then blossomed a green radiance, and a puff of white smoke appeared as though the now-disparate mechanic had worked his old Ford magneto one last time in farewell.

Howard's roused himself from the fighting chair, unnerved by Frank's short flight into sentiment. He opens the ice chest, hovers over the cans of beer, orange soda, Coke, and chooses a Coke, I think, to keep his edge.

It's the second such meander Frank's made in the past hour. He'd remembered a blind man earlier, one of a charter party, who was scared when he came aboard. Mundus said he was amazed by the man's spatial sense on Cricket's cramped and rolling backdeck and so refused to abide the man's fits of depression. The man became a friend and shark fisherman who saw more than most when hooked into a fish. And this led him to the subject of kids and overbearing fathers. Frank said he made a practice of first ordering such fathers to shut up — 'I'm the captain here" — then taking the kids aside and telling them, "If you listen to them long enough, they'll tell you what they don't know." It seems warmth is the iceberg beneath the tip of Frank's cold facade.

Blue sharks have found us again. There are three baits out, two small baits on the small reels, the line floated by Styrofoam chunks.

In addition, there's the terminal gear designed by Frank specifically for white sharks: a multiple wire leader made of eight stainless steel lines, each of 392-pound breaking strength and 20 feet long, with a ring at the top end onto which the Cricket's steel winch cable can be fastened. At the other end, a big 12.0 hook is secreted in a flank of blue shark Frank has freshly cut. The whole business dangles beneath a red plastic bobber the size of a soccer ball.

There is a big fish under the boat. Now I feel its presence, like Frank has all along. Long stretches of quiet pass with only the whistle of a decreasing wind and the rattle of the wooden ladle, like a dead piano, in the hollow of the chum box. Waves are still overhead. The shining path of the slick rises and falls like a magic carpet.

I wonder if Frank, now embarked upon the story of Harry Hoffman — a great white hunter, and, like Uncle Bud, a mechanic extraordinaire, brother in oil, and beloved charter Idiot, by the sound of it— realizes Howard has blasphemed by coming on this trip.

What I'd learned before boarding the Cricket — it was, besides the despair born of one too many obits, the reason I'm here — the curious fact that the people of Milolii, a fishing village a spitting distance from Honaunau where Frank's decided to retire and grow papayas, still worship *amakua* their ancestral spirits, which, they believe, live eternally as sharks.

In ancient times Honaunau was the City of Refuge. Today the ruins of a vast enclosure, its walls 20 feet thick, 15 feet high, 1,000 feet long, and 700 feet wide, survive. According to the old laws, the family of one murdered was awarded a chance for revenge. The murderer was let go on one side of the island and allowed a head start. There ensued a chase over mountains, through dense forest.

"Sometimes the race was kept up to the very gates of the temple, and the panting pair sped through long files of excited natives who watched the contest with flashing eye and dilated nostril," observed Mark Twain after a visit to the city in 1866, ruins even then. His story ran in the *Sacramento Union*.

The crowd would send up "a ringing shout of exultation when the saving gates closed upon him and the cheated pursuer sank exhausted at the threshold. But sometimes the flying criminal fell under the hand of the avenger at the very door, when one more brave stride, one more brief second of time would have brought his feet upon the sacred ground and barred him against all harm. Where did these isolated pagans get this idea of a City of Refuge — this ancient oriental custom?" asked Huckleberry's ink-stained father.

Where did Frank?

Once inside the walls, those escaping revenge — even rebels in arms, or aging shark fishermen with young vegetarian wives — were/are free. They can go forth without fear. To harm them is death. They are tabu.

It was Paul Strauch, a half-Hawaiian surfer of international stature, who told me during a visit to Montauk that he had never eaten shark meat, nor had any of his family. He knew of Frank's reputation, and when he learned it was to be Frank's last year fishing, the subject of retirement came up. I told him Frank had already bought his property on the Big Island near this place called Milolii. Paul's jaw dropped.

He said the Hawaiians of Milolii, fishermen mostly, believe, as did their ancestors, that offerings to the shark gods would assure the transformation of departed members of their family into patron sharks. Markings on a transformed shark are said to correspond, on occasion, to a physical characteristic of the dearly departed, even to an article of clothing in which the dead had been wrapped for burial.

Sharks are family, and as *amakua* are able to intercede for the safety of their fishing descendants — saving them from a capsized boat, for instance, or, on the bleaker side, seeking out and killing an enemy. Some *amakua* can take on either shark or human form. They are said to exchange souls.

Ku-hei-moana is thought to be the most important shark god and is described in legend as king shark (sometimes queen shark) of the broad ocean: a man-eater, in either case, 30 fathoms long, with a mouth as big as a grass shack.

There are legends throughout the Hawaiian Islands of shark-men, identified by the mark of a shark's mouth on their bodies. They can change back and forth. Sometimes a shark-man can go for years without anyone realizing, until it's noted that what seems like a disinterested warning to swimmers is always followed by a fatal attack by a man-eating shark.

I wonder about Frank's scarred arm, about the alleged roller-skating accident, and break out in a cold sweat.

This idea of an inter-species conspiracy has been lurking in me for a few years as fancy: microbes loosed by a mad scientist, a likely partnership. As horrible as such a plague would be, mad microbes might give survivors back the healthier outlook we once enjoyed as a minority on the planet, living without gunpowder in fear of lions and tigers. But here, looking at Frank's arm as he opens another can of chum, I figure the mad scientist is in us. Yes, it's clear; macroscopic or microscopic or both, something has brought us here to proffer melon and cookies on our islands of dead whales, with our own happy heartbeats beckoning the beasts to dinner.

In Hawaii, sharks have increased their attacks to an unprecedented frequency: one surfer per month last year, the surfers themselves summoned to the meal by the most beautiful waves in the world. With arms and legs dangling off surfboards, they look to tiger sharks like sea turtles. Or, perhaps the time has come when the tigers simply recognize something new on the menu. And then there was the islander in the West Indies who said he expected more white sharks because the people with "belly-full" (tourists) sweat more for their constant eating, and thus add salt to the ocean when they swim. Salt made the smaller fish hungrier, he said, which, in turn, attracted white sharks. He told me this rum-drunk after a campaign speech by a man running for local election on the anti-hotel plank. More stirrings.

Now Frank's retiring a few miles from the last flock of shark-worshippers, their minds miraculously left unconsumed by the white shark of Christianity. Has to be more than coincidence. So is Howard's charter.

Not surprising, perhaps, our Hawaiian builder of condos can ignore local beliefs in his quest for a great white — not surprising, but dangerous.

Maybe that's why he came halfway 'round the world to the village of extinct Indians, to fish with Frank — to get out of range. But, surely, the king or queen shark of the broad ocean must be able to sense this far with his or her ampullae.

And who or what exactly is Frank? I was told Eugenie Clark's son asked Frank to participate in a shark eradication program in Hawaii after so many surfers got eaten. Eugenie Clark is the shark researcher who had a suit of chain mail made of stainless steel to protect her. He refused. He's staring at the big bobber and handlining one of the smaller baits, teasing a blue shark, lovingly.

I'm summoning up the courage to pose the only question I really want the answer to:

"Hey, Frank," says I. "If you do fish in Hawaii, aren't you worried about the people who believe sharks are their ancestors?"

Mundus turns and faces me. Howard sits up on his throne.

"Those are the older ones. Their kids will kill their ancestors for a buck. Besides, I ain't gonna fish. Had enough — ALMOST enough," he says, looking at Howard, whose sudden frown at the thought of Frank's giving up brightens like the day with the captain's "almost."

But for me, he's let it out of the bag. Sharks, pheasants, buffalo, even brontosauruses disappearing is bad enough. But it's the fact we might as well be dead once we've lost the expectation of them — when it no longer occurs to us they should be here, as when young Hawaiians can't recognize their ancestors, or when the blind man is no longer pulled from his darkness by the muscle of a big fish, or when unemployed jockeys can no longer be frozen in fear, or when Mr. Banks is no longer moved to drop a flood warning on the corner of Broadway and 42nd Street. Without the possibility of all-fulfilling terror, we're just walking the plank.

As I see it, the long walk began in the late 17th and early 18th centuries when James II was King of England and Montaukett Indians manned the dories of the settlers' near-shore whale fishery as harpooners and oarsmen. Even before the English arrived, the Montauketts used the meat, oil, and bone from beached whales. They fished for them, too, venturing forth in canoes to stab at the grazing mammals with spears, hoping loss of blood would kill them before they could escape offshore.

Later the English showed them how to fasten their harping irons to the beasts, and the Montauketts joined in on the sleigh rides, which continued around the world over the next century as the industry expanded.

The settlers, of course, had harped fast to their new, whale-shaped world of Long Island. Inexorably, and despite the relatively good relations the English enjoyed with the area's native inhabitants, local Indians lost their land. Their share of the whale catch was paid in subsistence amounts of meat, oil, bone, and booze, the great Indian palliative.

The Montauketts were the muscle in an infant industry that gave the settlers their first source of profit, fired their lamps, and fueled one political and one industrial revolution of the big wheel. The Montauketts worked hard and sold off their land for a pittance. In all of these transactions, they insisted on only one thing — that they be given the fins and tails from the catch so they might offer their burnt sacrifice to the spirit of the whale.

Were they sure in their belief the Provider knew the difference between the smoke from the sacrificial tails and fins — the parts that gave the great animals their speed and direction — and the stench of the try works oiling the settlers' way?

Were they as sure of the whales' renewal as Howard is that his trophy will freeze the transcendent glory of his having faced a real monster, smelled its blood, and survived?

Howard will not build a fire under his white shark, if he gets one. It will be decapitated just behind the gill plates. The head will be wrapped in shrouds of wet Fiberglas, which will become a mold when hardened. Into the mold will be poured the epoxy. Only the original mount will have the shark's real teeth and jaw. There will be no magic smoke to propitiate the fearsome shark god and encourage him to make more in his image — only plastic fumes.

Thenceforth, Howard or his assigns need only order popouts from the mold. The only difference between the original white and its molded progeny will be the false teeth tapped into the plastic, the kind of thing our captain finds painful.

The waves whipping the Cricket sound like the dead laughing because we cast our souls in ice and insulating plastic, hoping to save them in our refrigerated hearts like woolly mammoths. Our ancestors vouchsafe a smile as we make gaudy glaciers of our one and only time, our vain stab to stop this melting until such time as we can grow gills.

Frank's laughing, smiling at me like he agrees with my thoughts. The only words I catch of the story he's telling are: "Ha! We are now disconnected from the outside world."

But now I've caught enough to know he's talking about the last white shark caught before the movie "Jaws" was released, before all hell broke loose and the myth outstripped him, the movie pouring Frank's great quarry into the Hollywood mold.

The story became monster versus man when the real tale, Frank's story, was more like silly bastards paying charter captain to play with a big fish. The story with the original teeth is the one about his idiots' mostly working-class fantasies, claustrophobic craziness, their primitive spark, which Frank knows how to kindle with the flint of his chum ladle and the steel in his gaze, conjuring the spark and the sharks simultaneously with the same slick.

The sparks, like the one igniting oily dinosaur vapor in the

Cricket's GM V-8 today, are what warms Frank. Takes us idiots out to ignite it. Foments chaos, like in Mr. Banks, like in Howard, in order to reassure himself the whole droning and sweating wave building onshore to the west is not as dead as it seems. Our explosion of life is something he must see again and again.

Frank knows there is no mastery over this great fish. It's like robbin' a bank. Most of the time the cops show up. But it's cops and robbers that's fun, not Saint George and the dragon. In order to get the idiots to see this, he must get them on board. And to get them onboard, he must first accomplish at every possible opportunity the Cricket's immaculate presentation of shark flesh at the dock.

"'Put a big fish on the dock, walk away, and say nothing, was always my advice," says Frank. "I always said just three words: Put them on the dock.'"

He's telling a fidgety Howard about a piston that just happened to blow on the trip when Harry Hoffman caught the last white, a 1,500-pounder, to be caught in these parts before *Jaws* was released and how he presented it, big, white, and scary, nonetheless. But I've heard this story before. It's Frank's parable of the immaculate presentation. Excuse me; I'm going to lie down, but I'll be within earshot.

"The deal was, I'd take Harry fishin', and he'd take care of my motor. One spring, Harry couldn't get down to check us out. There was a pay phone by the boat, so Dicky held out the phone, I started the engine, took the valve covers off, and he tuned Cricket over the phone. He was good, so whenever he wanted to go fishin', I'd take him fishin', three, four, five, six times a year.

"On the trip he caught the fifteen hundred pounder, we'd been drifting for two days. I'd take a bearing once a day, to see what it looks like. We had nice weather, slow drift. The third day, I go and take a bearing—no good. That's funny. So the hell with it. Fourth day, still can't get a bearin'. Fourth night, the fish shows up. Fifth day,

Harry catches his fish, just like *clockwoyck*. It was a blind strike, no sign of him in the slick."

Howard looks hard at the sea, wishing for X-ray eyes, a sixth sense, like his quarry has. I see him, even though I'm asleep.

"Okay, we start home," Frank continues. "We're rollin' along doin' 1500 r.p.m.s. Harry and I was on the bridge, towin' the white shark behind us. We're about a half hour from the fishin' grounds, on the way home.

"Harry says, 'Hey, I thought you was gonna call the wife if we done anything on this trip.'

"I says,' Oh yeah.' I hated like hell to push the buttons, but I gotta call home. I turned on the shit box to see if I can get the New York marine operator—nothing.

"Dead.

"At that time, I had a C.B. Turn the C.B. on — nothing. I could hear voices, but I couldn't get anybody come back for a radio check.

"So I laughed, shut it off, and said, 'Harry, we are now disconnected from the outside world.'

In my dream I'm on board the Exxon Valdez and we've lost communications.

"Fifteen minutes later, Bango, there goes the piston. Big cloud of black, oily smoke goes toward the sky. I pulled back on the throttle and I glance at the instrument panel and seen we still got oil pressure, but on the way down. I shut it off. Harry goes down; we lift the motor box. We were covered with oil.

"Everything, everybody. There was oil [Frank pronounces it earl] on the flyin' bridge. Couldn't stand on the flyin' bridge without slidin' back and forth.

I see everyone in the world covered with oil, dancing, rubbing, sinful. Detergent is our only prayer.

"I says, 'All right Harry—what is it, doctor?'

"Harry says, 'Well,' he says, 'you got a blown piston. There's a hole in the top of the piston.'

"'Ooooh, Jeez, whatawe do, Harry, watawe do, doctor?'

"'Well,' he says, 'how much oil you got?'

"I says, 'About six gallons, seven gallons.'

"He says, 'Well, fill it up, see how much it takes. But, he says, 'We'll run.' And I says, 'Yeah, okay,' so we put one gallon in, puts it up to the fill mark, and away we go.

"'Nowwww,' Harry says, 'where are we from land? We've been driftin' three days with no intruments.' 'Well,' I says, 'I think Block Island should show up just off the bow, on the starboard side. That's where I think Block Island's gonna pop up.'

"We go 20 minutes; one gallon a oil. Pull back on the throttle; there goes the oil pressure. Shut it off, put in another gallon, another 20 minutes, and that goes. 'At this rate, fellas, we are not going to make this.'

"After an hour and three more gallons, Dicky goes up on that mast and finds Block Island. It's a clear day, crystal-clear day.

"I says, 'Thank God for that; that's one in our favor. BUT, if it's this clear, we're a long way off.' Frank drones on, telling Howard, "I see a white dot on the horizon. The white dot gets bigger, and it's the Viking, Paul Forsberg, comin' back from Cox's. We get lined right up to him, so he has to cut us in half. We have dumped in our last gallon of oil and we're lined right up to him. He's within three boat lengths of us before he pulls back on the throttle. I'm laughin'.

"Forsberg looks, says, 'Oh my God, they're on fire. No, they can't be on fire — if they was on fire, they'd be puttin' the fire out. They're all standin' there, wavin'. Sumpin' else is wrong.'

"So he pulls back on the throttle, pulls up alongside of us, and I put my thumb like a hitchhiker. They threw us a rope. Broke that. Doubled up on it. Broke that. Tripled up on it — then he could tow us.

"Well, the Cricket II went faster than it ever went. Being towed, this white shark was floppin' behind us like a little blue shark. The wave action was just too bad that I couldn't pick him up. I can pick up 1500 pounds, no problem, but I couldn't put him in the cockpit, so we just let him drag along behind.

"I told Forsberg, when he started towin' us, 'Just get us to the inlet and turn us loose. We can run. Just idlin' speed — nobody will know the difference. So when you get to the inlet, let us go.' He said, 'Okay.'

"As luck would have it, we had a case of Ajax with us. We started cleanin' all the oil off the Cricket. We cleaned all the way home. We got the boat spankin' clean. When he turned us loose, I mashed on the starter, and we chug-a-lugged in towards the inlet. We stopped in front of the inlet, calm spot, and we lifted the fish up. We putted over to the Deep Sea Club, weighed him in, and we ran back to the slip. Nobody even knew we were broke down. Just as proud's a peacock."

... and again he sent forth
the dove out of the ark;
and the dove came in to him
in the evening; and, lo,
in her mouth was an
olive branch plucked off...

[GENESIS 8,11]

Chapter

18

COME HELL OR HIGH WATER

IT'S THE AFTERNOON OF THE FOURTH. One day to go. The sky is blue

in patches for the first time since we left Montauk. The waves, still

towering, look blacker for the brightening, cloud-streaked sky.

Howard's laughing, says I hollered 'cuts grease!' in my sleep. □ I

make my way through the bunk room strewn with wet sleeping bags

reeking of chum to the head. I have to go bad. Howard's intent on the

soccer ball. Down the companionway, struggling to get my oilers off

as Frank winds up the tale of Harry Hoffmann's blown-engine catch

that was saved by the soap with the Greek warrior's name. □ Ajax, as

I recall, taking the seat, was once the hero of the Trojan War, the mighty

suicide who fell on his sword after Odysseus beat him out for the honor

of inheriting the armor of fallen Achilles. Crybaby. Now he's the foam-

ing cleanser. If he hadn't fallen on his sword, Homer might not have written about him. He'd have sunk into quiet obscurity, leaving a lesser mortal to be reincarnated as suds. We can only hope his spirit soars like an eagle for having an abrasive detergent as avatar. And for saving Frank from the disgrace of an oily deck—girding his weak spot, the ignominy of a blown engine, just at the moment Harry's white monster was lifted high to wow the masses. This was most important, as it was the last monster before the movie.

Whew, finally. The storm kept me from going before. I couldn't have stayed on the bowl for the waves until now.

POW!—what was that?

POW!—the rifle, something's happening, and I'm on the bowl, story of my life. POW, right next to me. It's not the rifle. It's bombs bursting in air.

I struggle with my oilers and lurch topside, where Frank is caught in the past, regaling Howard with stories of how it used to be on the Cricket. Paul Smith lights another M-80 firecracker.

The sun is all the way out now. A freighter of some kind, the first boat we've seen in days, is a speck heading in our general direction. Jim's on the chum ladle, sleepy. The deck is warming. Howard sheds a layer of clothes. The buckets of monster mash will be coming to life —getting high, as they used to say of smells in the old days, the same words we now take to mean glimpsing Utopia via narcosis. Interesting.

It follows, like day the night, that Frank's now recalling how, when he was a boy, before marine radios were very reliable, a few old Italian gents enjoyed a thriving trade in homing pigeons down on the docks.

"It was when I was hangin' around the dock I seen the guys come down walkin' up and down the dock with a cage. 'Anybody want a pigeon? Twenty-five cents a bird.' Fishermen bought two birds.

"One bird [Frank says boyd] you set off once you was offshore, sayin', 'Havin a fine time — wish you was here.' The second one you saved for emergencies. It would go back to the guy that sold them, and if there was any kind of trouble, he'd go get help."

Since I've surmised Frank's purpose, whether he has or not, this story he's telling Howard and me about how one day two pigeons lighted on the Cricket far offshore comes as further evidence that he's been chosen.

Noah was adrift for 150 days after the rains fell for 40 days and 40 nights. God had opened floodgates on the ocean floor, as well, according to the Good Book, the quicker to drown all but two each of the hapless species unlucky enough to have walked the earth beside our omnivorous bipedal forebears. After the flood, there was nothing in sight but trackless ocean, like today on the Cricket.

After 40 days, Captain Noah released one member of the winged species he had on board — a crow, I think — and told it to go find land. After a time, the bird returned, tired and empty-beaked. Another seven days passed. Noah next released a dove to fly off and see if the waters had receded enough to have bared a chunk of land. The dove took its time but eventually flew back with an olive branch in its beak from the top of Mount Ararat upon which the sun was again shining.

Frank said how strange it was to see two city pigeons 50 miles offshore coming to rest on a shark fishing boat. Why strange? With discount furniture and auto-supply stores flooding the land, it's clear the pigeons took it on themselves to seek a meaningful outcropping somewhere and found the Cricket — the flood story backwards, reversed polarity. If, according to two-pigeon theory, just one pigeon had showed, it would have meant someone was having a fine time back in Babylon, watching coked-up topless girls at the Babylon Brook, for instance; 'Wish you were here.' But the second pigeon meant trouble like the kind of trouble on the Ark, as in 'Maybe there's no way out of here.'

I'm sure the second pigeon was meant to return to Babylon with one of Frank's Monster Fishing business cards, the ones with the Cricket's green fire-breathing dragon logo on it, an olive branch from the deep.

He said he used to mix his cards in with the butterfish chunks. The sharks would eat them. Once caught, Mundus would gut the sharks and reveal the cards to his customers as some kind of proof.

"It was 1960," Frank's recalling innocently, not realizing the gravity of his words. He says he brought the pigeons back to Montauk and gave them, poor bastards, to Bob Fitzgerald.

"We picked up two pigeons out there fishin' when we was in Montauk. Both of them landed on the boat, on the flyin' bridge, and we brought them home. Bob Fitzgerald had chickens and pigeons on the roof of his bar at Fitzgerald's dock. He decided he was gonna raise chickens, but they're a pain in the ass, so he put the chickens up on the flat roof to get rid of 'em. He thought they was gonna stay there with the pigeons.

"His hobby was raisin' homing pigeons. Fishermen never used Fitzgerald's pigeons, even in the old days. Those pigeons probably wouldn't a made it—hangin' around him, they was probably drunk all the time. They didn't get along with the chickens, and there was a chicken rebellion. Chickens can fly a little bit, so they come down off the roof. Most of them survived that much at least.

"Bob was runnin' the bar, and his brother Dick was runnin' the dock. You could go in there anytime with a dollar bill, put it on the counter, and make believe you was payin' for your drink and he'd keep fillin' your glass up, and you'd wind up leavin' the dollar and walk out stoned. But that was the place to go. You talk about the happy house a horrors—that was nothin' compared to Fitzgerald's bar.

"There was spitoons, but everyone just spit on the floor. One time, a dog was chasin' a chicken outside, come in the back door. The chicken jumped on the bar, ran the full length of the bar. The dog jumps up on the bar, runs after it, knockin' everything down. He had a guy playin' a piano.

"The doors was open, and this honky tonk music was playin'. I was workin' on the boat, but I hadda stop, and I go in there — holy shit, just listenin' to this guy, one tune right after the other, *binginy, binginy, binginy.*

"It was closin' time. He had a half a dozen people in there, and they wouldn't go home, so Fitzgerald just took his Army fold-up cot from out in back and brought it out and opened it up in front of the bar and said, 'The hell with you guys. I'm goin to sleep. Help yourself. Put the money in the jar.'

Frank's wound up, back in time, remembering Montauk and its saloons pre-flood, before the yuppies bought out the endangered indigenous drunks, raised the prices, Varathaned the floors, hung plants instead of fish, and kicked out the dogs.

"Fitzgerald was great for raffling off stuff. Someone'll come in with a 10-pound fluke, he'll hang it up at the bar. The flies is all over it. 'Okay, fellas, today we're rafflin' off that fluke, 25 cents a chance.' And whoever won, they had to buy everybody a drink. The money never went noplace.

"We come in with the dead chicken. It's his chicken. I put it in a black plastic bag, and I walk in and says, "Here, Bob, I got somethin' for you. You can raffle this off.' He opens up the bag and says, 'It's one of my chickens—you shot one of my chickens. I'm gonna charge you for the chicken, I'm gonna charge you $5 for the chicken.' I says, 'Get outta here—I didn't shoot him, I'm bringin' him back. You can eat it. I'll charge you $10 dollars for eatin' him.

"The chickens got to be a pain in the ass. I was there once, I seen Bob half drunk, somebody mentioned about the chickens—how they was comin' and goin' in and out the door all the time. He had no screens on there; the chickens would wander in and he'd shoo 'em out. Somebody would make some kind of a joke about the chickens or kinda insult Bob about 'em.

"He had a 30-30 rifle in the corner, and he goes outside, and everybody puts their fingers to their ears and he goes bang, bang, bang three shots. Now it's quiet. In come Bob, staggerin', with the smokin' 30-30 rifle in one hand and the wounded chicken in the other hand. He'd just blew one wing off, blood goin' all over the place, and he throws the chicken in the corner and says, 'There, there's one of the sons-a-bitches won't bother me no more. I don't know why I mess wid em.'" A gust of wind strums the cross-tree shrouds. Frank goes on:

"There was this one guy, a real nut, a real idiot. He was dangerous, this guy, Joe, one of my customers. He wants to catch a chicken and put it in our fish box as a joke. The chickens were wanderin' all over the sand dunes.

"He runs around after a live one and wants to put it on my boat, but he didn't want to chase it around. So he shot it. He had a .38 pistol and decides to go up over the sand dunes and shoot a chicken. *Bang, bang, bang.* When he comes walkin' back over the sand dunes, he's still got the smokin' .38 in his right hand, and in his left hand this chicken that he's shot.

"In the parkin' lot—which wasn't any parking lot at the time—a car was parked with my customers; three cops and two F.B.I. guys what was goin' fishin' with me. They was sleepin' in their car, waitin' for me to show up. They hear this *bang bang* and it wakes them up, and they look, and here comes this guy over the sand dune with this .38 and the chicken. One of the cops hollers out, 'What's goin' on?' Joe says, 'It's okay—everything's all right, fellas go back to sleep.' So they look at this nut, they stretch their necks and go back to sleep. He goes and puts the chicken on my boat.

"Now these guys figure if they turn him in they're gonna lose their fishin' trip, aaaaargh? So they say, 'The hell with it—we'll just let this guy go. Something's wrong wid 'im.'

"Eventually we heard that the same guy shot his father-in-law in the head with a pistol in the city and stole a hundred thousand dollars in cash, put the $100,000 in a black plastic bag, and sent it to a friend of his back in Montauk. The guy in Montauk was so scared he went to the dumps and threw it in. He didn't know if it was counterfeit or not, threw the money in the dumps. The F.B.I. shut the dumps down and picked through everything, and found the money. He's probably still servin' time. That took care of him."

This sounds like the good ole days to me, the fun days Before *Jaws*: 1960 B.J. (Before *Jaws*, Before Jacques). Frank brought the pigeons back when the flood of mediocrity was still a trickle, the colorless wave of the future still a gentle swell. Fitzgerald and what chickens he hadn't shot were still alive. Mr. Banks was a regular charter customer. It was the age of innovation—the externally cooled Superior—and of discovery: essence of pilot whale for white-shark chum and the first paralyzing contact with the monsters themselves. It was the age of strong drink and calliope music on the Cricket—even, as I sense I'm about to learn, goat sacrifices.

I'm worried now about how the Cricket will fare after Frank leaves for Hawaii.

Higher clouds, backlit by a stronger sun, have formed a vault now, a bubble in which the Cricket drifts along with her memories and manifestations.

She has blazed trails, endured much. She survived at least 10 white sharks over 1,000 pounds, countless tigers, makos, and duskies. Sharks below, idiots above. She survived torpedoes, 90-caliber anti-aircraft shells, the Dr. Frankenstein of mechanics, and a strict but caring captain. She was his shelter down in Virginia before she was whole.

Even before her planking went on, Frank threw a tarp over her ribs for a tent at night, during the time old Cockrell was making her tight, real tight, as though he could see into her future. And she was his shelter later, at the dock, on the nights he didn't go home or was told to leave. And now he's leaving her flat, talking out loud about the fruit orchard and the macadamia nut trees he'll soon have in Hawaii. Still, she continues to meet his gait across the deck even as he contemplates that twin-hulled slut the Double D, which might as well be a damned piece of fetid land worthy of flooding for her full-sized refrigerator, wide-screen tv, fully stocked bar, and kitchen.

Left alone will the Cricket be, just a slow boat without the king of the slow drift. Too slow, like a weekly newspaper, to compete with the fast, plastic-hulled fishermen going they're not sure where, leaving history in their wakes, racing with the fast and faster current.

Cricket will be only half without Frank, he half without her. He's stirring his jaws in the bleach bucket along with his stories, so we can hear. Five in the bucket so far. After the bleach, they will go through a secret process, winter work done before dawn in his garage. Before dawn because fishermen can't reset clocks wound offshore to the rhythm of swordfish feeding at night under the moon. Clocks set for makos and the "golden hour," the whole place coming alive when molten morning pours her golden bead to mark the indefinable horizon.

The final step is to block the jaws with Styrofoam and cardboard to keep their intimidating shape, so as someday to take big, refreshing bites out of a dull den or office. He gets $40 for small jaws, $300 for big makos; as much as $500 for individual white shark teeth.

Frank straightens up, moves the chum buckets around, each move wedded to Cricket, perfectly synchronized with his partner, who bore him home straight through the drinking days, towing his sharks behind. They are one.

"On a regular day-trip, why, we'd have three or four doubles before we'd leave the house in the mornin'. Vodka and juice, then, when we'd get down to the boat, we each had a half-gallon jug on the chart table. That chart table musta housed truckloads a booze in its day. On a regular day-trip, we'd get down to the boat before the charter would. So we'd pour another one in a coffee cup, always a coffee cup, vodka and coke.

"That would hold us on the way out to the fishin' grounds. Then once in a while, Dicky would say, 'Gotta go down and take a bearing; 'cause we had the loran down below. That was my excuse too—when we only had an hour to go to the fishin' ground, I'd go down. The party would be all anxious out in the cockpit. I'd go down, take a bearin', pour myself a couple a shooters.

"Then you'd have somethin' to eat, and then it would be afternoon, on your way home, and the party would say, 'Hey, Frank, want a drink?'

"'No, no, no, you know I don't drink. When we can see the lighthouse, then we can drink.' So we'd see the lighthouse, and I'd say, 'Okay, pour me a drink, and don't be cheap about it—you know, a decent drink.' So we'd drink all their booze. When we get to the dock, then we'd decide to do a little serious drinkin' at the bar. So otherwise we was teetotalers."

Howard laughs. POW!, another mini-depth-charge explodes off the port side, in a flash of green submarine light.

"We were the first ones to find out that sound attracts sharks," Frank brags to Howard. "We would use the M-80s—they're hard to get now. In the shark tournaments, you'll hear 'em throwin' the M-80s. But you only need four or five. As fast as you can throw them, you light one and throw it, light one and throw it, and then they go off, *bang, bang, bang.* The reason for that is—you know yourself if you're in a dark room and you hear a noise; 'Where'd it come from?' you ask.

"Bang, it come from there — you turn your head, and it goes again, bang; oh, no, it's over there, *BANG*, oh, no, it's over there, *bang, bang, bang*—you're honed in on it.

"But these tournament guys, they throw a whole case. A whole case of M-80s is stupid, because there's nothin' there. You can't raise 'em if they ain't there. Four will tell you within five minutes if there's anything there. Four will do it. They always come up. Big sharks. All-size sharks.

"If it's a flat calm day and you see a mako going across the stern out there about 30, 40 yards, you know he missed the slick, aaargh? So you take your foot or a gaff handle and you bang on the deck steady, *bang, bang, bang*. Now you're watchin' him. He's goin' away from you. He disappears. He went down. Where is he? Somebody says, 'Here he is — look.' You look down, and he's right at your feet. The bigger the noise, the farther away they hear it."

And Cricket endured the war games, and if the pyrotechnic theory is right, the war games drew the sharks to Frank just as he was being drawn to them. I feel I'm in sync with the master. He's going to tell us about big guns.

"When we used to have the firing range on the cliffs by Montauk Point, after the war, the Navy also had torpedo practice, so's they would chase you from the torpedo practice, down into the firing range.

"We'd be outside the range minding our own business, fishin', and there was destroyers, escorts, flat-tops would show up, submarines pop up, P.T. boats come buzzin' along side of us. One day one comes up alongside and says, 'Ahoy, the Cricket II,' and I said, 'What the hell do you want?' This really makes him mad. I'm supposed to be nautical about this. He says, 'We suggest that you clear outta this area 'cause we're gonna have torpedo practice.

"'Where the hellya want us to go?'

"'To the west.'

"'I can't go to the west 'cause the Air Force is having firing practice at the range.' He says,' We don't have any jurisdiction over the Air Force — we're Navy.'

"I says, 'You mean to tell me you want us to go west?'

He says, 'Well, you can't go east because between here and the east, we're gonna have our torpedo practice.

"Okay, I make a right-hand turn; there's two or three boats behind me. I turn the radio on; everybody's screamin', 'Look, Mundus has gone mad — he's goin' down through the firin' range.'

"I says, 'Hey, boys, you better follow me down through the range, because you see all this action I got around me. It's because the Navy's gonna have torpedo practice. You better follow me. Somebody better call them at the point and tell 'em to stop shootin'. Otherwise, we're gonna get our ass shot.'

"Somebody called in, and they stopped firing. The Air Force was mad at us, but a small parade of boats went through. It was a wonder they didn't kill somebody. They'd tow a sleeve behind a plane and the guys would have practice up on the hill; *bang, bang, bang,* with their hot .90s. They was supposed to start southeast, and stop when they got to the southwest but they always said, 'One more, one more, one more.'

"John Gnagy and I..." Frank begins, and I jump, because I remember John Gnagy from when I was a kid in Levittown. He was the goateed tv sketching instructor in the '50s who tried to teach art on the tube. I liked him, but I liked Winky Dink better. The "Winky Dink" show was a learn-to-draw show. Your mom sent away for a green plastic sheet that stuck to the television via static electricity. You traced a televised farm scene or whatever onto the green plastic. It's unsettling to think that while our faces were melding to the television sets, being bombarded by electrons — our *ampullae* of Lorenzini, as it turns out — Gnagy and the Monster Man were fishing and dodging real artillery shells off Montauk Point. What a difference a tube makes. Already we were set adrift by our Zenith and Motorola *ampullae,* swimming, no longer touching the ground, opting for the flood while it was still a trickle, sniffing the dying Leviathan electronically, its commodious cushions of blubber.

"So we're driftin', and I heard bang, bang, bang. I can hear 'em startin' to shoot, and sure enough, here comes the airplane towin' the sleeve. I jumped up, looked at the compass, looked at the Lighthouse. I was to the west-southwest of the lighthouse, and I was startin' to worry about how, if those things don't go off on a timing fuse, they go off when they hit the water — here comes the whistle [Frank whistles the falling-shell whistle] — *BOOOOOM !* It lands about 100 feet from the boat. Aaaaargh?

"The schrapnel rolls along the surface of the water. John Gnagy sees this and dives on deck and slides along on his face. So I says, 'John, I don't know what you're divin' for. That one's already right there in the water; there's the hole. So I mash on the starter button, and I put it in gear from down below— I wasn't gonna wait— and I jumped up on the bridge, and I got on the radio— Dusty Drobecker, he had the Rip Tide at that time— I give Dusty a call, I says, 'Dusty, are they gonna shoot today?'

"He says, 'Yeah, don't go down through the range.'

"I says, 'I'm not in the range. I'm to the west-southwest, and they just dropped one within 100 feet of me.'

" He says, 'You gotta get outta there.'

"I says, 'You're late again, because I'm on my way.' It was flat calm, and you could see the half-circle still in the water from where the Cricket left, and here come another one. Here comes the whistle, and I still had time to say to my mate— his name was Oli—I says, 'Oli, I wonder where this one's gonna hit?' and he dove in the corner of the flyin' bridge — don't know what the hell he was gonna do in the corner, but, anyhow, he was in the corner, and *BA BOOMBO*— that one landed right in the hole, right where we was. If they was shootin' at us, they couldn'ta come any closer. A lot of the boats had close calls. Why they didn't really hit a boat, I don't know.

"And torpedo practice. Yeah, old man Drobecker, he had the Skip II. For a hull, he had double three-eighths plywood. Now, he was out there. Who does he have on the flyin' bridge but Jim Hurley, the reporter from the *MIRROR*. Flat calm day, and they're ridin' around, tuna fishin'. Jim Hurley looks off to one side and sees this thing comin' under the water, straight at the boat, and it goes *zooooom*, Right under the boat and keeps right on goin.' He says to Walter, he says, 'What the hell was that?' Drobecker says, 'Oh, a torpedo— they're havin' torpedo practice somewhere around here.'

"'Well, says Hurley, 'isn't that rather dangerous?

"'Yeah.'

"'Well, why don't you call the Coast Guard?'

"Walter says that won't do no good. But he insists Walter push the button on the radio. Walter calls the Coast Guard. Now, when the Coast Guard was raised when they was kids they was only taught two words: one was STAND; the other was BY. That's all they know is stand by. So they're standin' by, and in about 20 minutes, they call back, and he tells Walter he had nothin to worry about 'cause they was only dummies. ONLY DUMMIES," shouts Frank. "They'd go through anything, any dragger around here, like cheese."

I'm on the chum ladle, spelling Howard, who's lying on the icebox amidships. And from the Cricket the music fell like rain. Let me hear you say it!

"Then we started with the underwater speaker. We went bananas with the underwater speakers. Gordon Rynders, he had a lotta time on his hands, bein' a newspaper photographer, so I asked him to make up some kinda underwater speaker. So he took an ordinary speaker and put a diaphragm on it the best he could, so it wouldn't get wet, and we could just hang it down in the water.

"Well, the first day we hung it down the water, we had a white shark show up. Music is made up of nothing but noise: high, low and medium. Everything is in music. Don't make no difference what song you play—you got all the notes."

Amen, music defined.

"We don't know what's the best. We got tapes. First day we hang it in the water, there's a white shark, about 1500 pounds. Now, we don't get him. The next day, Gordon has to go back to the city. He wanted to use the speaker on his boat. That was Friday. On Sunday, Gordon comes back to the Cricket, puts the speaker back in the water; another white shark. We rose them both on Johnny Cash.

"We tried riggin' up our own waterproof speaker, and believe me, we went through all my contacts and all their contacts tryin' to get waterproof speakers. The only one we come up with was the ones that's in swimmin' pools. They was $150, and they'd last us about two months, not even. You hadda watch it constantly. Blue sharks will come right up, and if you don't get it out, he's gonna grab that thing. It definitely worked.

"We had tapes from all over the world. Because we had these speakers on there and the cassette—why, when things got dull, I'd put on one of his crazy tapes.

"We had one sound-effects tape—everything from a chicken, a cow, all the animals recorded from the real live thing, Big Ben strikin' twelve times, glass breaking, crowds laughing, a railroad train soundin' like it's goin in one side of the boat and comin' out the other when you turn it up loud, outer space sounds, oooohweeeoooooweee, so when somebody'd come on the boat with a hangover, I would tell them, you lay here [next to the speaker] and relax — it'll be a while before the fish come up. Then I'd put on the sound effects, turn it up loud, and the poor bastard. Big Ben — *bong, bong,* here comes the train, *whooooo whooooo.* We played it underwater, too, but music was better because it has more of a variety. On some of his tapes, he had a calliope, and when we were comin' in the inlet, he'd turn that damn thing on, blastin', and it sounded like a circus boat comin' in ...

"Well?" says I.

Frank grins, the first real sincere smile in my direction, as if to say, 'There's hope for you yet, obituary-drone.' The terrestrial sounds descending into the depths must have felt like a warm rain on the lateral lines of fish beneath the Cricket, an alien message like madness to us — or proof of a higher, other-worldly existence, some of it recognizable as the sounds, the mooing and oinking, which first vibrated through the planking of Noah's Cricket, but then weirder through the ages, with the ever-growing roar of war, the buzz of hunting boats, the sibilance of ashes.

Descending. Still on the ladle.

I think the tilefish squid baits were to Luby, in his backdeck ballet, like the notes of Beethoven for the symphony on the backdeck. Hour after hour, his and the other mates' hands synchronized perfectly as the stainless steel longline was wound upon its big reel mounted amidships, 36 miles of it, set and retrieved each day, in sections buoyed at each end, and flagged for detection.

Hands synchronized perfectly to snap on the snoods, hooked shortlines, every few fathoms to swim perpendicular to the longline. Each snood with a circle hook that won't let go of the tile througout its death struggle and 100-fathom ascent, eyes bugged in surprise.

The synchronous movements of a string section as each tile is gutted and put below on the small Kilimanjaro of ice and again when the miles of stainless steel are sent out again, the baiting like clockwork, snapping on snood, after snood with their circle hooks and white-fleshed squids, their tentacles waving melodiously as they go below. Quick flicks of the wrist, squid after squid, master baiters from dawn until the middle of the night, two hours off every four, working to a state that would be exhaustion to any but backdeck musicians, play-ing their own siren song with tight string, hooks, and the alluring notes of meat.

Capt. Krusa has a mate called Johnny Angel, now toothless, who tied his last, a front one, to a snood and snapped it onto the longline as it was being set—farewell.

"I still got a lot of the tapes," Frank's saying. "I mean we had North American, real Indian dances. Once, down in St. Maarten, the house I was rentin' was a new house, and right behind it was the little house of my landlady. She had two of her grandchildren, six and eight years old. The grandfather lived in another shack. She wouldn't say good morning to him, she would say, 'Are you still with us?' cause he was about 80 some years old. Down there, we had to depend on the rain for our water, it filled up the cistern behind the house. She didn't have any runnin' water in her place, so she'd come out— right under-neath the kitchen window. There was a hand pump, and she'd pump whatever she needed. I was doin' the dishes, and she looked up at me, and they have a habit of tellin' a story to tell you somethin'.

Like you, says Howard.

"She says, 'Mornin.' She's pumpin' away and hears me turn the water on, and she says, 'You know, we haven't had rain in a long time.' I says, 'I know— I'm watchin' it. I'm goin' very easy on the water.' She says, 'I hope we get some rain.' I says, 'Why didn't you tell me? I could play a North American Indian rain dance.' She looks up at me and says, 'Could you?'—they're very superstitious—I says,

'How much do you want? I got to know how much to order.' She says, 'A lot.'

"I says, 'Okay, I'll order a lot.' I turn on the tape and it's goin' aaeeooohh, aaaeeeoooh, and I'm jumpin' around the kitchen. The two little boys is lookin' up at me, their eyes poppin' outa their heads. 'Wokay,' I says, 'that oughta do it—hang on.'

"The next day, it rained. The next night, it rained. The next day, it rained. The next night, it rained. It rained three days and three nights. She comes to me, and she says, 'Frank, can you turn it off?' I says, 'I can't—I already put my order in. 'You asked for a lot; you didn't say how much.' It come down the mountain — it flooded, the drains flooded, what a mess. Finally it's over, and I'm gigglin to myself."

Yeah, like God in Noah's time — like He's giggling now.

"I was gettin' ready to come home to Montauk, and she says, 'Frank, you think you could order some more rain before you go?' I says, 'Sure — all right, how much you want? Because remember last time.' She says, 'A little, just enough to hold us till you get back.' I says, 'I can't order a little. How 'bout a couple hours of hard rain?' She says, 'That would be nice.' I put on the tape: *aaaeeeoooh, aaaeeeoooh,* shut it off, okay, that was just about enough. Don't you know the next day we got two hours of hard rain, so help me.

"The next time I came back, the next year, I seen her, and she wanted me to order some more. I says, 'No, I can't, I don't have my music.' I didn't dare try it one more time. And them two little dark-skinned boys, they walked way around me like I was God Himself. Their eyes would bug out every time they'd see me; they'd go as far as they could to the next building and slide along on their backs."

Frank's made his way up the mast by this time and is standing spread-legged and staring off, looking for something or at something I can't see, and I find myself looking up to him like the dark-skinned, bug-eyed boys — Caliban upon Setebos. He descends again.

"What killed Dicky" Frank's saying, "was the fact he never ate nothin'. He drank continually. I drank continually, too, but I also ate continually. That's the only thing that kept me alive. The more I drank, the more I ate. He was the opposite.

"One of the funniest stories was down in Atlantic City. He was startin' to get heavy on it then. We was layin' flush to the dock, and the boat's bangin' the way the wind was. We was in there gettin' supplies—we was out more than we was in, so we was in gettin' supplies and the boat was bangin'. So I says, 'Dicky, for God's sake, don't you feel the boat bangin'? I says, 'Go put a spring line on her, hold her away from the cussed dock.'

"I was down below, doin' something, puttin' groceries away, something, and I hear the pitter-patter of little feet goin up to the bow, back down to the stern, pitter patter, fumblin', draggin' lines. He comes down below. It was still bangin'. No sense me sayin' nothin', I gotta go out and check up. I go out, and I look.

"What he done, he took a piece of half-inch nylon and made it fast to the Samson post on the bow, went to the stern, pulled it as hard as he could, and made it fast to the stern bits. The line never went to the dock. He'd pulled as hard as he could pull, good and tight— it was holdin' that boat together. You know he was out of his mind."

Luby comes to mind again, forces himself aboard with Dicky, and Jack Curtin, his friend. Jack is a captain now. He was a deckhand and Tom Luby's best friend on the backdeck of Deliverance and in the waterfront bars of Montauk when the boat was in.

Jack told me he was mad as hell at God the day they lowered Luby down in the sea of tombstones in Queens, the heavy metal and glass of New York City towering behind the clutch of mourners, adding to the gravity. He said it was then he realized Luby was what he called his "ghost."

"I could have gone either way," he said as though poised on the side rail of Deliverance 100 miles at sea, looking down, still poised years after Luby was laid low. "I could have gone either way," he said, going on to describe the days-long drug and alcohol binges that had no purpose, no end in sight, but which were, he said, a sort of search, nonetheless, for a shoreside equivalent to pulling fish from the sea, with its constant rushing alongside; only Deliverance and her crew with no other vessels on the horizon for days, just wind and water, stories and fish.

Onshore they referred to their upcoming trips as "the sentence." But once at sea, the names of the week dissolved quickly, becoming the Beginning, the second day, the third, fourth, until — especially when "fishing fine"— they would tell their captain, "Don't stop us now. We've got the blood," like the scene aboard the Pequod Jack said he remembered from 'Moby Dick', the movie.

They fished themselves down to peanut butter and some crackers one time, not wanting to come in. Forced ashore by hunger, but unable to entirely disembark the backdeck, its miles of hooks, its mountain of ice like Kilimanjaro below, waxed cartons and their treasure of yellow-spotted tiles.

Jack said he thought Luby, like himself, was "confused by civilization." He said for his own part he had tried joining the carpenters' union—but never built a wall, then stepped back and said to himself, 'Wow, look at the size of that wall,' the way he was amazed when a big fish came in over the rail. As for Tom, he'd grown up in the Bronx, in a bad neighborhood. He had come to Montauk to get away from it.

Jack said when he thought of Luby, it was hard to think of all of him. There were so many parts.

He recalled the time in the engine room, as it steadily filled with water, the first time he took Deliverance offshore as her captain. Jack had cleaned up, made the decision to better himself, and he had.

The impeller on the pump that cooled the engine had blown. He called ashore, and Captain Krusa told him to put the deck hose into the expansion tank, cut down the flow to the pump by restricting it through the sea cock. But the engine overheated again and the pump blew up and he couldn't get the sea cock closed. Jack remembered it was he and Luby alone in the engine room, up to their waists, burning themselves on overheated engine parts as they scrambled with wrenches to close the cock. There was the thought shared between them with a look so quick, yet so long: "we are going down"—just before the cock closed.

There was the chant of "Holy Shit, Holy Shit," the day on a back-deck, before Deliverance, when he and Tom watched a white shark glide by the boat, Provider, a shark so big they could not grasp its length in one glance. And, there was the productive fishing spot named for Luby— or, more precisely, for his tale of a wild girl. The Knotted Nylon is in 81 fathoms between Veaches and Atlantis Canyons. Jack said there was not a fisherman worth his salt who didn't know the place, otherwise unmarked on the featureless expanse, for a ribald confession told one day for warmth and which glowed there still.

Jack said he looked up to Luby because he could come and go. He was a great fisherman, in demand. Anyone would have him, and he could come and go at will. He could leave the boat and go back to school and then come back to the boat again and be welcome. He could still get an academic scholarship to N.Y.U., despite his low orbiting. He was an astronaut and a fisherman who would always come back after carefully creeping out onto the edge where golden euphoria drops off into night. Balancing the fulfilling dawns aboard Deliverance. Who can say? He might have discovered it's not an edge at all out there but yet another globe with distant lands to discover just beyond sunrise, with Indians there to be saved. Jack said Luby still came to him, but only offshore.

I'm hot and smell to high heaven. Don't feel well. Experiencing Deja Vu. Fish must have it all the time — all animals except the omnivorous bipedal humper. I know what Frank is going to say before he says it. He's going to tell how Cricket found Atlantis.

Frank's eyes widen. I look to the slick. Nothing. The float dangling terminal gear fit for two tons of white shark has not moved. And when I look back, the captain is stuffing his cheek with tobacco and smiling. He told me he'd come home after a double-overnighter and the next morning he woke up tired, with a quick pulse. He went under the sink for a double shot of vodka, but it didn't work. He told that day's charter customers, "See those leaves blowin'; you don't want to go out."

Then he called his doctor, who told him to get someone to drive him in. He was in intensive care for two days —"heavy blood, high blood pressure. The suction was jammed, the heart wanted to pump but couldn't," he said in the same way he described trouble with the aluminum Superior. The doctor told him to keep his weight down and not to drink to "excess." Frank said he told him, "You're not talking English. Don't offer me a drink — offer me a bottle." He never drank again.

Our Fourth of July celebration continues apace— *Pow!*— in the chum— *Pow!*— slick every ladle or so. A few more blue sharks have joined us, circling. All we need is some Johnny Cash, some "burnin' ring of fire," echoing off the reef of artillery shells beneath us, massaging the lateral lines of little fish, jingling the odaliths of larger ones, letting freedom ring like the Avon lady chumming at the front door of Mrs. White.

What more can we offer? Maybe drag out the fishing kite with old Ben's key. Dangle it on the surface like an electrical skip-bait, challenging Zeus in the clouds to tickle your *ampullae* with one of his bolts.

Are you near? Would you sooner come to the evenly fired pistons of our beating hearts? Should we hang over the side for you to feel them? What do you want? Whom do you want?

"Speaking of Atlantic City," says Frank, eyeing me and sensing happy horse manure. He says the words "Atlantic City" (the once peaceful seaside resort, now gaudy ziggurat to wishful thinking), but I hear it as Atlantis. Lost Utopia is what he really means. Is perfection rising up, or are we sinking toward it, or is it the same thing?

Are we to be lost beneath the waves on this trip? Will Atlantis appear to us? Perhaps when Dicky tied the Cricket bow-to-stern, he thought she had found Atlantis and tied off to the mirage, the same one that appeared to Tom Luby and our other pioneers of the rush-in-no-particular-direction-but-down.

" ... mudding up," I hear Frank say. "Ask any of the guys that harpooned any amount of swordfish ..." Frank's dispensing another piece of fishing advice to Paul. He doles it out regularly to the man meant to inherit Cricket, but this mudding up sounds contiguous with my drift.

"The worst thing in the world you can do is to harpoon a swordfish in the gill plates so it goes through this side and buttonholes the other, holds it closed. They can't breathe through one side because it don't work right, so they're being choked to death. It happened to us once," he tells Paul, with Howard hanging on every word.

"The swordfish tail-walked, jumped, stayed on the surface, it went down, it come up immediately, back up, stayed in the air. I couldn't figure out what the hell was wrong with this swordfish. Eventually, why, he got tired of this and did what swordfishermen call mudded up. He mudded up. He hooked up wide open and kept right on goin' down past the bottom. He jams his bill and his whole head right into the bottom. They do that when they can't breathe. Giant tuna will do it, too, a lot of them up in Maine. When they come back they got a flat nose, a flat face, head and everything else from hitting the rocks, from goin' so fast when they hit the rocks."

Frank's back in Atlantic City after his mudding-up digression, still staring at me and talking about not being able to trust journalists. It's Jerry Kenney of the *News* again who betrayed him.

"Somehow Jerry found out about it and called me up two days before we was getting ready to leave and wanted to know about this Atlantic City trip and the white shark. I said, 'If I tell you the information, you'll promise me you won't say anything until we get back?'

"We get there, somebody hands us the paper, and he's got this whoooooole thing—the Cricket went to Atlantic City and up the Great Egg Harbor River to catch a white shark. We needed that like we needed a hole in the head," Frank says disingenuously, for my benefit, choosing to stress the pesty part of a gadfly business—the one he'd learned to play like a fiddle.

"So'd the guy who tended the drawbridge over the river. He was bothered more than what we was because we'd chase them away," Frank says of the curious who swarmed to witness the joust.

"People read about it, would go down to the bridge and see the boat, and stop and talk to the bridge tender to ask him all of these damn-fool questions.

"The way it happened was: I get a phone call from this guy down in Atlantic City. He wanted to know what white shark teeth looked like, so I told him what they looked like over the phone. He says, 'Yeah, that musta been one.'

"He said it bit the bow of a boat. I wormed the story out of him, and he says a friend was out fishin', and he brought the boat back and said a shark grabbed a hold of the bow of his boat, and he said they picked the teeth out. He says they was in the boat a quarter of an inch. 'How do you go about catchin' him?'— that's what he called me for.

"I says, 'You can find out if he's there by puttin' out test baits. Put a buoy out with a half-a-dozen mackerel on it over there and another buoy over here with a half-a-dozen mackerel on it. Go back the next day and see if they're gone.

"He calls me back the next day, and he says, 'Yeah, he's there, because he took the baits, the whole thing and chopped the line.'

"I says, 'No skeletons or nothin'?'

"'No, nothin', the whole thing's gone.'

"I'm shakin' my head. I'm thinkin' about this all right, and it so happens Mr. Banks had the boat chartered. We went fishin' and I mentioned it to Mr. Banks, what this guy said.

"Mr. Banks turned to me and says, 'Head this boat to Atlantic City. We're goin' to *Atlaaaaantic City.*' I says, 'When?' He says, 'Tomorrow.'

"'Can't, I got two charters for next week.'

"He says, 'Give 'em away to someone else.'

"'If I can, I'll try.' Right away dollars and cents started to come into my head. I got a week's charter here against two charters. Soooo, I says, 'look, let's not be too hasty. Here's the guy's number; we'll call him up tonight.'

"So we call him up and asked him a bunch of questions, and the answers he was givin' sounded all right, sounded good. Mr. Banks says, 'Okay, we're on our way.' He said, 'If we get him, there's an extra $10,000 in it for ya.'

"Sokay, down we go. We asked the guy if he could get goats for bait. A white goat. 'Yeah,' he says, 'no problem. That'll be about $35.'

"I says, 'No problem—have a goat for us when we get there.' We got there; he shows up with a white goat. We put the goat on the boat, aaargh?

"We spread a piece of canvas there, tie him up with a short string. Nowww, if a white shark shows up, we got a good bait."

Howard's doubled up laughing.

"The public didn't like it too much. There was a lot of *aaahin'* and *ooooin'* and *gee whizzzzz* and here they was bringin' down apples and stuff for the goat's last meal and feelin' sorry for him and all this kinda happy jazz.

"Sokay, he gets us the goat, talks to us for five minutes, says he has to go but he'd see us the next day. He tells us about where the boat was when it got hit, and we went to work right away. We went out and dropped anchor.

"We musta had 50 cans a chum with us. Why we didn't get arrested for pollution, I don't know. There we was inside the river, inside the inlet, and inside the bridge, aaargh?

"There we are chummin', and we got swarms of seagulls and big birds and everything else over the top of us, with a goat. Now the harbormaster, he hadda come along and tie up to the boat to find out what was goin' on. So a little bit a bribery — I give him a copy of the *Monster Man* book what Boggsy wrote about me and told him what we was doin'. He was happy, and away he went.

"We didn't see a shark of any kind. We chummed in there for five days. A day goin' down, a day comin' back, chummed in there for a seven-day trip, and all that time, we never seen nothin'. We never seen that guy again either. We called his number a lotta times, never got an answer. If he got us down there on a wild-goose chase, he should be workin' with Sherlock Holmes. He had all the answers; he had the stories. He sucked us in."

Sounds like some kind of turning point, the first time old Mundus was played like he played his Idiots. Oh, how he's played them.

I know this because he revealed to me up on the flying bridge yesterday how he dealt with the impatience of fishermen — the greatest force, after gravity, in the world, after all, and one now exuding from Chong like the reek of chum.

"I tell them, 'I want the fish now,'" Frank says of the impatient, "and that generally confuses them, throws them off guard — a diversion, like buildin' a fire in front of the police station while you rob a bank around the corner."

"Keeps 'em busy tryin' to figure it out. Instead of them being impatient, sayin' 'Where's the fish?' I beat 'em to the punch, in other words. If I can beat 'em to the punch and hit 'em with the words with what they were gonna hit me and twist 'em around, now I got the bastard confused — that's my job. The more time that they know they have comin' up, the less impatient that they are. The impatient ones are the ones that know they have to go back to the dock tonight, know that the day is runnin' short.

"Those are the ones that if they're gonna get impatient, they're gonna get impatient the last two hours of the fishin' time. They're sittin' around like pregnant nuns. Father Time is against us, aaargh?"

Howard, of course, didn't hear this, although he sure as hell looks pregnant-nun-ish right now.

I turn my face to the sun to absorb its warmth. The beauty is that all this makes sense on the Cricket, and by the Cricket, I mean Frank and his boat as one being — marine Minotaur.

All of it: the high chum and bubbling butters, music reinvented, big white sharks lured by Johnny Cash, the Fourth of July celebrated, complete with the sanguine smells of gunpowder and death, the assurance we are closing with the enemy, the promise of impending carnage to be wrought upon oppressors. We have Great White gods, and thanks to a con man from Atlantis, we have white goats to sacrifice to them. We have jaws in the bucket. All we want is a dead Leviathan.

Is there any doubt the whites and other carnivorous sharks have become attracted, grudgingly, to our chaos—our ever-climbing-tide, the incessant slap-slap of hungry thighs—just as we have become fatally attracted to them? Frank knows he's been the matchmaker, is tired of the strain. It's taken its toll. He nearly killed himself with booze, perhaps in an unconscious and fruitless attempt to douse his magnetism.

"The suction was jammed. The heart wanted to pump but couldn't," he'd said, making his heart sound — *kachunk* — — like the Cricket's diesel. He quit drinking two years after Jaws was released.

His first wife Janet had left him the same year. "I have to be honest and give my mother her due," Frank's daughter, Patti, had told me. "For all the stories about Harry Hoffman, Mr. Banks, Peter Gimbel, and so forth, there existed a parallel story off the boat. All of these characters spilled over into our life, some literally. Peter Gimbel had his first cage in our back yard. I can remember, as a kid, the summer kids used to come over, and we'd sit around a low table behind the house, playing cards. Each of us sat on an enormous whale vertebra like little stools. We never thought anything strange about it.

"My poor mother was deeply involved with the PR work. She ground chum, drove the truck all over town to pick up bunker, sanded bottom paint, and hand-laid on the coat of Fiberglas Cricket still wears. She kept the dinner hot until my father swerved home from the bars. She was a waitress on the dinner shift at Gosman's [where Frank towed his first big white ashore]. I had to play under or around the dock, supervised from afar by two dozen waitresses, until the boat came in. As soon as Cricket passed the restaurant, I became officially under the babysitting care of my father, and as you can imagine, he took the responsibility a bit more lightly. Emotionally, I'm still on the steps of Fitzgerald's, listening to the fishermen tell stories and lies. Sometimes the draggermen would feel sorry for me and give me a huge fluke to use as ammunition. 'Tell him you caught this on your rig at the end of the dock, honey.'"

When booze rose up against him, *Jaws* was consuming his life, like he said the Pope (John XXIII) had already consumed what faith he'd managed to drag offshore day after day, month after month, year after year, toward old age. He's ruminating about it again:

"We had nuns on the boat down off Jersey, a charter: one priest and four or five nuns out mackerel fishin'. At that time, then, they had full habits. Well, then they change the laws as they go along. That's what made me mad about it. I was brought up strict Catholic. Aw, yeah, we spent a lot of time sittin' in church, but as we got older, why, they started changin' the laws around. I says, 'What's this deal here?' Got me upset. S'posed to be laws that were made by the Good Lord. Now the laws are made by the Pope. He says nuns can walk around lookin' like everybody else, 'cept they got a little white bib on. They never could drive a car; now they can drive a car, all this kinda happy stuff; make their own laws..."

As I recall, John XXIII had pissed off a lot of fishermen. He took a big chunk out of their business when he rescinded the fish-on-Friday law. It took years to recover.

"...I was a *choych-goin'* man until they started switchin' the laws around. They started switchin' things around when Patti was first goin' to school in Montauk," says Frank, either not seeing or denying what had been in store. Frank's descent continued.

After the God he'd known disappeared, the whales were taken away. No God, no more royal chum. Then the wife went. Then his booze. Next the black maw of human-fed extinctions loomed over his monsters. The Pope took the God, the God took the blubber, the blubber took the booze, the booze took the wife. Even the monsters were deserting Frank Mundus, either because the goat was never sacrificed in Atlantic City, or more likely because the wimpy god of the new room disapproved of goat sacrifices. The cheese stood alone until Big Guy and the girl from Manchester, England, showed up and the vision of hula-dancing fruit trees swayed in his head.

Cricket has encouraged everyone who's trod her deck to be free, to pull out the stops, do anything their hearts desire except lie to themselves. Cricket's told me this, too: don't lie to myself, or else your nose will grow longer than Rotten Ronald wished his penis was. Don't lie, she says, or that which made you will be doomed to live deep in the dark of the shark's belly, never to see daylight again.

She's right. I can't keep up. There, I've said it. I don't want to. My days as a reporter are numbered.

"I was on my hands and knees.
He was solid as what the deck is,
his gas was pumped right
into him, right solid tight, like
an automobile tire."

[FRANK MUNDUS]

Chapter

19

T E R M I N A L   G E A R

"BLACKFISH WHALES, BLACKFISH WHALES," shouts Paul Smith, who's

halfway up the mast with one arm around the crosstrees, the other

pointing to a pair of pilots moving fast, their rounded backs slipping

like obsidian torpedoes into the invisible world. □ Howard is reborn.

Frank, excited, reminds us the presence of blackfish whales is a sign

only slightly less promising than a dead floater, that white sharks are

in the area. And he says this could explain why there has been

absolutely no sign of life in the slick for hours—that is, we have drift-

ed onto a path of temperature-perfect, food-promising, magnetically-

true whale migration, with its predators lying in wait, looking up. The

Cricket herself and her tired and high-smelling crew are under clearing

skies, looking up for our own sweet chariots. Frightened to death, at the

same time, like the lesser sharks who fly before the king of the hill.

"It's his sled," says Frank with a blank stare filled with the reflection of bleeding dinosaurs, submerged forests, the dead seed of spent armies, and the big, triangular teeth of today. He's rigging a new bait made of two small sharks.

"Make it look like one's chasin' the other, in case we got some wise asses down there. If it's the same fish that took that bottom bait, he's movin' right along with us," Frank says, now certain we've had company the entire Fourth of July.

An hour passes, maybe two. Our shining path is shinier in the sunlight. The ball and the big rod's dangling terminal gear are doing the work of a panic-stricken goat treading desperately with its throat cut in the middle of the road of whales. One day the road will pass over 42nd and Broadway, as Mr. Banks foresaw in his instinctual desire to drop a pilot at the famous intersection. But for the moment, the ball is riding from wave peak to valley to peak, with its obscene danglement representing our best, most heartfelt prayer for the immediate future.

"Over the river and through the woods to grandmother's house we go," Frank is singing into the quiet of July Fifth. "That was my favorite statement the last few years as I climbed on the boat, mashed on the starter button, and went up on the bridge when we left the dock. 'Over the river and through the woods to grandmother's house we go, the Cricket knows the way...'"

Frank's in gear: "Just one more over 1,000 pounds would be nice," says he.

"Did you see pilot whales the day you caught the last big one?" asks an anxious Howard.

"No, it was a floatin' whale. Donny Braddick was runnin' a boat called the Fish On. They were ridin' around tuna fishin'. We were on our way home. They bump up against the whale. 'So,' Donny says, 'give him a call on the radio.' Mike, who used to work for me, says 'Don't bother — he never has the radio on.' So they're ridin around.

"The Cricket II is easy to spot in the distance, so he says, 'There's Frank over there.' They turn and buzz over to us and holler to us that there's a dead whale and where it is. I was on the way home and the whale was only five or 10 degrees off to one side, so I said, 'Okay, thanks. 'We'll take a look at it.'

"So we go down there. He beats us to the whale, naturally, 'cause he's a lot faster. I see him spin around the whale, and I see Mike run up to the pulpit, take the harpoon. I say, 'No, no, no, no—aaaaaah, he did.'

"I see the stick stop when he threw it. I say, 'Shit, they harpooned one.' All right, it took us another five minutes to get where he was, and that's all it took for them to lose the white shark.

"There was another boat there too called the Early Light. The Early Light was the name of the boat that took people home. My charter and Donny's, once we decided to get into it.

"The Early Light had harpooned a white shark before we even got there. So there was two sharks that never showed again. You wouldn't have any trouble spottin' them because they would be draggin' 10 feet of white line behind 'em. When I put the people on his boat, he says, 'If you see one that's swimmin' around with a hunk of harpoon warp in it,' he says, 'Well, that one was mine.' I says, 'Yeah, okay,' and to myself: 'If I do find one, I ain't gonna give it to you.'

"There was a bunch a white sharks feeding on the whale that day, all of which we was trying to bait. There was a pecking order. We was playin' with them all the time.

"If you add up as many times as what one showed up and watched how long it was there, you'd notice something. One would go, and the next would come, and you play with him, and he would go, and the next one would come, I'd play with him, he'd go, and the next would come. I mean, it was a continual circle. One was allowed to go up a very short time. He was allowed so many minutes up there, then he hadda come down, and if he was late comin' down, they'd send up the next one — then we'd have two at one time.

"I'd say, "That's funny — now we got two at one time.' I'd no sooner get the words outa my mouth when the one that just came up *pussshed*, slammed into the side of this one as much as to say, 'Get the hell outa here — your time is up.' He'd disappear. It was a peckin' order.

"There was only one other time, that was shortly after daylight, when the twins showed up: two of 'em, just a little over 1,000 pounds. They showed just for two minutes; then one was gone. They started about one o'clock that mornin'. It was continual, but we didn't notice the pattern until I started baitin' 'em at daylight. Well, we got everything ready. We was all rigged up. I ain't gonna bait at nighttime. So when daylight came, I said, 'Okay here we go.' First light I throw one the bait.

"*Sheeeit,* that was a joke, throwin' him the bait. Just looked at it, wanted no part of it. If it wasn't for the side pulpit where I could stand out on the end of the pulpit, and swing the bait back and forth, we woulda been outa luck. I'd throw it ahead of him, and by the time he got to the bait, — almost touched him, a lot of times — I'd then pull it away and get him mad.

"When we got there the day before, it was four o'clock in the afternoon. Then we tied up to the whale and pulled the boat right tight against the side of him.

"I said, 'Let me see how solid he is.' I had a pair of shorts, and I went out and walked up on him. I was the first one to go out. I was on my hands and knees. He was solid as what the deck is, his gas was pumped right into him, right solid tight like an automobile tire.

"And when I stood up, I found I could walk on him with no trouble. It wasn't slippery at all. When I stood up, I said, 'Where the hell did all the sand come from?' I looked down, and all the grooves were loaded with sand. When they die they automatically go right to the bottom, on account of their weight. Then they bounce and roll, roll and bounce on the bottom and pick up a lot of sand, like Topsider shoes. And then, in 24 hours, the gases from whatever they got in their stomachs blows them up, and up they come to the surface. But he was so fresh that all the grooves was still full of sand; it wasn't washed up yet. And then I go walkin' around on him, no problem. There was one shark around then, and we fed it melon and cookies from the whale. That was the only time we had to make nonsense because that afternoon they all started showin' up. Actually, the first one that hit, I was down below — I told Teddy I was goin' to bed.

"He said, 'I'm gonna stay up.'

"I said, 'Go ahead, stay up; you'll know when he's there.'

"He did. A big shark came up and hit the whale sideways, and the whale hit the boat sideways. It was a *boom boom,* you could feel it because it was flat calm. John DiLenardo, he came on the Cricket from Donny's boat, he says 'Haaaaa, there's one here; here he is.'

"I said, 'That's nice. I got up and looked and said, 'That's nice. Tell him to come back at daylight.' Nothin' you could do.

"Like I said, at daylight, there was one there most of the time. Matter of fact, we slacked the Fish On, slacked that boat off on about a 50-foot piece of three-eighths line, tied to us. We was tied to the whale.

"Donny wanted to go over to his boat to get somethin' during the day, so we pulled his boat in. Teddy jumped on with him. He turned on his fathometer, and every once in a while they'd holler, 'Hey, there's another one at 100 feet. 'Hey, there's another one at 100 feet, 110 feet, 100 feet, 110 feet. They was stacked up like airplanes. Goin' around and holdin' at 100 feet.

"There was eight that we know of. We had on one of the twins — it was just between 1,000 and 2,000, no bigger than that. John had that one on for about an hour and it bit through the one-eighth flex cable. We lost that one. Went back to the whale, and that was when Big Guy showed up.

"We was about— oh, I don't know — about 50 yards from the whale, and he decided he was gonna take one big bite out of the whale, forced his body up so that his dorsal fin was up out of the water before he grabbed. When he relaxes, the weight of his body and the shake of his head pulls it off ..."

Frank has skipped over something here, in this telling. I know because I interviewed Donny Braddick the day after the Cricket towed the big shark back to Montauk. Donny told me how, at one point when he was jockeying his boat around, before he climbed onto the Cricket, a line got wrapped around the propeller.

"I looked at Mike," Donny had said, "but I never said, 'Get in the water because you're the scummy mate.' He dove down and freed the line, and when he came up, his eyes were the size of silver dollars. Then the line got caught again."

"The second time, Mike didn't want to go in. He said, 'Hold my ankles.' I said, 'That's a good idea, Mike—that way, when the shark comes, he'll bite your head off.' Two of us held his ankles."

Now Frank's telling Howard how the big white chose the Cricket. "Every time he come up— when it was his turn in the wheel, then he come up— I got him madder. He was so mad that toward the end, before he actually took it, when he come up to the whale, he didn't come up toward the area where they was generally bitin' — he came up right underneath the side pulpit because he was lookin' for that thing what was makin' him mad. The last two times, when he come up, he wasn't like the other ones. The other ones would come up and slide down, but if they was gonna bite, they would bite as soon as they showed up. They'd go around and make one turn, go straight for the whale, wag their tails one time to give themselves a little push and *BOPPO*...hit hard in an upward direction, then shake and fall back. Now, when that happened, they would not look at the bait at all because they had a bushel basketful of food.

"But this guy here, the one we caught, the tip of his tail looked like he'd gone under a low bridge, just ticked it—there was a little white spot on it. The last two times he come up, I got him so mad; I wouldn't give him the bait. When his time was up he had to go so he couldn't play with me no more, so he'd go back down. Without eatin', he'd go back down. Then one of the other ones, Scarface, would show up. He had scratch marks down the side of his face. Then one of the twins would show up.

"When it was his turn again, he come right up *straaaaight*. He came up straight right up under that side pulpit. I hollered, 'Teddy, look at this—he's not comin' up over there, he's comin' up over here. He's aimin' directly for it.' I'd throw the bait in the water and say, 'Here it is,' and he'd keep right on comin'. Then I'd take it away from him, slide it across the water, slide it, slide it, and he'd come up, open up his mouth, and I'd take it away from him, and he'd turn and go that way, come back, put his head out further, open up his mouth more, almost let him touch it, then take it away from him, and it was time for him to go.

"So he'd go. The other ones would come up and half-heartedly look at it and wouldn't touch it. And then another would come, another one would come, and then finally, why, *Woop*, here comes White Tip again. 'Watch this, guys—stand by, now, Donny.' Donny was sittin' in the chair. Pole was in the chair-holder. I had a hold of the cable.

"So when Big Guy decided he was gonna get that bait; I could not take it away from him. I was pullin' it, and all of a sudden, he had it. Other times where I could see he was comin' after it, and I could pull it away from him, but this time, he just had it.

"I dropped the cable and screamed to Donny, 'He's got it.' We disconnected from the whale, cut the other boat loose. The hell with that, just let it drift. There was a boat driftin' on the ocean with nobody on it.

"After it was cut loose, I had problems backin' up and goin' forwards because the line was underneath the whale. At one time it looked like the line was stuck on the whale's pectoral. So we had a litle trouble gettin away from him, gettin' clear. Once we got clear, we was all right.

"They're fast, even the big fish. He took off like a bullet, leavin' a nice wake. He peeled off better than half the line on that 130 on one run, and Donny started to holler. We're gettin' low,' and I had just mashed it in gear and was spinnin' around and was goin' in that direction, and he stopped.

"Then he went down deep, down to the bottom, and sulked, rolled, banged, thrashed, then comes back to the top. Then he made a hard right the other way, took half the spool off again, and by the time we turned around and got goin' towards him, he calmed down and we got all the line back. He went down the bottom again. He come back to the top and charged the boat. He come *straaaaight* in our direction and he was comin' real fast."

Donny had recalled the white shark was charging the Cricket, no question about it, and he was getting scared. "Frank had it in the corner," Donny'd said, meaning he'd pushed the Cricket's throttle all-ahead-full. "I was down crankin', kept sayin' 'He's gone, he's gone...'"

"...We had a lot of slack. I started to go ahead," Frank says, "but the line come tight. He went to the bottom again, and when he come to the top, there he was. Poked his head out of the water real quick. We had everything planned on doin' it different, but now, 'Okay, here we go fellas, we're robbin' the bank and the cops showed up...'"

Donny said that when the shark surfaced, it was wrapped in the leader. "The belly was facing the boat, his pectoral fin pointing to the sky. He was mad, and his jaws kept snapping, *bam, bam, bam ...*"

"He done somethin' we didn't expect," Frank goes on, "so now we gotta change the plan. I jammed it in reverse. I don't like takin' a fish that way, but I put it in reverse, wide open, and I holler to John and say, 'Take the first flyin' gaff — he's on your side — take the first flyin' gaff and hit 'im. I don't care how, just hit 'im.'

"John hit 'im with the first flyin gaff just about the time that I'm puttin' the boat in motion to go ahead — we're still goin' back — to stop the motion of the boat. Otherwise I woulda run right over the top of him. So he got the first flyin' gaff into him that come tight, and he's rollin' and snappin', then Teddy got the second flyin' gaff into him, and he's rollin' and snappin'.

"I could stay up on the bridge, and I was hollerin':

'Look out — he's gettin' ready to come up on the other side,' so they'd run to the other side. I didn't have to go down there because I had Teddy, I had John, Mikey, and then Donny.

"He'd got down outa the chair. I had four good mates, in other words. I had all the help I needed down there, and it worked out perfect.

"Now the cable. But because we had two flyin' gaffs in him, the cable could not go past the flyin' gaffs, aaaaarh? We got the loop on him, but instead of the loop bein' a reverse tail rope, now the loop turned into a head choker because you could only pull it tight on his gills and hang on. That was as far back as we could go.

"If we didn't have a good crew, I never woulda caught that fish. I could only be in one place at one time. They saved the fish right at the last, 'cause when he poked his head out of the water, he only had three feet of leader wire left. All the leader wire was around his gill plates. Donny kept a tight line on him all the time. When he rolled, he was chokin' to death, and that's why he stuck his head out of the water. All fish will stick their heads out of the water when they're chokin to death if you hold a gill plate closed on one side."

Frank tells us again about fish mudding up. He's forgotten he'd told us before, or he thinks it's worth underscoring the fact that fish would sooner kamikaze than drown in the cruel gravity of fresh air.

"So we got the head choker on him," Frank continues, now back with the monster white, "and now he decides he don't like what's goin' on, and he's pullin' and thrashin', and I'm pullin' ahead slow, with the boat in a tight circle, trying to flatten him out. Eventually, why, they did get a tail rope on him, but that wasn't easy. And lucki-ly, nobody got hurt.

"The big ones don't thrash like the little ones. The big ones *rolll-lll, booooooom* this way, *booooooom,* that way. We started towin him backwards. We had three-and-a-half hours to get in."

Howard's praying to the grapefruit. His eyes are sharp little blades slitting the throats of goats. He's donating his virgin daughter to Aztec priests, giving up a lucrative condo project to his competition.

"That was a beautiful night," says Frank of his most immaculate arrival in Montauk. "Did I tell you about the party we had for that night? We'd just got in. Just got tied to the dock, and there he is. This guy jumps on the boat and says, 'Frank, congratulations on your fish,' he says, 'I'm your party for tonight. Think we're gonna make it?'

"I shook my head and said, 'I doubt it. The fish is not even out the water yet, never mind weighed in. It's a rod-and-reel fish; we gotta weigh him in. Then we're gonna have to take pictures; and blah, blah, blah, and I says, 'It's 11:30 now,' I says. 'I doubt it. I'm awfully sorry.'

"He says, 'I'm sorry for myself, but I'm glad for you.' He says, 'I guess I'll have to turn around and go back to Chicago.' "

Howard thinks of his own return ticket, his own empty hands, and gives Frank the most beseeching look I've ever seen; it's the fresh realization that his chartered captain had stepped onto the whale's sandy beach like a conquistador claiming lost Atlantis; the last tourist taking one more small step for man, then strolling carefree along the last beach upon the last island of extinguished life, and from that exalted place, reaching down to feed the world's sleek inheritors genteel rations of melon and cookies as they consume his oasis by bushel-basket bites — all this in preparation for that last, wet leap for mankind.

God saw this and said it was good, a scene that bore repeating in the not-too-distant future, a most fitting end on some future Fourth of July. Then God told Mundus to take one last white shark, a big one, and then retire, grow papayas, and say nothing, especially to reporters.

All at once, the ball is gone. Paul grabs the rod from its holder. Howard takes the throne. Jim straps him in the harness, and Paul hands him the rod.

"There's the prettiest sight in the ocean: the hole in the water where the cork was," says Frank, on his way up the mast to the bridge, from which he will direct the action. I go below to get my camera. The big reel screams as a very large animal goes deep.

Here comes our imagination. I can feel it in my intestines. Frank was just saying how he had timed the Cricket's movements between drifts, and we have just about enough fuel to make it home. The big rod is bent like a snapper pole and screams. A pod of blackfish whales has just passed. Whales ... whites ... bent rod ... coincidence?

Howard was hyperventilating but now is settled down. The reel has stopped screaming, and he's started to wind.

Frank yells: "Wind, Howard, keep it smooth, use your legs, pump with your legs not your back. I like the way the line's moving, Howard."

Jim is directing the fighting chair as the line slices wide arcs through the waves. Frank mashes on the starter. The Cricket growls. Whatever line Howard had gained the fish is taking back zzzzzzzzzzzzz, and then some. *"Wooooooh,"* says the angler, King Chong.

The sun is bright now. It's hot, and Howard's drenched with sweat. I swing the camera strap like a bandoleer so my hands are free. I jump on Cricket's rail, then crawl on my hands and knees out onto the starboard platform, only 12 inches wide, for the omniscient view.

Out here, 15 feet from Cricket's center, I'm levered and holding onto the platform's stainless steel wire railing for dear life. Waves alternately lower me to the green sea surface and raise me on high. From there the Cricket looks small and far away. At once I can see Frank standing spread-legged on the bridge, watching Howard, and Howard's hunched back, his rod bent, U-shaped, like a magnet.

The chair turns to starboard. The line points down in my direction. The fish is directly under me somewhere.

"Can you see anything?" Frank shouts to me.

I see everything but scream, "Not yet." I'm walking the plank. I'm hanging 10, soaring like a shearwater out here — down as the Cricket rolls into a trough, up as she falls off the other side of each successive swell. Close to the water I can see myself in reflection and quickly below that a glint — golden armor. It's the flank of Howard's catch, and below that, the sun's rays reach for the dark forges of eternal Atlantis.

On the way up, I'm even with Cricket as she slips into a trough. Her flank flashes white in the welcome sun. Above her now and climbing, I see the play in its proper perspective: A monster pulling from below, Howard humped, and Frank above him, the hierarchy. I'm even now with Frank, who's watching over his angler from the bridge, spread-legged, commanding angler and mates. Jim's unlimbering the monster shackle. Paul's gripped an axe-handled gaff.

Now I'm above Frank and climbing. Cricket's smaller from here, her entire crew a happy multitude: The present company, of course, but Teddy, too, and Oli, Davy Crockett, the frozen jockey, the son-of-a-bitch Otto, the restored blindman, Rotten Ronald, Bea with her bite marks, good old Mr. Banks, Uncle Bud, a Montaukett with his iron, Tom Luby, my stowaway, and Captain Hader of the Devilfish. Below sea level is the future perfect, says Hader, where one day life as we know it will have been. One day, when, in the course of human events, it becomes necessary to dissolve, we will all know, says he.

Cricket-level is the way it is now. Above her is the way she was, the way she was in her glory and perhaps ours. Higher still, Excelsius, Cricket's an antique speck — the ark. We should go no higher than the moon and gently, if we want to stay on earth.

On the way down again — a flash deep down. Here comes my imagination. Any closer to the surface, and I could jump on her beautiful, arching back, with red hair streaming halfway down to her powerful tail of blue.

"Frank, I see him," I yell. Howard's been straining, fighting hard.

"Watch the reel, Howid," Frank screams. "If it slips, stop reelin', you're wastin' energy ... Still don't know what the hell you got." The angler's straining in his harness, pushing against the fighting chair's foot rest, letting his legs — as he was told to do — take the punishment.

I see what he's got. It's a big blue shark, looks like 300 pounds. It's foul-hooked in the side, just before the pectoral fin, uninhibited, which is why the fish is pulling so hard.

"You got two good runs," says Frank, calming his charter. "Stay there, Howid. He's comin' your way. His head's turnin'", says the master, reading the line. I know Frank knows the fish is foul-hooked, probably knew it from the start. It's likely to go at any time.

The shark's close to Cricket now, just inches from the surface. I'm rising and falling directly over its cold, angry eye and yawning jaws. I shoot a picture from on high, from on low, journalism at its objective best. I want the picture caption to read something like: "New Disney ride causes sixth visitor to jump this week."

Jim's ready with the stainless steel noose, too late to fetch the rifle from its scabbard. Howard's holding strain. Pow! the hook pulls loose. The shark disappears in a swirl of red for the blood, white for her belly, and blue for her powerful slender back as it blends with the deep.

Howard is excited and, yes, happy, without his great white, even without his great blue. Silence from the bridge for 10 expectant minutes, and then:

"La-di-da, you plan it like a bank job, and then the cops show up. As long as you had fun playin' the game, Howard. When the shark loses, he loses his life. When you lose, you lose a fish."

"Growlrowl, growlrowl, growlrowl," Cricket speaks as the captain heads her home to the summer-crowded village of extinct Indians. Jim and Paul begin to clean up. Mundus stays topside. The sun has been totally revealed by the trailing edge of the passing front's cloak of clouds. We're peeling off our heavy clothes.

I've begun to write some of this down, sitting in the monster chair. I can write something pretty good about the end of an era, but there's no future in obituaries. I know Frank would agree. I've already decided to take Captain Hader up on an offer he made before he died. Hader said that Bill Masin — who has a boat — and I could have Burials At Sea, split it down the middle, if we wanted. I figure we can raise the price to $80 a box, split two ways, with no overhead and a little advertising. I'll reach out to funeral homes with a mailing, a clever letter about how loved ones can allow their departed to share in the timeless beauty that is Montauk. First thing I'll do when I get back is call Masin, then my wife and daughter, the paper last.

Frank's left Cricket to steer herself. "Them poor bastards on the beach are doin' some sweatin' now," he says of the heat, but I know he means the heat and everything else. I don't want to go back or, to be more precise about my emotion, I don't want this peace to end.

"Got to get rid of them chum buckets, or they'll explode," Frank tells his mates.

Amen, I tell mine.

"The little old lady
from Pasadena walks to
church on Sunday.
She has no muscles.
She knows she has no muscles,
so she listens to me
and catches fish."

[FRANK MUNDUS]

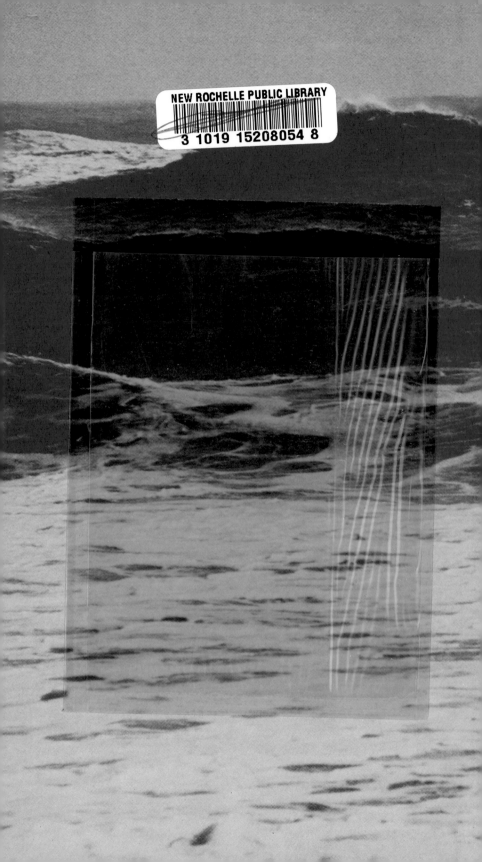